THE SERMONS OF
ST. FRANCIS DE SALES

FOR

LENT

St. Francis de Sales
1567-1622
Bishop, Founder of the Visitation,
and Doctor of the Church

THE SERMONS OF

ST. FRANCIS DE SALES

FOR

LENT

GIVEN IN THE YEAR 1622

Volume III in the Series

Translated by Nuns of the Visitation

Edited by Father Lewis S. Fiorelli, O.S.F.S.

"Our entire good consists not only in accepting the truth of God's word, but in persevering in it."

—St. Francis de Sales

TAN BOOKS AND PUBLISHERS, INC.
Rockford, Illinois 61105

Nihil Obstat: Rev. Msgr. John H. Dewson
                   Censor Librorum

Imprimatur: ✠ Most Rev. Robert E. Mulvee
                   Bishop of Wilmington
                   Wilmington, Delaware
                   December 12, 1986
                   Feast of St. Jane Frances de Chantal

Library of Congress Catalog Card No. 87-50084

ISBN: 0-89555-260-4

Further volumes in preparation.

Printed and bound in the United States of America.

TAN BOOKS AND PUBLISHERS, INC.
P.O. Box 424
Rockford, Illinois 61105

1987

My advice is that henceforth
we live no more in ourselves, but that
in heart, intention, and confidence
we lodge forever
in the pierced side of the Saviour.
—*St. Francis de Sales*

The Sermons of St. Francis de Sales

Volume I   On Prayer
Volume II   On Our Lady
Volume III   For Lent

TABLE OF CONTENTS

About St. Francis de Sales............................ xiii

Preface... xvii

Translator's Note..................................... xxiii

1. Fasting
   Sermon for Ash Wednesday, February 9, 1622,
   concerning the spiritual fruits of fasting and the
   conditions which make fasting pleasing to God: fasting
   universally, that is, with all the senses and with the
   understanding, memory, and the appetites of the will;
   how completely the primitive Christians fasted; fasting
   through humility rather than through vanity, fasting
   through obedience rather than through self-will,
   following the community customs in fasting rather than
   seeking to be singular, fasting only to please God and
   not for the esteem of men, and the evil of subjecting
   the commands of God and our superiors to our own
   human discretion................................. 1

2. Temptation
   Sermon for the First Sunday of Lent, February 13,
   1622, concerning the universality of temptation, the
   spiritual danger of idleness, faith as a prime weapon
   against temptation, slothful souls, presumptuous reliance
   of beginners on the strength from their sensible fervor,
   attachment to the consolations of God, Our Lord's
   example in undergoing temptation from the devil,
   battling one's faults with patience and perseverance, vain
   hopes which distract the soul from practicing solid
   virtue, the folly of avariciously chasing after a
   multiplicity of devotions, and vain complacency in God's
   consolations...................................... 15

3. Faith
   Sermon for Thursday after the First Sunday of Lent,
   February 17, 1622, concerning faith as the adhesion of
   the understanding to the truths revealed by God or the
   Church, living faith which produces the fruit of good
   works vs. dead or dying faith, vigilant, penetrating faith
   vs. dormant faith, the supernatural prudence which
   accompanies vigilant faith, attentive faith, confidence in
   prayer, perseverance in prayer, patience in prayer, and
   humility in prayer............................... 34

4. Eternal Happiness
   Sermon for the Second Sunday of Lent, February 20,
   1622, concerning our inability to comprehend eternal
   happiness, the ability of the soul in Heaven to use its
   faculties to understand clearly and to love ardently, the
   soul's joy in heavenly conversations with the angels,
   saints, Our Lady, Our Lord, and with the Most Holy
   Trinity, the soul's great joy in recalling Our Lord's
   mercies to it, His Passion and death, and in seeing the
   love of His Heart for it, each soul's great delight in
   receiving a secret name known to God alone, the kiss
   given by God to the blessed soul, and the endlessness
   of the joys of eternity............................ 52

5. Election and Reprobation
   Sermon for the Thursday after the Second Sunday of
   Lent (coinciding with the Feast of St. Matthias),
   February 24, 1622, concerning the danger which all
   Christians live in of refusing to receive the grace of
   salvation, the danger of even specially favored souls
   falling from God and being damned, why we must
   always have a great fear of damnation—even in the
   religious life, the avarice of the evil rich man, two
   kinds of avarice and especially that of clinging to what
   we possess, using God for one's own benefit, non-
   material avarice, using riches vs. idolizing riches, the
   avarice and treachery of Judas, the beginnings of
   spiritual downfall, the salutary fear of sin, availing
   ourselves of the grace to mortify our evil inclinations,
   the replacement of those who die or defect from the

Apostolic College or from the religious life, and the
choice of St. Matthias to replace Judas............. 66

6. Mutual Charity
Sermon for the Third Sunday of Lent, February 27,
1622, concerning Our Lord's commandment of love of
neighbor, His desire that we be united with each other,
the relationship between love of God and love of
neighbor, in what way the Commandment of love of
neighbor is new, Our Lord's example of love of
neighbor, Our Lord's restoration of man to God's image
and likeness, seeing and loving Our Lord in our
neighbor, the extent to which we should love our
neighbor, how it is better to be spent for our
neighbor's sake than to spend ourselves for him in the
way we choose, union with God and our neighbor in
the Most Blessed Sacrament, love of neighbor as the
Commandment which God stresses to us the most
earnestly, and how we should love our neighbor with
the same incomparable ardor and constancy with which
Our Lord loved us on the Cross.................. 83

7. Proper Conduct in Illness
Sermon for the Thursday after the Third Sunday of
Lent, March 3, 1622, concerning the cure of St. Peter's
mother-in-law, the celibacy of St. Peter, the Communion
of Saints, God's lordship over all things, two methods
of meditating, the wonderful submission to God and
resignation into the hands of her superiors of St. Peter's
mother-in-law as she lay ill with fever, over-eagerness in
seeking cures from God, St. Bernard's words that
religious must not be concerned with their bodily
illnesses, over-eagerness in seeking remedies for illness,
the admirable submission to God's will of St. Peter's
mother-in-law and how we should imitate her, using
one's health to serve God, and the practice of true
evangelical poverty in time of illness............... 99

8. God's Spiritual Providence
Sermon for the Fourth Sunday of Lent, March 6, 1622,
concerning God's special spiritual care of those who

have withdrawn from the world to follow the Saviour
on the "mountain" of perfection, how God's Providence
is greater in proportion to the soul's lack of anxiety for
its own needs, how we must diligently use the ordinary
means to attain perfection and how, if these fail, God
would sooner work a miracle than leave us without
assistance, how God tests souls, anxiety to be rid of
spiritual pains rather than trusting God to console us as
He wills, the twin virtues of humility and generosity,
how Our lord reproduced the five loaves and two
fishes, how religious souls must be satisfied when God
gives them only a sufficiency (or even less), and how
God will continually renew the spiritual goods which
we have. 116

9. Proper Fear of Death
    Sermon for the Thursday after the Fourth Sunday of
    Lent, March 10, 1622, concerning Our Lord's raising of
    the son of the widow of Naim, Our Lord's motives for
    performing this miracle—and in this manner, burial in
    the Old and in the New Law, God's creative power in
    raising the dead, the error of some ancient philosophers
    who say we should not fear death, the holy Fathers'
    teaching that we must fear death without fearing it, how
    even saintly souls should fear death, St. Paul's desire
    for death and Job's desire for death, the secret language
    of love, that it is good to fear death, how this fear
    should be combined with confidence in God's
    Providence, how in order to die well we must lead a
    good life, how we should daily remind ourselves that
    we shall die, and how we should always bear in mind
    the account we must someday render to God, and keep
    ourselves in the state we would wish to be found in at
    death. 129

10. Hearing the Word of God
    Sermon for Passion Sunday, March 13, 1622, concerning
    the goodness which should be practiced by those who
    preach God's word, how we should esteem God's word
    even if it is taught by a sinful person, how a person's
    refusal to believe Our Lord's word proves the evilness

of that person—not of Our Lord, how all sin is a
result of defection from truth, how God's word is
Truth, how Lucifer's sin as well as that of our first
parents resulted from a choice of vanity over truth, how
we should remain attentive to the truths of faith, our
culpable failure to live according to the truths of God's
word, the dispositions with which we should hear God's
word and the unimportance of distractions and dryness
in the lower part of our soul as long as the higher
part of the soul is devoted and reverent toward God's
word... 147

11. Humility and Obedience
Sermon for Palm Sunday, March 20, 1622, concerning
the perfection and imperfection found in every creature
(except the Blessed Virgin)—including the angels in
Heaven and the lives of the saints, how we should take
note of and profit from the imperfections in the lives of
the saints, how we should not use the faults of the
saints to excuse our own failings, worldly prudence vs.
the folly of the Cross, fraternal correction, the ass and
colt upon which Our Lord entered Jerusalem and what
they represent, Our Lord's humility and patience and
submission, perfect obedience vs. obedience full of
worldly prudence, the proper answer to make to the
objections of worldly prudence, Our Lord's confounding
of the maxims of the world, and our blessedness in
imitating Him.................................. 160

12. The Passion of Our Lord and What It Means
Sermon for Good Friday, March 25, 1622, concerning
the brass serpent which saved the Israelites, the
sinlessness of Christ, the manner in which He redeemed
us, the two natures of Christ and our three "natures,"
Our Lord as Saviour, how our salvation comes from
looking upon our Saviour, Our Lord's seven last words,
His prayer for forgiveness for those crucifying Him, His
pardon of the good thief and of St. Peter, and the bad
thief's and Judas' damnation; the danger of damnation
and how we should both fear and hope, Our Lord's
confiding of Our Lady and St. John to each other, the

darkness on Good Friday, Our Lord's great sorrow over those who would not profit from His Passion, His feeling of abandonment by His Father, His thirst, His obedience in remaining on the Cross and how we should imitate Him, the Cross as the one way of salvation, and Our Lord's perfect commending of Himself into His Father's hands and how we should do likewise, making no reservations............... 177

Index..209

ABOUT ST. FRANCIS DE SALES

St. Francis de Sales, the holy bishop, founder, and Doctor of the Church, is known throughout the Church for his great sanctity, learning, theological knowledge, gentleness, and understanding of the human soul. Through these marvelous gifts he converted and guided innumerable souls to God during his own lifetime, and re-converted 70,000 from Calvinism. He continues to direct many souls through his spiritual writings and published sermons. Today St. Francis de Sales is known as one of the great figures of the Catholic Counter-Reformation and of the 17th-century rebirth of Catholic mystical life.

St. Francis was born in 1567 in the castle belonging to the de Sales family in Thorens, Savoy, located in what is now southeastern France. His mother, Francoise, was only 14 years old when Francis, her firstborn, came into the world. This maternity was a dangerous one, the labor was long and difficult, and it was marvelled that both mother and child did not die. It is most noteworthy that a month before the birth Francoise had consecrated her unborn child to Our Lord in the presence of the Holy Shroud, which at that time was kept in the Sainte Chapelle in Chambery, France.

Later, Francis was to have a great devotion to the Holy Shroud because his mother had been delivered much better than expected through her veneration of this holy relic. He considered the Shroud to be his country's shield and greatest relic. It was his favorite devotional picture, and he had numerous images of it painted, engraved and embroidered, placing them in his room, chapel, oratory, study, reception rooms and breviary. St. Francis de Sales wrote that his devotion to the Holy Shroud was due to the fact that "my mother, when I was still in her womb, dedicated me to Our Lord before this holy banner of salvation."

As he grew older, St. Francis de Sales studied literature, law, philosophy and theology in Paris and Padua. Upon finishing his studies, he received a doctorate in civil and canon law. Though he could have had a brilliant secular career, he set his soul on following the call of God to the priesthood, and was ordained in 1593 at the age of 26. He was consecrated Bishop of Geneva at age 35, and was to remain Bishop of Geneva for the remaining 20 years of his life. Some years after St. Francis de Sales took charge of Geneva, King Henry IV suggested to him the possibility of a transfer to a diocese with more worldly advantages; the saint replied in words that soon became famous all over Paris: "Sire, I have married a poor wife and I cannot desert her for a richer one."

Shortly after becoming a bishop, St. Francis met St. Jane Frances de Chantal, a widow; between these two saints there grew a deep spiritual friendship. St. Francis became the spiritual director of Jane Frances, and with her, he founded in 1610 the religious order of nuns known as the Order of the Visitation, or the Visitandines.

Both of these saints loved the Heart of Jesus, and conceived this Heart as the particular treasure confided to the nuns of the Visitation. It is most remarkable that 60 years before the great revelations of the Sacred Heart of Jesus to the Visitandine St. Margaret Mary Alacoque (1673-1675), St. Francis de Sales and St. Jane Frances de Chantal had very often spoken to their spiritual daughters of this sacred love. St. Francis de Sales stated that the Visitandines who followed the Rule would receive the privilege of bearing the title, "Daughters of the Sacred Heart of Jesus," and he gave to this institute, as coat-of-arms, the Heart of Jesus crowned with thorns. The religious wear this emblem emblazoned on their pectoral crosses.

Although devotion to the Heart of Jesus was at this time very little known, God was drawing these two souls to prepare the Visitation as a holy sanctuary to receive the famous revelations to come. Also, the annals of the Order show that several Visitandines had experienced spiritual attractions toward, and even mystical favors from, the Heart of Jesus. Then, years later, with His revelations to St. Margaret Mary at the Visitation of Paray-le-Monial, God called this order to share with the entire Church that precious gift which had been its own special portion.

Among St. Francis de Sales' private papers collected after his death by St. Jane Frances de Chantal, there are many striking references to the Visitation's special calling to dwell in the Heart of Jesus and to love and imitate the two special virtues of His Heart, meekness and humility. "Learn of Me that I am meek and humble of Heart." In his sermons, too, St. Francis makes reference to the Heart of our Saviour and to the sacred Wound in His side. With the wisdom of hindsight, the reader can see how God in His Providence had chosen St. Francis de Sales to be, as it were, His "precursor," a preparer of hearts in anticipation of the great forthcoming revelation of His own Divine Heart.

The saintly bishop has left a description of an occasion in 1613, the feast of the Holy Shroud, when he was invited to be one of the prelates who exposed the holy relic for the veneration of the faithful. (It had been moved to Turin, Italy in 1578.) In a letter to St. Jane Frances de Chantal, he wrote: "A year ago, about this hour of the day, I was at Turin, exhibiting the Holy Shroud in the midst of a great crowd. Several drops of sweat, falling from my face, dropped upon the Holy Shroud itself, and thereupon, within my heart, I uttered this prayer: 'O Saviour of my life, deign to mingle my unworthy sweat with Thine and infuse into my blood, my life, and my affections the merits of this sacred moisture.' My dear Mother, the Prince Cardinal was angered because my sweat fell upon the Holy Shroud, but it came into my mind to tell him that our Saviour was not so nicely sensitive, and that He only shed His own sweat and blood in order to mingle them with ours, so as to give them the price of eternal life. And so may our sighs be joined with His that they ascend

before the Eternal Father like the smoke of fragrant incense."
As a spiritual director, St. Francis de Sales was for a time
the confessor of Blessed Marie of the Incarnation (Madame
Barbe Acarie). This saintly woman was a wife, mother of
six children, Parisian hostess, mystic, and foundress of five
Carmelite convents.

St. Francis de Sales wrote two of the greatest Catholic
masterpieces on the spiritual life: the *Introduction to the Devout Life* and *Treatise on the Love of God*. The former shows
how holiness is possible for all people in the state of grace,
including people living in the world. This book was a best-
seller in the 17th century and is still popular today. The *Treatise on the Love of God* covers all aspects of the virtue of
charity, the supernatural love of God. St. Francis de Sales'
pamphlets against the Calvinist heresy have been gathered
together into a book and given the title *Controversies*. The
arguments presented in this book are just as unanswerable
today as when they were written. Because of his writings,
St. Francis de Sales has become the patron of writers and
journalists; he has also been designated patron saint of the
Catholic press.

St. Francis de Sales died at age 55, in the year 1622. His
beatification, which occurred the very year he died, was the
first formal beatification ever held in St. Peter's Basilica. He
was canonized in 1665, and was declared a Doctor of the
Universal Church by Pope Pius IX in 1877. With this decla-
ration the Church presented the teachings of St. Francis de
Sales to all the faithful as a sure guide to true Catholic doctrine and the ways of the spiritual life—a sure guide to Heaven.

PREFACE

While Bishop of Geneva, St. Francis de Sales was in demand as a preacher both within and outside his diocese. As a result, four volumes of Sermons from the 26 volumes which comprise the Annecy edition of his works stand as written testimony to the manner in which he responded to those requests and the seriousness with which he viewed his duty as bishop to preach the Gospel of Christ. These sermons, compiled from the saint's own working notes, texts of sermons and fragments, cover every aspect of the liturgical year, as well as associated occurrences in the community life of the Visitation Order, which he co-founded with St. Jane de Chantal.

As a young priest and preacher St. Francis was consumed by a burning desire to proclaim the love of God to all people, regardless of social class or intellectual distinction. Therefore, he chose in preaching to adopt the homily as his style, long out of vogue in his day. From his experience in hearing the popular orators of Paris churches, St. Francis saw that if he were to be an effective preacher he would have to speak in a manner which the people could understand clearly, devoid of the accustomed elaborate rhetorical devices and seemingly endless Latin and Greek quotations. In using the homily form of preaching, St. Francis could reach out to everyone in a way which was simple and direct. However, in doing so, he risked his reputation and even prompted the following criticism from his father:

> Provost, you preach too often; I hear the bell ring for sermons even on weekdays. In my day it was not so, preachings were much rarer; but what preachings, God knows! They were erudite, well thought out; more Latin

and Greek were quoted in one than you quote in ten;
everyone was enraptured and edified; people used to
go to sermons in crowds. Now you have made preaching so common, this will no longer happen and no one
will think very much of you!

On the contrary, experience proved that it was this intimate
and familiar form of preaching "from the heart" which
strengthened the faith of the believer, caused many to return
to the Church, and distinguished St. Francis as an outstand-
ing preacher. Later in life he would advise a preacher to
resist a preoccupation with form and endeavor to have a "heart
to heart conversation" with the hearer, in which love itself
would be the form and love itself would assure results:

> I would not like people to say at the end of a sermon:
> "What a great orator he is!" "What a wonderful mem-
> ory he has!" "How learned he is!" "How well he
> speaks!"....I would prefer that the hearer whose heart
> has been touched would testify to the preacher's power
> solely by an amendment of life.

When St. Francis became bishop in 1602, this simple style
practiced as a young priest, along with his growing popularity as a spiritual director and writer, guaranteed him a hearing and served as an effective means of bringing Christ to
people and people to Christ!

The Council of Trent had taught that it was the bishop's
principal duty to preach. As bishop, St. Francis vowed to
fulfill this task scrupulously whenever requested. When his
own brother complained that other episcopal duties made it
difficult for him to accept preaching engagements, St. Francis
reminded him of his duty and emphasized that preaching must
be accessible to all:

> You are now a bishop and this is the time for you to
> learn what it is to which that title binds us. We must
> not be like those little trickles of water that spring from
> artificial rocks in the garden of great folk and to which

one scarcely dares approach. Such water is drawn only
in silver goblets or goblets of crystal, and very little
at a time, for fear of disturbing or checking the flow.
To fulfill our office we must be like the great and open
fountains from which water is taken in abundance, not
only for men, but also, and even more frequently, by
beasts—everything, even snakes, having free use of
it...We must never repulse anyone, even though our
peace and comfort may have to suffer a little.

As important as the preaching of others might be, St. Francis
was convinced that the bishop *in his person* held special power
to inspire others through his preaching:

It is marvelous what great power a bishop's preaching
has in comparison to that of other preachers...Abundant
as are the rivulets, people like to drink from the source
itself.

The Lenten Sermons of St. Francis de Sales afford a rare
opportunity to witness his dedication as bishop to his duty
to preach, his unique homiletic style in the presentation of
theological truths, and the love and devotion which inspired
and gave power to his words.

In the 17th century, tradition had made Lent a special time
in the Church year when a bishop would be invited by another bishop or a nobleman to preach a series of sermons
to the people of a diocese or region. In the years of his epis-
copacy St. Francis had occasion to preach almost 20 such
Lenten series, allowing him to touch a wide range of persons
from every walk of life and social status. It was at just such
a Lenten preaching engagement (1603) that he first encountered Madame de Chantal, with whom he would share a deep
spiritual friendship. A biographer described the success of
his Lenten sermons:

He spoke in his heart with God, and was therefore able
to speak from his heart to the hearts of all who would
hear him.

In his famed letter, *On the Preacher and Preaching,* St. Francis voiced the conviction which was the source of his effectiveness:

> Our words must be set aflame not by shouts and unrestrained gestures, but by inward affection. They must issue from our heart rather than from our mouth. We must speak well, but heart speaks to heart, and the tongue speaks only to people's ears.

The "heart to heart conversation in love" shown in St. Francis' own preaching found its logical beginning and nourishment in the Eucharist, the Sacrament of Love. In Christ's Living Presence he could rekindle the divine intention in preaching by recalling Christ's own purpose: "I have come that they might have life and have it more abundantly!" And through this personal encounter with the Eucharistic Christ, he likewise gained inspiration and guidance to bring that intention to fruition in himself and those who would hear him. The Lenten series of sermons preached at Chambery (1606) attested that his personal holiness was the basis of his effectiveness as a preacher.

In a letter, St. Francis recounted that he had made a rather unpromising beginning and had moved very few of those who heard him. What appealed to the heart of his hearers was internal to his person. To intimidate the bishop, the Senate of Chambery had publicly issued a threat concerning his property, a threat which he met with Christian fortitude. His patience and charity in the matter so excited the imagination of the people that churches became full for his sermons. The charism of his personal holiness broke down all resistance, as one biographer comments:

> Tradition says that the contrast between the humility and gentleness evident in the Bishop of Geneva and the characteristics assigned to Catholic bishops by Calvinist legend broke down the prejudice which was the surest defense against his genius of persuasion...the personal

integrity of Francis de Sales being unassailable, and his patience under suspicion, deepened the impression of his personal life on his contemporaries.

St. Francis stated it even more simply: "To love well is sufficient for speaking well!" Besides this point, the story also illustrates that the disposition of the hearer is equally essential in the "heart to heart" communication on which St. Francis based his preaching.

A contemporary writer has accurately insisted that "More than half of every successful sermon is preached by the congregation." According to an incident which is said to have taken place during the Lenten series preached at Annecy, St. Francis agreed wholeheartedly.

> The Saint had the habit of pausing at the beginning of a sermon and looking across the assembly ranged before him for a few silent moments. A member of the cathedral chapter ventured to ask him what his silence signified. "I salute the guardian angel of each one of my audience," he answered, "and I beg him to make the heart under his care ready for my words. Very great favors have come to me by this means."

Judging from his popularity as a preacher, St. Francis' prayer for his congregation brought the desired result—namely, that the heart of his hearer became "more animated" and "gained in strength and vigor," which was seen in an amendment of life. The "heart to heart conversation" of the homily, preacher and hearer, thus bore fruit because of the union effected by Christ's Love.

The Lenten sermons which follow, translated by the Visitation Sisters and edited by Fr. Lewis Fiorelli, O.S.F.S., were obviously meant to be heard, not read. Therefore, a great part of St. Francis' "heart to heart" preaching which made them so effective is undeniably and regrettably lacking. However, the fact that these sermons result from the loving efforts of persons intimately living St. Francis de Sales' spirit, as his spiritual sons and daughters, can be perceived as something issuing from his own heart. If it were not for their labor of love, very few indeed would have even this opportunity of experiencing the personal charism of the saint.

As noted, the dispositions of the reader are equally important if the spiritual profit originally intended by the author is to be gained through these sermons. The emphasis of Vatican Council II on preaching, in particular the homily, reflected in the saint's teaching and practice, should in its own way lead to a receptivity in the reader's heart.

Though the selection of Lenten sermons was intended for cloistered religious, their message is equally valuable to the lay reader, who has only to use his judgment in making application according to his state in life. In fact, the lay reader has the rare opportunity of profiting from the fatherly counsel of St. Francis de Sales which reveals his "secret heart" in the informal setting of the convent and garden of his spiritual daughters. The virtues encouraged for religious are also required for the laity, if both are in their own way to respond generously to the Council's Universal Call to Holiness. Other reasons of disposition must be left to personal interest. However, in approaching these sermons the reader can in faith proceed with the assurance that the heart has already been uniquely led to a beneficial posture through the family of St. Francis de Sales, who, after the saint's example, have offered preparation through prayer! LIVE + JESUS!

Rev. John A. Abruzzese, S.T.D.
Secretariat of the Synod of Bishops
Vatican City State

TRANSLATOR'S NOTE

The twelve sermons for Lent contained in this book were translated from St. Francis de Sales' *Oeuvres,* vol. X (Annecy: Niérat, 1892-1964).

The first volume of this series, *Sermons of St. Francis de Sales on Prayer,* includes an Introduction on the Origins and Value of the Sermons which was also taken from the Annecy edition.

Studio Fotografica Nazionale, Fratelli Dutto

The Holy Shroud, the burial sheet of Our Lord Jesus Christ, showing the great outflow of blood from His pierced right side—see the white area at left. (*Grateful acknowledgements to Father Peter Rinaldi, S.D.B. for obtaining this beautiful photograph.*)

"What will we do, what will we become, I ask you, when in Heaven, through the Sacred Wound of His side, we perceive that most adorable and most lovable Heart of our Master, aflame with love for us— that Heart where we will see each of our names written in letters of love!"

—St. Francis de Sales

— 1 —

FASTING

*Sermon for Ash Wednesday, February 9, 1622, con-
cerning the spiritual fruits of fasting and the conditions which make fasting pleasing to God: fasting
universally, that is, with all the senses and with
the understanding, memory, and the appetites of
the will; how completely the primitive Christians
fasted, fasting through humility rather than through
vanity, fasting through obedience rather than
through self-will, following the community customs
in fasting rather than seeking to be singular, fasting only to please God and not for the esteem
of men, and the evil of subjecting the commands
of God and our superiors to our own human discretion.*

These first four days of the holy season of Lent serve as
a preface to indicate the preparation that we ought to make
in order to spend Lent well and to dispose ourselves to fast
well. That is why I thought of speaking to you, in this exhor-
tation, of the conditions which render fasting good and
meritorious. I will speak as briefly and as familiarly as possible, not only today but in the discourses that I will address
to you every Thursday during this Lent. All will be as simple
and proper for your hearts as I can make them.

To treat of fasting and of what is required to fast well,
we must, at the start, understand that of itself fasting is not
a virtue. The good and the bad, as well as Christians and
pagans, observe it. The ancient philosophers observed it and
recommended it. They were not virtuous for that reason, nor
did they practice virtue in fasting. Oh, no, fasting is a virtue

only when it is accompanied by conditions which render it pleasing to God. Thus it happens that it profits some and not others, because it is not undertaken by all in the same manner.

We find some people who think that to fast well during the holy season of Lent it is enough to abstain from eating some prohibited food. But this thought is too gross to enter into the hearts of religious, for it is to you I speak, as well as persons dedicated to Our Lord. We know very well that it is not enough to fast exteriorly if we do not also fast interiorly and if we do not accompany the fast of the body with that of the spirit.

That is why our Divine Master, who instituted the fast, greatly desired in His Sermon on the Mount to teach His Apostles how it must be practiced [*Matt.* 6:16-18], which is a matter of great profit and utility (for it would not have been becoming to the greatness and majesty of God to teach a useless doctrine. That could not be.). He knew that to draw strength and efficacy from fasting, something more than abstinence from prohibited food is necessary. Thus He instructed them and, consequently, disposed them to gather the fruits proper to fasting. Among many others are these four: fasting fortifies the spirit, mortifying the flesh and its sensuality; it raises the spirit to God; it fights concupiscence and gives power to conquer and deaden its passions; in short, it disposes the heart to seek to please only God with great purity of heart.

It will be very helpful to state clearly what must be done to fast well these forty days. For although everyone is bound to know it and to practice it, religious and persons dedicated to Our Lord are more particularly obliged to it. Now, among all the conditions required for fasting well, I will select three principal ones and speak familiarly about them.

The first condition is that we must fast with our whole heart, that is to say, willingly, whole-heartedly, universally and entirely. If I recount to you St. Bernard's words regarding fasting, you will know not only why it is instituted but also how it ought to be kept.

He says that fasting was instituted by Our Lord as a remedy for our mouth, for our gourmandizing and for our gluttony. Since sin entered the world through the mouth, the mouth must do penance by being deprived of foods prohibited and forbidden by the Church, abstaining from them for the space of forty days. But this glorious saint adds that, as it is not our mouth alone which has sinned, but also all our other senses, our fast must be general and entire, that is, all the members of our body must fast. For if we have offended God through the eyes, through the ears, through the tongue, and through our other senses, why should we not make them fast as well? And not only must we make the bodily senses fast, but also the soul's powers and passions—yes, even the understanding, the memory, and the will, since we have sinned through both body and spirit.

How many sins have entered into the soul through the eyes, as Holy Scripture indicates? [*1 Jn.* 2:16]. That is why they must fast by keeping them lowered and not permitting them to look upon frivolous and unlawful objects; the ears, by depriving them of listening to vain talk which serves only to fill the mind with worldly images; the tongue, in not speaking idle words and those which savor of the world or the things of the world. We ought also to cut off useless thoughts, as well as vain memories and superfluous appetites and desires of our will. In short, we ought to hold in check all those things which keep us from loving or tending to the Sovereign Good. In this way interior fasting accompanies exterior fasting.

This is what the Church wishes to signify during this holy time of Lent, teaching us to make our eyes, our ears and our tongue fast. For this reason she omits all harmonious chants in order to mortify the hearing; she no longer says *Alleluia,* and clothes herself completely in somber and dark colors. And on this first day she addresses us in these words: Remember, man, that you are dust, and to dust you shall return [*Gen.* 3:19], as if she meant to say: "Oh man, quit at this moment all joys and merrymaking, all joyful and pleasant reflections, and fill your memory with bitter, hard and sorrowful thoughts. In this way you will make your mind fast together with your body."

This is also what the Christians of the primitive Church taught us when, in order to spend Lent in a better way, they deprived themselves at this time of ordinary conversations with their friends, and withdrew into great solitude and places removed from communication with people. For the same reason, the ancient Fathers and the Christians of the year 400 or so were so careful to spend these forty days well that they were not satisfied with abstaining from prohibited meats, but even abstained from eggs, fish, milk and butter, and lived on herbs and roots alone. And not content with making their bodies fast in this manner, they made their minds and all the powers of the soul fast also. They placed sackcloth on their heads in order to learn to keep their eyes lowered. They sprinkled ashes on their heads as a sign of penitence. They withdrew into solitude to mortify the tongue and hearing, neither speaking nor hearing anything vain and useless. At that time they practiced great and austere penances by which they subjected their body and made all its members fast. They did all this with full liberty, neither forced nor constrained. Note how their fast was accomplished whole-heartedly and universally; for they understood very well that since not only the mouth has sinned, but also all the other senses of our bodies and powers of our soul, the passions and appetites are full of iniquities. It is thus reasonable that, in order to make our fast complete and meritorious, it should be universal, that is to say, practiced in both body and spirit. This is the first condition to be observed in order to fast well.

The second condition is never to fast through vanity but always through humility. If our fast is not performed with humility, it will not be pleasing to God. All our ancient Fathers have declared it so, but particularly St. Thomas, St. Ambrose and the great St. Augustine. St. Paul in the epistle that he wrote to the Corinthians [*1 Cor.* 13], which was read last Sunday, declared the conditions necessary for disposing ourselves to fast well during Lent. He says this to us: Lent is approaching. Prepare yourselves to fast with charity, for if your fast is performed without it, it will be vain and useless, since fasting, like all other good works, is not pleasing to God unless it is done in charity and through charity. When you discipline yourself, when you say long prayers, if you have not charity, all that is nothing. Even though you should work miracles, if you have not charity, they will not profit you at all. Indeed, even if you should suffer martyrdom without charity, your martyrdom is worth nothing and would not be meritorious in the eyes of the Divine Majesty. For all works, small or great, however good they may be in themselves, are of no value and profit us nothing if they are not done in charity and through charity.

I say the same now: if your fast is without humility, it is worth nothing and cannot be pleasing to the Lord. Pagan philosophers fasted thus, and their fast was not accepted by God. Sinners fast in this way, but because they do not have humility it is of no profit at all to them. Now, according to the Apostle, all that is done without charity is not pleasing to God; so I say in the same way, with this great saint, that if you fast without humility your fast is of no value. For if you have not humility, you have not charity, and if you are without charity you are also without humility. It is almost impossible to have charity without being humble and to be humble without having charity. These two virtues have such an affinity with one another that the one can never be without the other.[1]

But what is it to fast through humility? It is never to fast through vanity. Now how can one fast through vanity? According to Scripture there are hundreds and hundreds of ways, but I will content myself with telling you one of them, for it is not necessary to burden your memory with many things. To fast through vanity is to fast through self-will, since this self-will is not without vanity, or at least not without a temptation to vanity. And what does it mean to fast through self-will? It is to fast as one wishes and not as others wish; to fast in the manner which pleases us, and not as we are ordered

or counseled. You will find some who wish to fast more
than is necessary, and others who do not wish to fast as
much as is necessary. What causes that except vanity and
self-will? All that proceeds from ourselves seems better to
us, and is much more pleasant and easy for us than what
is enjoined on us by another, even though the latter is more
useful and proper for our perfection. This is natural to us
and is born from the great love we have for ourselves.

Let each one of us examine our conscience and we will
find that all that comes from ourselves, from our own judgment, choice and election, is esteemed and loved far better
than that which comes from another. We take a certain complacency in it that makes the most arduous and difficult things
easy for us, and this complacency is almost always vanity.
You will find those who wish to fast every Saturday of the
year, but not during Lent.² They wish to fast in honor of
Our Lady and not in honor of Our Lord. As if Our Lord
and Our Lady did not consider the honor given to the one
as given to the other, and as if in honoring the Son by fasting
done for His intention, one did not please the Mother, or
that in honoring the Virgin one did not please the Saviour!
What folly! But see how human it is: because the fast that
these persons impose on themselves on Saturday in honor
of our glorious Mistress comes from their own will and choice,
it seems to them that it should be more holy and that it
should bring them to a much greater perfection than the fast
of Lent, which is commanded. Such people do not fast as
they ought but as they want.

There are others who desire to fast more than they should,
and with these one has more trouble than with the first group.
On this matter the great Apostle complains [*Rom.* 14:1-6],
saying that we find ourselves confronted by two groups of
people. Some do not wish to fast as much as they ought,
and cannot be satisfied with the food permitted (this is what
many worldly people still do today who allege a thousand
reasons on this subject; but I am not here to speak of such
things, for it is to religious I am addressing myself). The

others, says St. Paul, wish to fast more than is necessary. It is with these that we have more trouble. We can easily and clearly show the first that they contravene the law of God, and that in not fasting as much as they should, while able to do it, they transgress the commandments of the Lord. But we have more difficulty with the weak and infirm who are not strong enough for fasting. They will not listen to reason, nor can they be persuaded that they are not bound by it [the law of fasting], and despite all our reasons they insist on fasting more than is required, not wishing to use the food we order them. These people do not fast through humility, but through vanity. They do not recognize that, being weak and infirm, they would do much more for God in not fasting through the command of another and using the food ordered them, than in wishing to abstain through self-will. For although, on account of their weakness, their mouth cannot abstain, they should make the other senses of the body fast, as well as the passions and powers of the soul.

You are not, says Our Lord, to look gloomy and melancholic like the hypocrites do when they fast in order to be praised by men and esteemed as great abstainers.[3] [*Matt.* 6:16-18]. But let your fasting be done in secret; therefore, wash your face, anoint your head, and your heavenly Father who sees what is hidden in your heart will reward you well. Our Divine Master did not mean by this that we ought to have no care about the edification of the neighbor. Oh, no, for St. Paul says [*Phil.* 4:5]: Let your modesty be known to all. Those who fast during the holy season of Lent ought not to conceal it, since the Church orders this fast and wishes that everyone should know that we are observing it. We must not, then, deny this to those who expect it of us for their edification, since we are obliged to remove every cause of scandal to our brothers. But when Our Lord said: Fast in secret, He wanted us to understand: do not do it to be seen or esteemed by creatures; do not do your works for the eyes of men. Be careful to edify them well, but not in order that they might esteem you as holy and virtuous. Do not be like the hypocrites. Do not try to appear better than others in practicing more fasting and penances than they.

The glorious St. Augustine, in the Rule that he wrote for his religious (later adapted for men religious), orders that one follow the community as much as possible, as if he wished to say: Do not be more virtuous than the others; do not wish to practice more fasting, more austerities, more mortifications than are ordered for you. Do only what the others do and what is commanded by your Rule, according to the manner of living that you follow, and be content with that. For although fasting and other penances are good and laudable, nevertheless, if they are not practiced by those with whom you live, you will stand out and there will be some vanity, or at least some temptation to esteem yourself above others. Since they do not do as you do, you experience some vain complacency, as if you were more holy than they in doing such things.

Follow the community then in all things, said the great St. Augustine. Let the strong and robust eat what is ordered them, keeping the fast and austerities which are marked, and let them be content with that. Let the weak and infirm receive what is offered them for their infirmity, without wishing to do what the robust do. Let neither group amuse themselves in looking to see what this one eats and what that one does not eat, but let each one remain satisfied with what she has and with what is given to her. By this means you will avoid vanity and being particular.[4]

Let no one introduce examples here to prove that there is not so much wrong, after all, in not following the common life. Do not tell me, for instance, that St. Paul the first hermit lived for ninety years in a grotto without hearing Holy Mass, and therefore that instead of going to the Office I must remain retired and in solitude in my room in order to have ecstasies and ravishments there. Oh! do not cite that to me, for what St. Paul did was done through a particular inspiration which God desires to be admired but not imitated by all. God inspired him to go to this very extraordinary retreat in order that deserts might become better esteemed, for at that time they were uninhabited.[5] Later they became inhabited by many holy Fathers. It was not, however, so that everyone should actually follow St. Paul's example. Rather, it was that he might be a mirror and marvel of virtues, worthy to be admired but not imitated by all. Do not bring up the example of St. Simon Stylites either. He remained forty-four years on a column, making two hundred acts of adoration each day while genuflecting. Like St. Paul, he acted in this manner by a very special inspiration. God wished to show in this a miracle of holiness, how we are called to, and can lead in this world, a life all heavenly and angelic.

Let us, then, admire all these things, but do not tell me that it would be better to retire apart in imitation of these great saints and not mingle with others or do what they do, but to give oneself up to great penances. Oh, no, says St. Augustine, do not appear more virtuous than others. Be content to do what they do. Accomplish your good works in secret and not for the eyes of others. Do not act like the spider, who represents the proud; but imitate the bee, who is the symbol of the humble soul. The spider spins its web where everyone can see it, and never in secret. It spins in orchards, going from tree to tree, in houses, on windows, on floors—in short, before the eyes of all. In this it resembles the vain and hypocritical who do everything to be seen and admired by others. Their works are in fact only spiders' webs, fit to be cast into the fires of Hell. But the bees are wiser and more prudent, for they prepare their honey in the hive where no one can see them. Besides that, they build little cells where they continue their work in secret. This represents very well the humble soul, who is always withdrawn within herself, without seeking any glory or praise for her actions. Rather, she keeps her intention hidden, being content that God sees and knows what she does.

I will give you an example of this, but familiarly, for this is how I wish to deal with you. It is concerning St. Pachomius, that illustrious Father of religious, about whom I have often spoken to you. He was walking one day with some of those good Fathers of the desert, conversing on pious and devout subjects. For, you see, these great saints never spoke of vain and useless things. All their conversation was about good things. Now, during this conference one of the religious, who had made two mats in one day, came to stretch them out in the sun in the presence of all of these Fathers. They all saw him, but not one of them wondered why he did it, for they were not accustomed to pry into the actions of others. They believed that their Brother did this quite simply and so they drew no conclusion from it. They did not censure the action of the other. They were not like those who always sift the actions of the neighbor, composing books, commentaries and interpretations on all they see.

These good religious thought nothing, then, about the one who stretched out his two mats. But St. Pachomius, who was his superior and to whom alone belonged the duty to examine the intention that motivated him, began to consider this action a little. And as God always gives His light to those who serve Him, He made known to the saint that this Brother was led by a spirit of vanity and complacency over his two mats, and that he had done this in order that he and all the Fathers might see how much he had labored that day.

You see, these ancient religious gained their livelihood by the labor of their hands. They were employed not at what they wished or liked, but rather at what they had been ordered. They exercised their bodies by manual labor and their minds by prayer and meditation, thus joining action to contemplation. Now, their most ordinary occupation was the weaving of mats. Everyone was obliged to make one a day. The Brother of whom we are speaking, having made two of them, thought for that reason that he was better than the others. That is why he came to stretch them in the sun before everyone, so that they would know it. But St. Pachomius, who had the spirit of God, made him throw them into the fire, and asked all the religious to pray for him who had labored for Hell. Then he had him put in prison for five months as a penance for his fault, in order to serve as an example to the others and to teach them to perform their tasks with humility.

Do not allow your fast to resemble that of hypocrites, who wear melancholy faces and who consider holy only those who are emaciated. What folly! As if holiness consisted in being thin! Certainly St. Thomas Aquinas was not thin; he was very stout. And yet he was holy. In the same way there are many others who, though not thin, nevertheless fail not to be very austere and excellent servants of God. But the world, which regards only the exterior, considers only those holy who are pale and wasted. Consider a little this human spirit: it takes account only of appearances and, being vain, does its works to be seen by others. Our Lord tells you not to do as they do but to let your fast be done in secret, only for the eyes of your heavenly Father, and He will see you and reward you.

The third condition necessary for fasting well is to look to God and to do everything to please Him, withdrawing within ourselves in imitation of a great saint, St. Gregory the Great, who withdrew into a secret and out-of-the-way place where he remained for some time without anyone knowing where he was, being content that the Lord and His angels knew it.

Although everyone ought to seek to please God alone, religious and persons who are dedicated to Him ought to take particular care to do this, seeing only Him, and being satisfied that He alone sees their works, content to await their reward only from Him. This is what Cassian, that great Father of the spiritual life, teaches us so well in the book of his admirable Conferences. (Many saints held it in such esteem that they never went to bed without reading a chapter from it to recollect their mind in God.) He says: What will it profit you to do what you are doing for the eyes of creatures? Nothing but vanity and complacency, which are good for Hell alone. But if you keep your fast and do all your works to please God alone, you will labor for eternity, without delighting in yourself or caring whether you are seen by others or not, since what you do is not done for them, nor do you await your recompense from them. We must keep our fast with humility and truth, and not with lying and hypocrisy—that is, we must fast for God and to please Him alone.

We must not make use of much learned discussion and discernment to understand why the fast is commanded, whether it is for all or only for some. Everyone knows that it is ordered in expiation for the sin of our first father, Adam, who sinned in breaking the fast which was enjoined upon him by the prohibition to eat of the fruit of the tree of knowledge. For this our mouth must do penance by abstaining from prohibited foods. Many have difficulties on this subject. But I am not here to address them, still less to say who are obliged to fast. Oh, no! for no one is ignorant that children are not bound to fast, nor are persons sixty years of age.

Let us rather continue, and see by way of three examples how dangerous a thing it is to wish to make deliberations of all sorts on the commandments of God or of our superiors. Two are drawn from Holy Scripture and the other from the Life of St. Pachomius. The first is that of Adam, who received from God the commandment not to eat the forbidden fruit under pain of losing life itself. The serpent came and advised Eve to break this commandment. She listened to him and prevailed over her husband. They discussed the prohibition which was made to them, saying: "Indeed! even though God has threatened us with death, we shall surely not die, for He has not created us to die." They ate it, and died a spiritual death.[6] [*Gen.* 3:1-6].

The second example is that of certain of Our Lord's disciples who, when they heard Him speak of giving them His flesh and His blood as food and drink, scrutinized and wondered, and questioned how anyone could eat the flesh and drink the blood of a man. But since they desired to deliberate so much about it, our Divine Master rejected them. [*Jn.* 6:61-67].

The third example is drawn from the Life of St. Pachomius. When leaving his monastery one day for some affair that he had in the great abbey of his order, where three thousand monks lived, he recommended that his Brothers take special care of several young religious who had come to him under a particular inspiration. As the holiness of these desert Fathers spread, poor young children would come and beg the saint to receive them into this life. Knowing they were sent by God, he received them and gave them very special care. That is why when he was leaving he very carefully recommended that they should take recreation and eat cooked herbs. Think of all the attention that was given to these children! But once the holy Father had left, the old religious, pretending to be more austere, no longer wished to eat cooked herbs, but were satisfied rather with eating raw ones. Seeing this, those who prepared them thought it would be a waste of time to cook them, since no one took them but these children.

Now, when St. Pachomius returned, they came out like bees running before him. Some kissed his hand and some his robe, welcoming their dear Father. Finally, one young religious came and said to him: "Oh, my Father, how I longed for your return, for we have not eaten cooked herbs since you left!" Hearing this, St. Pachomius was very much touched, and called for the cook. He asked him why he had not cooked the herbs. The latter answered that it was because no one except the children would eat them, and that he thought it a waste of time. But he insisted that he had not taken any rest either. Rather, he had made mats.

Hearing this, the holy Father gave him a good correction in the presence of everyone. Then he commanded that all his mats be cast into the fire, saying that it was necessary to burn all that was done without obedience. "For," he added, "I knew well what was proper for these children, that they must not be treated like older ones, and yet you wanted, against obedience, to make these kinds of deliberations." This is how those who forget the orders and commandments of God and who make their own interpretations, or who wish to reason about the things commanded, place themselves in peril of death. For all their labor, accomplished according to their own will or human discretion, is worthy of the fire. This is all that I had to tell you regarding fasting and what must be observed in order to fast well. The first thing is that your fast should be entire and universal; that is, that you should make all the members of your body and the powers of your soul fast: keeping your eyes lowered, or at least lower than ordinarily; keeping better silence, or at least keeping it more punctually than is usual; mortifying the hearing and the tongue so that you will no longer hear or speak of anything vain or useless; the understanding, in order to consider only holy and pious subjects; the memory, in filling it with the remembrance of bitter and sorrowful things and avoiding joyous and gracious thoughts; keeping your will in check and your spirit at the foot of the crucifix with some holy and sorrowful thought. If you do that, your fast will be universal, interior and exterior, for you will mortify both your body and your spirit. The second condition is that you do not observe your fast or perform your works for the eyes of others. And the third is that you do all your actions, and consequently your fasting, to please God alone, to whom be honor and glory forever and ever.

In the name of the Father, and of the Son, and of the Holy Spirit. Amen.

NOTES

1. Cf. *The Spiritual Conferences of St. Francis de Sales* (Westminster, Md.: Newman Press, 1962), Conference VIII, "On Self-Renouncement," p. 136; *Sermons of St. Francis de Sales on Our Lady,* Vol. II of this series (TAN Books, 1985), "The Annunciation," Mar. 25, 1621, p. 147.

2. Cf. St. Francis de Sales, *Treatise on the Love of God* (Rockford, Ill.: TAN Books and Publishers, Inc., 1975), Book X, chap. 9; *Sermons on Our Lady,* "The Purification," Feb. 2, 1622, p. 184.

3. Cf. p. 2 of this sermon.

4. Cf. *Spiritual Conferences* I, pp. 12-13.

5. St. Francis de Sales is speaking of the early stages of monastic life, centered in the desert, and of the special people who, under inspiration from God, were instrumental in establishing this form of religious life.

6. Cf. *Sermons on Our Lady,* "The Purification," Feb. 2, 1622, pp. 179-181.

— 2 —

TEMPTATION

Sermon for the First Sunday of Lent, February 13, 1622, concerning the universality of temptation, the spiritual danger of idleness, faith as a prime weapon against temptation, slothful souls, presumptuous reliance of beginners on the strength from their sensible fervor, attachment to the consolations of God, Our Lord's example in undergoing temptation from the devil, battling one's faults with patience and perseverance, vain hopes which distract the soul from practicing solid virtue, the folly of avariciously chasing after a multiplicity of devotions, and vain complacency in God's consolations.

> *"My son, when you come to serve God, prepare your soul for temptation."*
> —Ecclus. (Sirach) 2:1

This is an admonition of the Sage: "My son, if you intend to serve God, prepare your soul for temptation," for it is an infallible truth that no one is exempt from temptation when he has truly resolved to serve God. This being the case, Our Lord Himself chose to be subjected to temptation in order to show us how we ought to resist it. Thus the Evangelists tell us: He was led into the desert by the Spirit to be tempted. [*Matt.* 4:1; *Mk.* 1:12; *Lk.* 4:1]. I shall draw lessons from this mystery for our particular instruction, in as familiar a manner as I am able.

In the first place, I note that although no one can be exempt from temptation, still no one should seek it or go of his own accord to the place where it may be found, for undoubtedly he who loves it will perish in it. [*Ecclus. (Sirach)* 3:27]. That is why the Evangelist says that Our Lord was led into the desert by the Spirit to be tempted; it was not then by His choice (I am speaking with regard to His human nature) that He went to the place of temptation, but He was led by the obedience He owed to His heavenly Father.

I find in Holy Scripture two young princes who furnish us with examples on this subject. One sought temptation and perished in it. The other, without seeking it, encountered it but left the combat victorious.

At the time when kings should go to war, as his own army faced the enemy, David strolled about on the roof of the king's house, idling his time away as though he had nothing to do. Being idle in this way, he was overcome by temptation. Bethsabee, that inconsiderate lady, went to bathe in a place where she could be seen from the roof of the king's house. Certainly, this was an act of unparalleled imprudence which I cannot excuse, even though several modern writers wish to render it excusable by saying that she did not think of that. To bathe in a place where she exposed herself to view from the roof of the royal palace was a very great indiscretion. Whether she thought of it or not, young Prince David began by allowing himself to gaze on her, and then perished in the temptation which he had sought by his idleness and sloth. [*2 Kgs. (2 Sam.)* 11:1-4]. You see, idleness is a great help to temptation. Never say: "I do not seek it; I am not doing anything." That is enough in order to be tempted, for temptation has a tremendous power over us when it finds us idle. Oh, if David had gone out on campaign at the time that he should have gone, or if he had been engaged in something good, the temptation would not have had the power of attacking him, or at least of overcoming and vanquishing him.

In contrast, young Prince Joseph, who was later viceroy of Egypt, did not seek temptation at all, and so upon meeting it he did not perish in it. He had been sold by his brothers [*Gen.* 37:28], and his master's wife exposed him to danger.

But he had never indulged or heeded the amorous glances
of his mistress; rather, he nobly resisted her advances and
was victorious, thus triumphing not only over the temptation
but also over her who had been the cause of it. [*Gen.* 39:7-12].
If we are led by the Spirit of God to the place of temptation, we should not fear, but should be assured that He will
render us victorious.[1] [*1 Cor.* 10:13]. But we must not seek
temptation nor go out to allure it, however holy and generous
we may think ourselves to be, for we are not more valiant
than David, nor than our Divine Master Himself, who did
not choose to seek it. Our enemy is like a chained dog; if
we do not approach, it will do us no harm, even though
it tries to frighten us by barking at us.

But wait a little, I pray you, and see how certain it is that
no one who comes to serve God can avoid temptations. We
could give many examples of this but one or two will suffice.
Ananias and Saphira made a vow to dedicate themselves and
their possessions to the perfection which all the first Christians professed, submitting themselves to obedience to the
Apostles. They had no sooner made their resolution than temptation attacked them, as St. Peter said: Who has tempted
you to lie to the Holy Spirit? [*Acts.* 5:1-3]. The great Apostle
St. Paul, as soon as he had given himself to the divine service and ranged himself on the side of Christianity, was immediately tempted for the rest of his life. [*2 Cor.* 12:7]. While
he was an enemy of God and persecuted the Christians he
did not feel the attack of any temptation, or at least he has
given us no testimony of it in his writings. But he did when
he was converted by Our Lord.

Thus, it is a very necessary practice to prepare our soul
for temptation. That is, wherever we may be and however
perfect we may be, we must rest assured that temptation will
attack us. Hence, we ought to be so disposed and to provide
ourselves with the weapons necessary to fight valiantly in
order to carry off the victory, since the crown is only for
the combatants and conquerors. [*2 Tim.* 2:5; *Jas.* 1:12]. We
ought never to trust in our own strength or in our courage

and go out to seek temptation, thinking to confound it; but if in that place where the Spirit of God has led us we encounter it, we must remain firm in the confidence which we ought to have that He will strengthen us against the attacks of our enemy, however furious they may be.

Let us proceed and consider a little the weapons which Our Lord made use of to repulse the devil that came to tempt Him in the desert. They were none other, my dear friends, than those the Psalmist speaks of in the Psalm we recite every day at Compline: *"Qui habitat in adjutorio Altissimi"* ["Who dwells in the aid of the Most High"]. [*Ps.* 90 (91)]. From this Psalm we learn an admirable doctrine. He speaks in this manner as though addressing Christians or someone in particular: "Oh how happy you are, you who are armed with the truth of God, for it will serve you as a shield against the arrows of your enemies and will make you victorious. Therefore, do not fear, O blessed souls, you who are armed with this armor of truth. Fear neither the terrors of the night, for you will not stumble into them; nor the arrows that fly in the air by day, for arrows will not be able to injure you; nor the business that roams in the night; much less the devil that advances and reveals himself at noon."

O how divinely well armed with truth was Our Lord and Master, for He was truth itself. [*Jn.* 14:6]. This truth of which the Psalmist speaks is nothing other than faith. [*1 Thess.* 5:8]. Whoever is armed with faith need fear nothing; this is the only armor necessary to repel and confound our enemy; for what can harm him who says *Credo,* "I believe" in God, who is our Father, and our Father Almighty? In saying these words we show that we do not trust in our own strength and that it is only in the strength of God, "the Father Almighty," that we undertake the combat, that we hope for victory. [*Ps.* 17 (18):30; 43 (44):6-7; *Heb.* 11:33-34; *1 Jn.* 5:4]. No, let us not go on our own to meet temptation by any presumption of spirit, but only rebuff it when God permits it to attack us and seek us out where we are, as it did Our Lord in the desert. By using the words of Holy Scripture our dear Master overcame all the temptations the enemy presented to Him.

But I want it to be understood that the Saviour was not tempted as we are and that temptation could not be in Him as it is in us, for He was an impregnable stronghold to which it did not have access. Just as a man who is vested from head to foot in fine steel could not be injured in any way by the blows of a weapon, since it would glance off on either side, not even scratching the armor; so temptation could indeed encompass Our Lord but never enter into Him, nor do any injury to His integrity and perfect purity. But we are different. If, by the grace of God, we do not consent to temptations, and avoid the fault and the sin in them, ordinarily we are nevertheless wounded a little by some importunity, trouble, or emotion that they produce in our heart.

Our Divine Master could not have faith, since He possessed in the superior part of His soul, from the moment that He began to be, a perfect knowledge of the truths which faith teaches us; however, He wished to make use of this virtue in order to repel the enemy, for no other reason, my dear friends, than to teach all that we have to do. Do not then seek for other arms nor other weapons in order to refuse consent to a temptation except to say, "I believe." And what do you believe? "In God" my "Father Almighty."

St. Bernard, referring to these words of the Psalm which we have cited, said that the terrors of the night of which the Psalmist speaks are of three kinds. From this I will draw my third lesson. The first fear is that of cowards and slothful souls; the second, that of children; and the third, that of the weak. Fear is the first temptation which the enemy presents to those who have resolved to serve God, for as soon as they are shown what perfection requires of them they think, "Alas, I shall never be able to do it." It seems to them that it is almost an impossibility to attain to that height, and they readily say, "O God, what perfection is needed to live in this house, or in this way of life and in my vocation! It is too high for me: I cannot attain it!"[2] Do not trouble yourself and do not frame these idle fears that you are not able to accomplish that to which you have bound yourself, since you are armed and encompassed with the truth of God and with His word. Having called you to this manner of life and to this house, He will strengthen you and will give you the grace to persevere [*1 Cor.* 1:7-8; *1 Thess.* 5:24] and to do what is required for His greater glory and for your greater welfare and happiness, provided you walk simply in faithful observance.

Do not be astonished, therefore, and do not do as the slothful, who are troubled when they wake at night by the fear that daylight will come very soon when they will have to work. The slothful and cowardly fear everything and find everything difficult and trying because they amuse themselves in thinking, with the foolish and slothful imagination which they have created for themselves, more about future difficulties than what they have to do at present. "Oh," they say, "if I devote myself to the service of God, it will be necessary for me to work so much in order to resist the temptations which will attack me." You are quite right, for you will not be exempt from them, since it is a general rule that all the servants of God are tempted, as St. Jerome wrote in that beautiful epistle which he addressed to his dear daughter, Eustochium.

To whom do you wish, I pray, that the devil should present his temptations if not to those who despise them? Sinners tempt themselves; the devil already regards them as his own; they are his confederates because they do not reject his suggestions. On the contrary, they seek them and temptation resides in them. The devil does not work much to set his snares in the secular world, but rather in retired places where he expects a great gain in bringing about the downfall of souls who are secluded there serving the Divine Majesty more perfectly. St. Thomas used to marvel greatly at how the greatest sinners went out into the streets, laughing and joyful, as though their sins did not weigh on their consciences. And who would not be astonished at seeing a soul not in God's grace making merry? Oh, how vain are their joys, and how false their gaiety, for they have gone after anguish and eternal regrets! Let us leave them, I pray you, and return to the fear of the slothful. They are always lamenting—and why? Why, you ask? "Alas, we must work, and yet I thought that it would be enough to embark on God's way and in His service to find rest." But do you not know that sloth and idleness made poor David perish in temptation? You perhaps would wish to be among those garrison soldiers who have everything they wish in a good town; they are merry, they are masters of their host's home, they sleep in his bed and live well; nevertheless, they are called "soldiers," feigning to be valiant and courageous while they go neither to battle nor to war. But Our Lord does not want this kind of warrior in His army; He wants combatants and conquerors, not sluggards and cowards. He chose to be tempted, and Himself attacked in order to give us an example.

Ah, fear nothing, I pray you, since you are encompassed with the armor of truth and of faith. [*Eph.* 6:11-16]. Rise from your bed, indolent one, for it is time [Cf. *Prov.* 6:9; *Rom.* 13:11], and do not be frightened by the day's work, for it is natural that the night is given for rest and the day following for work. Rise, for mercy's sake, from your cowardice, and keep clearly before your mind this infallible truth: all must be tempted, all must keep readied for combat in order to win the victory. Since temptation has a remarkable power over us when it finds us idle, let us work and not grow weary, for we do not wish to lose the eternal rest which has been prepared for us as reward for our labors. Let us trust in God who is our "Father Almighty." By virtue of this fact all things will be rendered easy, although at first they may frighten us a little.

The second terror of the night, according to St. Bernard, is that experienced by children. As you are aware, children are very much afraid when they are out of their mother's arms. If they see a barking dog they suddenly begin to cry, and will not stop until they are again with their mamma.

In her arms they feel secure. They feel that nothing can harm them provided they are holding her hand.[3] Ah, then, the Psalmist says, why do you fear, you who are encompassed with truth and armed with the strong shield of faith which teaches you that God is your "Father Almighty"? Hold His hand and do not be frightened, for He will save you and protect you against all your enemies. Consider how St. Peter, after he made that generous act of throwing himself into the sea and began walking on the water in order more quickly to reach our Divine Saviour who had called to him, suddenly began to fear and at the same time to sink down, and cried out, "Lord, save me!" And at once his good Master stretched out His hand and took hold of him, thus saving him from drowning. [*Matt.* 14:29-31]. Let us do the same, my dear friends. If we feel that we lack courage let us cry out in a loud voice full of confidence, "Lord, save me!" Let us not doubt that God will strengthen us and prevent us from perishing.

There are some who, feigning courage, go someplace alone at night. When they hear a little stone fall from the ceiling, or just hear a mouse running, they cry out, "O my God!" We say to them, "What has happened?" "I heard something." "What?" "I do not know." We meet others who, when they go into the fields and from a distance see the shadow of trees, are very much frightened indeed, believing that it is someone waiting for them. Such great chimeras and childishness! Often persons who have just come into God's service are like these people. They affect fearlessness and seem never to feed enough on the crucifix. Nothing can satisfy them. They think of nothing but living always in tranquil rest. Nothing can overcome their courage and generosity.

This is what happened to poor St. Peter. Being but a mere child in the spiritual life, he made this act of generosity of which I just now spoke. But he made still another later on, and it cost him dearly. For when Our Lord announced to His Apostles how He was to suffer death, St. Peter, quick to speak but fainthearted and cowardly in acting, boasted:

"For my part, I will never abandon You!" [*Matt.* 26:31-35; *Mk.* 14:27-31; *Lk.* 22:33; *Jn.* 13:37]. And Our Lord went on, ". . . I shall be scourged." "And I too, for love of Thee." "I shall be crowned with thorns." "And I as well." In short, he would yield in nothing to his good Master. The more Our Lord expounded on the greatness of His afflictions, the more did St. Peter passionately insist that he would do as much. But how well he realized how completely he had been deceived when he found himself, at the time of his Saviour's Passion, so fainthearted and timid in the execution of his promises. It would have been much better for poor St. Peter to keep humble, relying on the power of Our Lord, than to trust vainly in the fervor which he felt at the time.

Thus it happens to those young souls who testify to so much ardor in their conversion. While these first sentiments of devotion last, they do wonders. It seems that in the way of perfection nothing is too difficult for them; nothing can lessen their courage. They greatly desire to be mortified, to be tested, in order to show their generosity and the fire which burns in their breast! But just wait a little. For if they hear a mouse, by which I mean if the consolation and sentiments of devotion which they have had until then happen to be withdrawn and if some little temptation attacks them, "Alas," they say, "what is it?" They begin to fear and to be troubled. Everything seems hard to them if they are not always in the Heart of their heavenly Father, if He does not give them consolations and speak sweetly to them. They simply cannot live in peace and contentment unless they receive endless consolations and no pain. "Oh, how miserable my condition is!" they say; "I am in the Lord's service where I thought I would live in peace, and yet all different sorts of temptations have come and only agitate me. My passions so annoy me that I do not have so much as an hour of real peace."

One could answer them, "My dear friends, do you really think that one never encounters temptations in solitude and retreat? Oh, how greatly mistaken you are! Our Divine Master was not attacked by the enemy while He lived among

the Pharisees and publicans but only when He retired to the
desert. There is no place where temptation does not have
access. Yes, even in heaven,[4] where it was born in the heart
of Lucifer and his angels, and at the same moment cast them
forth into damnation and perdition. The enemy brought it
to Eden, and with it made our first parents forfeit original
justice with which God had gifted them. Temptation entered
the very ranks of the Apostles themselves. Why, then, are
you astonished if it attacks you?"

Had you lived in Our Lord's time, during His mortal life,
and met His very holy Mother, our glorious Mistress, and
had she allowed you to live anywhere you wanted, you would
no doubt have questioned her in this manner: "My Lady,
where is your Son?" She would have replied, "My Son is
in the desert, where He must remain for forty days, continually fasting, watching, and praying." [*Matt.* 4:2]. "O my Lady,"
you might have answered, "I wish to live in no other place
but the desert where my Saviour is." But if the holy Virgin
asked you, "Why do you desire to dwell there?" you would
have replied, "Because where Our Lord is, all good things
abound; consolation is never lacking there and temptation
cannot find entrance."

O how completely mistaken you are! It is precisely because our Divine Saviour is there that temptation is found
there too. We might indeed have found it terribly frightening,
for the devil came there completely undisguised. He did not
act with Our Lord as he did with St. Pachomius and St.
Antony. He frightened them by hellish noise with which he
surrounded them, pretending to rend Heaven and earth before their very eyes. He did this to make them fear and tremble like children. Nevertheless, these holy Fathers fought him,
mocking him and his antics by reciting scriptural passages.
But seeing such strength, constancy, generosity, and confidence in the face of our dear Saviour, the devil thought he
would gain nothing by treating Him in this way. Therefore
he came visibly to Him, presenting his temptations with unparalleled impudence. This he did not only those three times

of which the Gospel makes mention, but at other times during those forty days that He dwelt in the desert. The Evangelists were simply content to single out these three [*Matt.* 4:3-10; *Lk.* 4:2-13] as being the greatest and most remarkable.

These young apprentices of perfection ask, "What shall I do? The passions which I thought I had mortified by my fervent resolution to follow them no more torment me greatly. Alas! it is so true that I become so disappointed that in a short time I feel there is no possibility of going on, and discouragement overcomes me." What a great pity that the desire for perfection is not itself sufficient for having it, but that it must be acquired by the sweat of our brow and hard work! Do you not realize that Our Lord willed to be tempted during the forty days He was in the desert precisely in order to teach us that we shall also be tempted during the entire time that we dwell in the desert of this mortal life, which is the place of our penance? The life of the perfect Christian is a continual penance. Console yourself, I pray, and take courage. Now is not the time for rest.

"But I am so imperfect," you say. I believe it, indeed! Therefore do not hope to be able to live without committing imperfections, seeing that this is impossible while you are in this life. It is enough that you do not love them and that they do not remain in your heart. That is, you do not commit them voluntarily and you do not want to continue in your faults.[5] That being so, remain in peace and do not trouble yourself about the perfection you so much desire. It will be enough if you have it in dying. Be not so timid! Walk confidently! If you are armed with the armor of faith, nothing can harm you.

The third terror of the night is that of the weak. These fear not only what can bring evil but what can in any way disturb or trouble their peace. They do not want any little noise whatever to come between God and them, since they have convinced themselves that there is a certain quiet and tranquillity which maintains those who have it in uninterrupted peace and happiness. Therefore, they want to enjoy

it at Our Lord's feet like Magdalen, to savor without inter-
ruption the comfort, the pleasure, and every sweetness that
falls from the sacred lips of their Master, without Martha
ever coming to rouse them or murmur against them, entreat-
ing Our Lord to make them work. [*Lk.* 10:39-40]. This
spiritual comfort makes them so able and so courageous, it
seems to them, that nothing is comparable to their perfection. Nothing is too difficult for them. In short, they would
like to melt away in order to please their Beloved, whom
they love with so perfect a love.

Yes, indeed, provided He continues with His consolations
and treats them tenderly! If He ceases to do so, all is lost:
there is no one so afflicted as they are, their misery is in-
sufferable, they never stop complaining. "O my God[6] [we
say to them], what has happened?" [They answer:] "What
is wrong? I have reason indeed to complain." "But what is
it that torments you so?" "It is because I am not holy." "You
are not holy! And who has told you that you are not? Perhaps you think you have returned to some fault again. If it
is that, do not make yourself so uneasy. Perhaps you have,
and someone has corrected you for it in order to aid you
toward perfection. You ought to know that those who have
true charity cannot endure to see any fault in their neighbor.
They try to remove it by correction, and especially in all
those whom they consider holy or very much advanced in
perfection, because they think them more apt to welcome
the correction. They also desire by this means to make them
grow more and more in self-knowledge, which is so necessary for everyone."[7]

"But that disturbs my peace." That is indeed well said!
Do you think that in this life you can have a tranquillity
so permanent as never to meet with disturbance? One must
not desire graces which God does not commonly give. What
He has done for a Magdalen, for instance, ought not to be
desired by us. Happy indeed shall we be if we have this peace
of soul at the time of death, or even only after our death![8]
Do not imagine that the Magdalen enjoyed this special

contemplation, which kept her in so sweet a peace, without first passing through thorny difficulties and severe penance and enduring the bitterness of a very great confusion. For when she went to the Pharisee's house to weep over her sins and to obtain pardon, she suffered the murmuring they uttered against her. They despised her and called her a sinner and a woman of evil life. [*Lk.* 7:37-39]. Do not imagine that you can become worthy of receiving these divine sweetnesses and consolations, of being lifted up by angels as she was several times a day, if you are not first willing to suffer together with her the confusions, contempt, and reproofs which our imperfections very much deserve and which will disturb us from time to time, whether we desire them or not. This rule is general: no one will be so holy in this life as not to be always subject to committing some imperfection or other.[9]

We must keep ourselves constant and tranquil in the knowledge of this truth if we will not be troubled with the unrealistic expectation of never committing any imperfection at all. We should have a strong and constant resolution never to be so cowardly as to commit any imperfection voluntarily. But we ought also to be unshaken in this other resolution: not to be astonished or troubled at seeing that we are subject to fall into these imperfections, even often. We must rather confide ourselves to the goodness of God who, for all that, does not love us less. "But I shall never be capable of receiving the divine caresses of Our Lord while I am so imperfect; I shall not be able to approach Him who is so sovereignly perfect." What relation, I pray you, can there be between our perfection and His, between our purity and His, since He is purity itself? In short, let us for our part do what we can and remain in peace about the rest. Whether God gives us a share in His consolations or not, we must keep ourselves submissive to His very holy will. That should be the mistress and guide of our life. After this we have nothing to desire.

The Psalmist, as interpreted by St. Bernard, assures us that he who has faith and is armed with truth will not fear these terrors of the night, nor the fears of the slothful, nor of children, much less the fears of the weak. But he goes further and says that he will no longer fear the arrow that flies by day, and this is the fourth lesson that I take from the Psalm quoted above.

These arrows are the vain hopes and expectations on which those feed who aspire to perfection. We find those who hope for nothing so much as to be Mother Teresa [of Avila] very soon, and even Sts. Catherine of Siena and Genoa.[10] That is good; but tell me, how long do you give yourself for this task? "Three months," you reply, "even less, if it is possible." You do well to add, "if it is possible," for otherwise you would be much deceived. Do not those fine hopes, notwithstanding their vanity, greatly console those who have them? But the more these hopes and expectations bring joy to the heart, while there is reason for hope, so much more does the contrary condition bring sadness to those fervent souls. Not finding themselves the saints they had hoped to be, but, on the contrary, very imperfect creatures, they are very often discouraged in the pursuit of the real virtue which leads to sanctity. "Gently," we say to them. "Do not hurry on so fast! Begin to live well, according to your vocation: sweetly, simply, and humbly. Then trust in God, who will make you holy when it pleases Him."

My dear friends, there are still other kinds of vain hopes, one of which is to desire continual consolation, sweetness, and tenderness in prayer throughout this mortal and fleeting life. This is surely a futile and foolish hope. As though our perfection and happiness depended upon that! Do you not realize that ordinarily Our Lord gives these "sweets" only to allure and gain us over, much as one does with little children in giving them sweets?[11] But let us go on, for we must finish.

In discussing what this business is which takes place in the night and of which the Psalmist speaks, St. Bernard observes that those armed with truth will not fear it. For my part (and this is the fifth lesson that I offer you), I consider that this business which takes place in darkness represents avarice and ambition, vices which traffic in the night, that is, in an underhand manner, and secretly. You see, ambitious people have no desire of being obvious in their pursuit of honors, prominence, charges or high offices. They proceed in secret, fearing to be discovered. Misers cannot sleep because they are always thinking of ways to increase their goods and fill their purses. But it is not of temporal misers that I wish to speak, but of spiritual avarice.

Regarding the spiritual danger of ambition, those who seek to be promoted to high office or authority and obtain them through their pursuit of them, or embrace them by their own choice—woe betide them, for they are seeking temptation! They will surely perish if they are not converted and, with humility, make use of that which they have embraced in the spirit of vanity. Of course, I am not speaking of those who have been raised up not by their own choice, but by their submission to the obedience they owe to God and to their superiors. They have nothing to fear any more than did Joseph in the house of Putiphar. If they are indeed in a place of temptation, they will not perish there.[12] Wherever we may be, provided we have been led there by the Holy Spirit, as Our Lord was into the desert, we shall have nothing to fear.

The spiritually avaricious are those who can never have enough of embracing and seeking after countless exercises of piety, hoping thereby to attain perfection all that much sooner, they say.[13] They do this as though perfection consisted in the multitude of things we do and not in the perfection with which we do them! I have already said this very often,[14] but it is necessary to repeat it: God has not placed perfection in the multiplicity of acts we perform to please Him, but only in the way we perform them, which is simply to do the little we do according to our vocation, in love, by love, and for love. One could well reproach these spiritually avaricious with that reproach which the prophet made to the temporally avaricious: "What do you want, poor men? You want to have this mansion now, because you say it faces yours. After that there will be another which adjoins it and because it is convenient for you, you will want that one too. This will go on and on. What! Do you want to become the sole master of the entire earth, with no one but yourself owning property?" [*Is.* 5:8].

Please consider the spiritually avaricious. They are never content with the spiritual exercises presented to them. If they think of Chartreuse, they say, "That, indeed, is a holy life, but they never preach." One must preach then. The life of the Jesuit Fathers may be filled with perfection, but they do not have the blessing of solitude from which one receives so much consolation. The Capuchins, as well as all religious orders, are very good, but they do not have everything that such people are looking for,[15] namely, the spiritual exercises of all mixed together into one. They ceaselessly struggle to find new ways of joining the sanctity of all the various saints into the one they would like to have. As a result, they are never content, since they cannot possibly embrace all they hope to. Whoever embraces too much enchains himself therein. They would always want to wear a hairshirt, take the discipline, pray continually on bare knees, live in solitude, and God knows what else! Still this would not satisfy them. You poor people! You do not want anyone to be holier than yourselves. You are not satisfied with the available sanctity, that gained not by making such a multiplicity of exercises, but by practicing well and as perfectly as possible those to which your condition and vocation oblige you. Enough cannot be said about how much this spiritual avarice impedes perfection, since it takes away the sweet and tranquil attention we ought to have in doing well what we do for God, as I have already said.

The sixth lesson is drawn from the same Psalm, where the prophet asserts that those so armed will not fear the noonday devil, that is, that spirit which comes to tempt us in broad daylight. I am very familiar with how St. Bernard explained this passage, but I wish to speak only on what is more to my purpose. This spirit which walks in broad daylight is that which attacks us in the fair noontide of interior consolations, at the time when the divine Sun of Justice [*Mal.* 4:2, Douay] so lovingly sends forth His rays upon us and fills us with so agreeable a warmth and light, a warmth which inflames us with so delightful and tender a love that we die to almost everything else so as better to enjoy our Well-Beloved. This divine light so illumines our heart that it feels itself entirely open to the Saviour's Heart, a Heart which, drop by drop, gives so sweet a liquid and so fragrant a perfume that it cannot be appreciated enough by this lover who is always languishing for His love. [*Cant.* 5:8]. She does not want anyone to come and trouble her in her repose which, in the end, terminates only in the vain complacency she takes in it. For she admires the goodness and sweetness of God, but in herself, and not in God. To her, solitude is very desirable at this time so as to enjoy the Divine Presence without any distractions. Yet she does not really desire it for the glory of God, but only for the satisfaction which she herself experiences in receiving these sweet caresses and holy delights issuing from this well-beloved Heart of the Saviour.

That is how the noonday devil deceives souls, transforming himself into an angel of light and causing them to stumble. [*2 Cor.* 11:14]. For they entertain themselves with these consolations and vain delights, in the complacency they draw from these tender feelings and spiritual delights. Yet whoever will be armed with the shield of truth and of faith will overcome these enemies as courageously as all the others, as David promises.[16] [*Ps.* 90: (91)5-6].

I doubt not that many prefer the end of today's Gospel to its beginning. It is said there that after Our Lord had overcome His enemy and rejected his temptations, angels came and brought Him heavenly 'ood. [*Matt.* 4:11]. What joy to find oneself with the Saviour at this delicious feast! My dear friends, we shall never be capable of keeping company with Him in His consolations, nor be invited to His heavenly banquet, if we are not sharers of His labors and sufferings. [*2 Cor.* 1:7]. He fasted forty days, but the angels brought Him something to eat only at the *end* of that time.

These forty days, as we said just now, symbolize the life of the Christian, of each one of us. Let us then desire these consolations only at the end of our lives, and let us busy ourselves in steadfast resistance to the frontal attacks of our enemies. For whether we desire it or not we shall be tempted. If we do not struggle, we shall not be victorious, nor shall we merit the crown of immortal glory which God has prepared for those of us who are victorious and triumphant.[17]

Let us fear neither the temptation nor the tempter, for if we make use of the shield of faith and the armor of truth, they will have no power whatsoever over us. Let us no longer fear the three terrors of the night. And let us not entertain the vain hope of being or wishing to be saints in three months! Let us also shun both spiritual avarice and the ambition which occasion so much disorder in our hearts and so greatly impede our perfection. The noonday devil will be powerless in causing us to fail in our firm and steadfast resolution to serve God generously and as perfectly as possible in this life, so that after this life we shall go to enjoy Him forever. May He be blessed! Amen.

NOTES

1. Cf. *Spiritual Conferences,* Conference XII, "Simplicity and Religious Prudence," p. 218.
2. Cf. *Spiritual Conferences,* V, "Generosity," pp. 82-83.
3. Cf. *Introduction to a Devout Life,* by St. Francis de Sales, Part IV, chap. 7; *Spiritual Conferences,* II, "Confidence," pp. 25-26; *Spiritual Conferences,* XII, "Simplicity and Religious Prudence," p. 227.
4. The "heaven" where Lucifer sinned was not the Heaven of glory and Beatific Vision, but was rather the abode of the spirit world during the period of probation; for no sin is possible in the land of the blessed. Elsewhere St. Francis de Sales assures us (cf. pp. 127-128, 152 and 184) that in Heaven we shall possess eternal glory securely, with no possibility or fear of falling through sin.
5. Cf. *Introduction to a Devout Life,* Part I, chap. 22; *Spiritual Conferences,* IX, "Religious Modesty," p. 162.
6. The expressions "O my God" and "O God" are very characteristic

of St. Francis de Sales, who lived and spoke in the presence of God.

7. St. Francis de Sales, knowing so well the temptations that attack beginners in the spiritual life, makes use of examples to warn the Sisters of some of the pitfalls of novices. Like any good preacher, he is trying to reach the real people who are before him.

8. Cf. *Spiritual Conferences,* XX, "Why We Should Become Religious," p. 393; *Sermons of St. Francis de Sales on Our Lady,* "The Purification," February 2, 1620, pp. 96-97.

9. St. Francis de Sales is familiar with the Council of Trent's teaching to the effect that because of the perduring consequences of the Fall, no Christian can go for long without sinning, at least venially, without a special grace from God.

10. Cf. *Spiritual Conferences,* IX, "Religious Modesty," p. 146.

11. Cf. *Introduction to a Devout Life,* Part IV, chap. 13.

12. Cf. pp. 16-17 of this sermon.

13. Cf. *Spiritual Conferences,* XII, "Simplicity and Religious Prudence," p. 214.

14. Cf. *Spiritual Conferences,* XIII, "The Spirit of the Rules," p. 247.

15. Cf. *Spiritual Conferences,* XIII, "The Spirit of the Rules," p. 237-239.

16. St. Francis is here criticizing those who in prayer are solely interested in the consolations of God, not in the will and glory of God who consoles.

17. Cf. p. 17 of this sermon.

— 3 —

FAITH

Sermon for Thursday after the First Sunday of Lent, February 17, 1622, concerning faith as the adhesion of the understanding to the truths revealed by God or the Church, living faith which produces the fruit of good works vs. dead or dying faith, vigilant, penetrating faith vs. dormant faith, the supernatural prudence which accompanies vigilant faith, attentive faith, confidence in prayer, perseverance in prayer, patience in prayer, and humility in prayer.

> *"Woman, how great is your faith. Let it be done as you desire."—Matt.* 15:28

On this day preachers praise the virtues of the Canaanite woman in various ways. For myself, I will treat of faith, showing you what it is. I will attempt to show the relationship between what I have to say to you with what occurred in the Gospel between Our Lord and the Canaanite woman. [*Matt.* 15:21-28]. In this way you will learn the qualities that faith should have.

When the Saviour said: Woman, how great is your faith, was it because this woman's faith was greater than ours? Certainly not as regards its object, because faith has for its object the truths revealed by God or the Church, and it is nothing else but an adhesion of our understanding to these truths which it finds both beautiful and good. Consequently, it comes to believe them, and the will comes to love them. For just as goodness is the object of the will, beauty is that of the understanding. In our day-to-day life, goodness is coveted through

34

our sense appetite and beauty is loved through our eyes. In our spiritual life, it happens in the same way in regard to the truths of faith. These truths are good, sweet and true, and are not only loved and desired by the will, but are also valued by the understanding because of the beauty it finds in them. They are beautiful because they are true; for beauty is never without truth, nor truth without beauty. Moreover, beautiful things which are not true are not really beautiful either. They are false and deceitful.

Now the truths of faith, being true indeed, are loved because of the beauty of this truth, which is the object of the understanding. I say loved, for although the will has goodness for the direct object of its love, nevertheless when the beauty of revealed truths is represented to it by the understanding, it also discovers goodness there, and loves this goodness and beauty of the mysteries of our faith.[1] In order to have great faith, the understanding must perceive the beauty of this faith. For this reason when Our Lord desires to draw some creature to knowledge of the truth [*1 Tim.* 2:4] He always reveals its beauty to him. The understanding, feeling itself drawn or captivated by it, communicates this truth to the will, which accordingly loves it for the goodness and beauty it recognizes there. Finally, the love that these two powers have for revealed truths prompts the person to forsake everything in order to believe them and embrace them. This is done spiritually. All this helps to explain how faith can be said to be nothing else but an adhesion of the understanding and will to divine truths.

With reference to its object, faith cannot be greater for some truths than for others. Nor can it be less with regard to the number of truths to be believed. For we must all believe the very same thing, both as to the object of faith as well as to the number of truths. All are equal in this, because everyone must believe all the truths of faith—both those which God Himself has directly revealed, as well as those He has revealed through His Church. Thus, I must believe as much as you and you as much as I, and all other Christians similarly.

He who does not believe all these mysteries is not Catholic and therefore will never enter Paradise. Thus, when Our Lord said: Oh woman, how great is your faith, it was not because the Canaanite woman believed more than we believe. It was, rather, that many things made her faith more excellent.

It is true that there is only one faith [*Eph.* 4:5] which all Christians must have. Nevertheless, not everyone has it in the same degree of perfection. To appreciate how the same faith can be more or less excellent, we speak of the conditions which enhance it and of the virtues which accompany it. To make all this clearly understood we must develop it slowly.

Faith is the basis and foundation of all the other virtues, but particularly of hope and of charity. Now what I say of charity applies also to all the many virtues associated with it. When charity is united and joined to faith, it vivifies it. And so it follows that there is a dead faith and a dying faith. Dead faith is faith separated from charity, a separation which prevents us from performing works conformable to the faith we profess. This dead faith is that which many Christians— the worldly—have. Indeed, they believe all the mysteries of our holy Religion, but since their faith is not accompanied by charity, they perform no good works which conform to their faith. Dying faith is that which is not entirely separated from charity. It performs some good works, although rarely and feebly, for charity cannot really be in the soul which has faith without performing works either little or great. It must either produce or perish, because it cannot exist without doing good works.[2]

Just as the soul cannot remain in the body without producing vital actions, so charity cannot be united to our faith without performing works conforming to it. [*Gal.* 5:6; *Jas.* 2:14-26]. It cannot be otherwise. Therefore, do you want to know if your faith is dead or dying? Examine your works and actions. The same happens with faith as with a person who is about to die. When he suffers a sudden weak spell or it appears he has expired, we place a feather on his lips and our hand on his heart. If the soul is still there, we feel his heart beating. From the movement of the feather over his mouth we see that he is still breathing. From all this we conclude with certainty that although this person may be dying, he is nevertheless not yet dead. Since his vital actions are functioning, the soul must of necessity still be united to his body. But when we notice that he no longer gives signs of life, then we conclude that evidently the soul has separated from the body and therefore this person is dead.

Dead faith resembles a dry tree that has no living substance at all. In springtime when other trees bud forth leaves and flowers, this one brings forth nothing, because it does not have sap, which those have that are not dead but only dormant. Now, here is another point. However much all other trees may look like this dead tree in winter, nevertheless, in their season they produce leaves, flowers and fruits. This never happens with the tree that is really dead.[3] It may look like the other trees, to be sure, but it is dead, for it never brings forth either flowers or fruit. Similarly, dead faith may indeed appear to be living faith, but with this important difference: it bears neither the flowers nor the fruit of good works, while living faith always bears them, and in all seasons.

It works the same way with faith as with charity. We know by the works which charity performs whether faith is dead or dying. When it produces no good works we conclude that it is dead, and when they are few and sluggish, that it is dying. But just as there is a dead faith, there must also be a living one which is its opposite. It is excellent. Joined and united with charity and vivified by it, it is strong, firm and constant. It performs many great and good works which deserve the praise: Oh, how great is your faith! Let all that you desire be done.

Now when we say that this faith is great, we certainly do not imply that it is something like fourteen or fifteen units long. We must not understand it that way at all. It is great because of the good works it performs and also because of the many virtues which accompany it, and which it governs, acting like a queen who labors for the defense and preservation of divine truths.[4] That these virtues obey her demonstrates her excellence and greatness—just as kings are not great only when they have many provinces and numerous subjects, but when, together with this, they have subjects who love them and are submissive to them. But if, despite all their wealth, their vassals pay no attention to their orders nor to their laws, we would not say that they are great kings, but rather very petty ones. So charity united to faith is not only followed by all the virtues, but as a queen she commands them, and all obey and fight for her and according to her will. From this results the multitude of good works of a living faith.

There is a vigilant faith which, again, depends on its union with charity. But there is also one which is sluggish, dull and apathetic, and it is the opposite of vigilant faith. It is lax in applying itself to the consideration of the mysteries of our Religion. It is completely torpid, and for this reason it does not penetrate revealed truths at all. It sees them, to be sure, and knows them, because its eyes are not altogether closed. It is not asleep, but it is drowsy or dozing. It resembles weary people who, although their eyes are open, see almost nothing, and although they hear talking, they neither know nor understand what is said. Why? Because they are quite overcome with sleepiness.

Thus, this dormant faith has its eyes open, for it believes the mysteries. It hears sufficiently what has been stated about them. But it is with—how shall I put it—a heaviness and dullness which hinders its understanding of them. Persons who have a dull and dreamy mind have their eyes open, appear very thoughtful and, it seems, attentive, but they are really oblivious to what is going on. It is the same with those whose faith is dormant: they believe all the mysteries in general, but ask them what they understand about them and they know nothing. This dormant faith is in great danger of being attacked and seduced by many enemies and even of falling over dangerous precipices.

But vigilant faith not only performs good works like living faith, it also penetrates and understands revealed truths quickly and with great depth and subtlety of perception. It is active and diligent in seeking and embracing those things which can increase and strengthen it. It watches and perceives from afar all its enemies. It is always on the alert to discover the good and to avoid evil. It guards itself against anything which could ruin it. Vigilant, it walks firmly, and easily keeps from falling over precipices.

This vigilant faith is accompanied by the four cardinal virtues: fortitude, prudence, justice and temperance. It uses them as an armored breastplate to put its enemies to flight, or to remain among them firm, invincible and unshaken. So great is its strength that it fears nothing, because not only is it strong, but also it is aware of its strength and by whom it is supported—Truth itself. Now there is nothing stronger than truth [*3 Esd.* 4:35][5], in which consists the valor of faith.[6] Men indeed have this strength. They have power and mastery over all animals. Yet because we do not always realize that this is in us, we often fear like weaklings and cowards, stupidly taking flight before the beasts. The strength of faith, on the contrary, consists partly in knowing its power. Therefore, it uses it on occasions and puts all its enemies to flight.

Faith employs prudence to acquire whatever can strengthen and increase it. It is not satisfied with believing all the truths necessary for salvation as these are revealed by God and made known by the Church. It is ever on the watch to discover new ones and, further, to so penetrate them as to draw from them the pith and substance by which it is supported, delighted, enriched and increased. Now, this prudence is not the same as that of many worldlings, who are very careful to amass wealth and honors and other such rubbish which enrich them and raise them in the eyes of men, but profit them nothing for eternal life. What false prudence that is! Even if it were to help me to gain towns, principalities and kingdoms, what would that profit me if despite all that I am damned? [cf. *Matt.* 16:26]. Of what use will my valor be if I use it only to acquire the transitory things of this mortal life? Certainly, even if I were the strongest and most prudent man in the world, and did not use this valor and prudence for eternal life, it would amount to nothing.

Despite that, there is no end to human prudence! It manifests itself in a thousand, thousand ways. And we certainly know that most of our evils come only from this false prudence. But for now let us speak only of that prudence which concerns faith.

The majority of Christians have the faith we must have, believing all that we must believe. Few things are really necessary for salvation: believe all the mysteries of our Religion and keep the commandments of God. [*Matt.* 19:16-17; *Mk.* 16:16; *Heb.* 11:6]. The prudence of worldlings is satisfied with this and wants to do no more than what is absolutely necessary for eternal life, and to flee only what can cause their damnation. You do not work for God, then, but only for yourselves in this, since your prudence extends no further than to doing what you know will keep you from being lost. You do not belong to those vigilant servants [*Lk.* 12:37] who always have their eyes on the hands of their masters [*Ps.* 122 (123):2], and who are extremely careful and attentive to do all that they know will render their services more pleasing to Him. By this they show clearly that they are not working for themselves, but rather for the love they have for their Master. They employ all their prudence not only to fulfill their duty towards Him, but also to do all that they discover is pleasing to Him. These are the faithful servants. [*Matt.* 25:21, 23]. Thus, they will have eternal life and, more, great glory and sweetness in the presence and enjoyment of the Divine Majesty.

There are many, writes St. Bernard,[7] who say: "I keep God's commandments." Very well, you will be saved; that is your reward. "I am not a thief." You will not be hanged. That is your reward. "I have not committed murder." You will not be executed. That is your reward. "I have dishonored no one." You will not be dishonored. That is your reward. "I do what I know is necessary in order to be saved." Very well, you will have eternal life. That is your reward. But in all this you will be deemed to be only a worthless servant. [*Matt.* 25:30]. Vigilant faith never acts in this way. It serves God not as a mercenary servant, but as a faithful one, employing all its fortitude, prudence, justice and temperance to do all that it knows and recognizes to be pleasing to our Lord and Master. It not only observes what is necessary for salvation, but it seeks out, embraces and practices faithfully everything that can bring it closer to its God.

To be attentive is the fifth quality of faith. Attentive faith is very great and excellent. In addition to being living and vigilant, it attains the highest point of perfection through this attentiveness. It is this faith that the Canaanite woman had. Let us reflect a bit on how the faith of this woman is great precisely because of its attentiveness.

While crossing the district and frontiers of Tyre and Sidon, Our Lord wanted to do so secretly so as not to manifest His glory. He considered retiring into a house so that He might not be seen or noticed. His popularity was increasing daily and He was followed by a great number of people who were attracted by His miracles and wonderful works. Wanting to hide Himself, He entered into one of the nearby houses. But notice this pagan woman standing among His listeners, carefully observing to see when the Saviour, about whom she had heard so many wonderful things, would pass by. She was as attentive as a dog carefully watching its prey, lest it escape. It is in this fashion that we can interpret the words of St. Mark the Evangelist. [*Mk.* 7:24-29].

When Our Lord passed by, or when He approached, or when He had entered into the house, or again, when He was leaving (this is a debated question, but I do not wish to enter into it here; as for me, I believe that this took place when He was in this house), the Canaanite woman, who had been watching to seize her prey, came to present her request to Him, crying out: Lord, Son of David, have pity on me! My daughter is cruelly troubled by the devil.

Reflect a bit on this woman's great faith. She asks our divine Master only that He have pity on her, and believes that if He does have pity, that will be sufficient to cure and deliver her daughter who was troubled by the evil spirit. Her faith would not have been so great had she not been so attentive to what she had heard spoken about Our Lord and to what she had concluded about Him. Those who followed Him or who lived in the houses near the one to which He had retired, had indeed seen and heard about the wonders and miracles He had performed, by which He confirmed the doctrine He taught. They had as much faith as the Canaanite woman, for a great part of them believed what was said of Him. But their faith was not as great as this woman's because it was not as attentive as hers.

We normally observe this among the ordinary people of the world. In a gathering where good, holy and lofty subjects are being discussed, an avaricious man will indeed hear what is said, but when it is over just ask him the subject of this conversation, and he will not be able to relate a word of it. Why? Because he was not attentive to what was said, his attention was on his treasure. The same is true of the sensuous, pleasure-loving man. Although he appears to be listening to the topic of conversation, nevertheless he remembers nothing about it because he is more attentive to his pleasure than to what is being discussed. But if someone is there who gives all his attention, and listens to what is said, oh, he indeed will relate very well what he has heard.

Why do we see so little profit derived from sermons or from the mysteries that have been explained or taught to us, or from those upon which we have meditated? It is because the faith with which we hear them or meditate upon them is not attentive. And so, we believe them indeed, but not with very great conviction. The faith of the Canaanite woman was not like that at all. Oh woman! how great is your faith, not only because of the attentiveness with which you hear and believe what they say of Our Lord, but also because of the attentiveness with which you pray to Him and present your request. There is no doubt at all that the attentiveness which we bring to our understanding of the mysteries of our Religion and that with which we meditate on and contemplate them renders our faith greater.

But what is prayer and meditation? It seems that these words have come from another planet since so few people want to understand them. What is meditation or contemplation? In a word, it is prayer. To make prayer is to pray. To pray with attention is to have a lively, vigilant, attentive faith like the Canaanite woman. This faith or attentive prayer is followed and accompanied by a great variety of other virtues described in Holy Scripture. But because they are innumerable I will be satisfied with touching on those which are more proper for you and which especially shone forth in the prayer of the Canaanite woman. Now, the particular virtues with which this woman accompanied her request were four: confidence, perseverance, patience and humility. About each of these I will say but a word, for I do not want to be too long.

She had confidence, which is one of the principal conditions that make our prayer great before God. "Lord," said this woman, "have pity on me. My daughter is greatly tormented by the devil." (In Latin this phrase means "sorely tried.") It is as if she meant to say: "This evil spirit torments her cruelly and excessively, and because of that, have pity on me." What great confidence! She believes that if the Lord has pity on her, her daughter will be cured. She doubts neither His power nor His will, for she cries out only: "Have pity on me!" I know that by this she meant: "You are so gentle and kind to everyone that I have no doubt that, begging You to have pity on me, You will do so, and as soon as You do, my daughter will be cured."

Certainly the greatest defect we have in our prayers and in all that happens to us, particularly in that which concerns tribulations, is our lack of confidence. Because of that lack we do not deserve to receive the help we desire and ask for. Now, such confidence always accompanies attentive faith, which is great or little according to the measure of our confidence. When St. Peter and the other Apostles were in the boat with their Lord, and noticed the storm come up, they became frightened and called upon His assistance. In that they did well, for it is to Him we should have recourse and from Him we should expect all our help. But when they saw the waves swelling higher and higher and their good Master still asleep, they became very excited and cried out, Lord save us! We are perishing! The Saviour reproved them, saying, "You men of little faith."[8] [*Matt.* 8:24-26]. By this He meant, "How little your faith is, since on this occasion when you ought to show it all the more, you lack confidence. Since your confidence is little, so also is your faith."

But the Canaanite woman had great confidence when she made her prayer—indeed, even amidst squalls and tempests, which were not capable of shaking that confidence in the least. For she accompanied it with perseverance, continuing to cry out resolutely, "Lord, Son of David, have pity on me!" Did she say nothing else? No, she had no other words on her lips but these, and she persevered in using them during the whole time that she kept crying out after Our Lord. How great a virtue is this perseverance! If you had asked that good religious, the gardener of St. Pachomius, if he had done nothing else but make mats and work in the garden, he would have replied, "Nothing else." This was his occupation from his entrance into the monastery, and he did not expect to have any other charge for the rest of his life.[9] What perseverance he had!

However, when I speak of perseverance I do not intend to treat of that final perseverance needed to be saved, but only of that which should accompany our prayer. How few people there are who really understand in what it consists! We see young girls who are only beginners in devotion (and young men as well, but we are not speaking of them here; we are speaking now only of girls, since it is to them that I address myself). We see some, then, who are only beginning to pray and to follow Our Lord, and who yet already ask for and desire delights and consolations. They cannot persevere in prayer, except by dint of sweetness and delight. If they experience some distaste in prayer, or if God withdraws or takes away the sweetness or usual facility that they have had in it, they complain and are afflicted. They say: "The fact is I am not humble, God is not the least bit interested in hearing me, He does not look at me, for He regards only saints, and what do I know!" They entertain other such nonsense and a thousand thoughts, abandoning themselves to anxiety and discouragement.

We grow weary of praying with this dryness and dejection of heart. And what do we want? Ecstasies, ravishments, sweetness and consolations. If God does not give us promptly what we ask, or does not indicate that He hears us, we lose courage, we cannot persevere in prayer, we quit it completely, then and there.

The Canaanite woman did not act in this way. For although she saw that Our Lord was paying no attention to her prayer, since He gave her no word of response and seemed in this to do her an injustice, nevertheless, this woman persevered in crying out after Him—so much that the Apostles were constrained to tell Him that He should dismiss her because she did nothing but cry out after them. Because of this, some are of the opinion that since our Saviour gave her no word of response, she addressed herself to the Apostles, asking them to intercede for her. This is why they said: "She keeps crying out after us." Others believe that she did not ask them, but that she continued to cry out to Our Lord. But I do not wish to delay here. As for myself, I hold this latter opinion, that when the Apostles said, "Lord, get rid of her," or rather, "Send this woman away, for she keeps crying out after us," they meant "after You," for she was crying out to them when she cried out to their Master.

Nevertheless, although Our Lord turned a deaf ear to all that, she did not fail to continue her usual prayer. In this she showed her perseverance, for it is no little virtue to persevere in always praying one same prayer and performing the same exercises. And what prayer shall we always say? Our

Lord dictated it with His own mouth. [*Matt.* 6:9-13; *Lk.* 1i:2-4]. Say, "Our Father, who art in Heaven." Shall we pray it every day, praying no other? No, I do not say that, but God has not enjoined any other on you. I know well that it is not wrong to diversify our prayers and meditations, for the Church herself teaches us this in the variety of her Offices. But over and above these prayers you will say one every day, which must be recited not only after Lauds, Prime and Vespers, but many times a day. And what will it be? "Our Father, who art in Heaven." Oh, how happy we will be if we accompany that prayer with perseverance. When we have repugnance and dryness in it, when the sweetness of prayer is taken away from us, we should persevere in praying without growing weary, neither complaining nor seeking to be delivered from it, contenting ourselves in all that with crying out unceasingly: Lord, Son of David, have pity on me!

Someplace in the writings of Cicero, I do not know just where, he says in the form of a proverb that there is nothing that wearies a traveler so much as a long road when it is flat or a short one when it is rugged and hilly. (I do not recall his exact words.) He adds many other things, but this is what he meant: perseverance is very difficult. Although the traveler walks along a beautiful, level road, nevertheless, its length wearies him. When he sees night coming on, he is troubled and disturbed. In a word, he would certainly have found more pleasure had this road offered the diversion of valleys and hills. In the same way, a rugged and hilly road, even if short, wearies and tires the pilgrim, since he is always doing the same thing. But it is short. No matter, he would prefer that it were longer, but going through a plain or valley.

What is this but the caprices of the human spirit, which has no perseverance whatsoever in what it undertakes? That is why worldlings who live according to their whims know so well how to diversify the seasons with their pastimes and recreations. They do not always play the same game, but several, otherwise they would soon weary of them. Just now, at Carnival time, they have ballets, dances, and masks. In short, they spend the seasons in a variety of amusements which are nothing but the whims and caprices of the human spirit.

This is why perseverance in always doing the same thing in religion[10] is a martyrdom, and may well be considered so. It is true that it is called a paradise by those who understand it well. But it can also be called a martyrdom, for the fancies of the human spirit and all self-will are continually martyred there. I ask you, is it not a martyrdom always to be dressed in the same fashion without having the freedom to dress up and fashion one's clothes as worldlings do? Is it not a martyrdom always to eat at the same time and almost the same kind of food?

Is it not great perseverance for peasants, who ordinarily have only bread, water and cheese for their nourishment? Nevertheless, they do not die any sooner but rather are in better health than the fastidious, for whom one does not know what food is right. They need so many cooks, so many different kinds of preparations! Then, present it to them and see what happens: "Oh," they say, "take that away from me, it is not good"; or "That will make me ill," and suchlike nonsense. But in religion we do not make use of such artifice. We eat what is given us! And this is a martyrdom, as is the constant following of the same exercises.

Let us persevere in prayer at all times. For if Our Lord seems not to hear us, it is not because He wants to refuse us. Rather, His purpose is to compel us to cry out louder and to make us more conscious of the greatness of His mercy. Those who understand the hunt know well that in winter, dogs cannot scent their prey. The cold air and frost prevent them from detecting their prey as easily as they do at other times. A similar thing happens in the spring. The variety and fragrance of the flowers takes away the facility of perceiving the animal's scent.[11] To remedy this the hunter puts some vinegar in his mouth, and holding the dog's head, squirts the vinegar into its nose. Now he does this not to discourage it from going in quest of its prey, but rather to urge and excite it to do its task. In the same way, when Our Lord deprives us of sweetness and consolation, it is not to refuse us or to make us lose courage, but He casts vinegar into our mouth in order to excite us to draw so much closer to His divine Goodness, and to encourage us in perseverance.

It is also to elicit proofs of our patience. This was the third virtue which accompanied the Canaanite woman's prayer. Seeing her perseverance, the Saviour desired to prove her patience, too. By this virtue we maintain, as far as possible, equality of mind among the inequalities of this life. That is why He responded to His Apostles, who begged Him to send her away, with a word which stung her deeply and which must have discouraged her greatly. It is not reasonable, He said, that I should take the bread of the children to give it to the dogs. I have not come for all stray sheep, but to find the lost sheep of the house of My Father.

"Ah, then, Lord, is this sheep not of Your Father's house? Will she be lost? Did You not come for everyone, for the Jewish people and for the Gentiles?" It is most clear that Our Lord came for everyone. This is very plain in Holy Scripture. But when He said, "I have not come for all stray sheep, but only for the lost sheep of My Father's house," He wished it to be understood that He was promised only to the Jews, who were called children of God, that is, that it had been foretold that He would come to Israel and walk with His own feet among this people, teach them by His own mouth, cure their sick with His own hands, perform miracles in His own person. [*Is.* 40:1-2, 10-11; 61:1; *Lk.* 4:18-21]. Therefore He must not take away the bread of the children of God, that is, of the Jewish people, and throw it to the dogs, or the Gentile people, a nation that did not know Him. It is as if Jesus Christ meant to say: The favors that I give to the Gentiles, for whom I have not been sent, are so small and so few in number in comparison with those that I bestow on the Israelites, that these latter have no reason to be jealous about it.

How then are we to understand that Our Lord came for the Gentiles as well as for the Jews? It is like this. Just as He had come to walk on His own feet among the children of Israel, He will walk among the Gentiles on the feet of His Apostles. He will cure their sick, not with His own hands, but through those of the Apostles. He will preach His doctrine to them, but through the mouth of His Apostles. He will recover their lost sheep, but by means of the labor of His Apostles. This is why He spoke to the Canaanite woman words which seem so rude and cutting, savoring so much of contempt and disdain for this poor pagan woman. Indeed, we ordinarily observe that nothing offends so much as cutting words spoken with contempt for those to whom we speak, particularly if they are spoken by persons of distinction and authority. We have seen men die of sorrow and grief because contemptuous words were spoken to them by their princes, even though they may have been said through the impulse or surprise of some passion. When this woman heard Our Lord, she did not lose patience at all. Neither was she offended nor saddened. Prostrating herself at His feet, she replied, "It is true. I am a dog, I admit it. But I take You at Your word, for the dogs follow their masters and feed on the crumbs that fall under their table."

This humility was the fourth virtue that accompanied the faith and prayer of the Canaanite woman—a humility so pleasing to the Saviour that He granted her all that she asked of Him, saying, Oh woman! how great is your faith. Be it done as you desire. Certainly all virtues are very dear to God, but humility pleases Him above all the others, and it seems that He can refuse it nothing. Now, this woman manifested the greatness of her humility in acknowledging that she was a dog, and that, as a dog, she did not ask the favors reserved for Jews, who were the children of God, but only that she might gather the crumbs that fell under the table.

There are many people who insist that they are nothing, that they are only vileness, misery and suchlike things (the world is full of this kind of humility); but they cannot bear to have another tell them that they are worth nothing, that they are fools, and similar contemptuous words. They will avow it as much as they wish, but you beware of saying it to them, for they will be offended.[12] I will add this further word in passing, since it comes to my mind. Confessors would be very happy if they could always bring their penitents to confess that they are sinners. But no! let them show them their faults; let them try to make them admit that they are wrong! Most often they neither wish to admit it nor can they believe it. As for our Canaanite woman, not only was she not offended at hearing herself called a dog, but she believed it, confessed it and asked only for what belonged to dogs. In this she manifested admirable humility which merited to be praised by the mouth of Our Lord—which He did, saying: Oh, woman, how great is your faith! Be it done as you desire. And in praising her faith He praised all the other virtues which accompanied it.

Courage then! Let us rouse our faith again, and give it life through charity, and the practices and good works performed in charity. Let us watch carefully to preserve it and increase it, both by the attentive consideration of the mysteries that it teaches us and by the exercise of the virtues about which we have spoken, particularly humility, by which the Canaanite woman obtained all that she desired. Let us imitate this woman as she persevered in crying out after our Saviour and Master: Lord, Son of David, have pity on me! He will say to us at the end of our days: Be it done as you desire; and because of what you have done, come, enjoy eternity.

In the name of the Father, and of the Son, and of the Holy Spirit. Amen.

NOTES

1. Cf. *Treatise on the Love of God,* Bk. 1, chap. 1; Bk. 2, chap. 14; Bk. 7, chap. 5.
2. Cf. *Treatise on the Love of God,* Bk. 4, chap. 2; Bk. 11, chap. 5, near

the beginning. Being so close to the Protestant Reformation and its understanding of justification by faith alone, St. Francis de Sales is careful to stress the Catholic view of faith informed by charity as found in the letter of James (*Jas.* 2:14-15) and in the teachings of the Council of Trent. Cf. also p. 159 of this volume, Notes 3, 5, 6.

3. Cf. *Treatise on the Love of God,* Bk. 11, chap. 12.
4. Cf. *Treatise on the Love of God,* Bk. 2, chap. 14; Bk. 8, chap. 6; Bk. 11, chap. 5 and 9.
5. In the Septuagint the two canonical books *Esdras* and *Nehemias* were united to form one called *Esdras B* (i.e., *Second*) and were placed immediately after the apocryphal book called *Esdras A* (i.e., *First*). (*Catholic Biblical Encyclopedia,* by Steinmuller & Sullivan). *1 Esdras:* In the Septuagint this book is called *3 Esdras* (or by modern scholars, "the Greek Ezra"), but it is placed before the other two. *3 Esdras* 4:35: So truth is great, and mightier than all other things. (*The Apocrypha,* Am. translation by Edgar J. Goodspeed, Vintage Books).
6. Cf. Sermon for the First Sunday of Lent, pp. 21-22 of this volume.
7. Cf. *The Spiritual Conferences of St. Francis de Sales,* Conference XI, "The Virtue of Obedience," p. 197 (8).
8. Cf. Sermon for the First Sunday of Lent, p. 22 of this volume.
9. Cf. *Spiritual Conferences,* X, "On Obedience," p. 167; XI, "The Virtue of Obedience," pp. 190-191.
10. That is, the religious life, in which one takes the three vows of poverty, chastity and obedience.
11. Cf. *Treatise on the Love of God,* Bk. 12, chap. 3.
12. Cf. *Introduction to the Devout Life,* Part III, chap. 5.

ETERNAL HAPPINESS

Sermon for the Second Sunday of Lent, February 20, 1622, concerning our inability to comprehend eternal happiness, the ability of the soul in Heaven to use its faculties to understand clearly and to love ardently, the soul's joy in heavenly conversations with the angels, saints, Our Lady, Our Lord, and with the Most Holy Trinity, the soul's great joy in recalling Our Lord's mercies to it, His Passion and death, and in seeing the love of His Heart for it, each soul's great delight in receiving a secret name known to God alone, the kiss given by God to the blessed soul, and the endlessness of the joys of eternity.

"I know a man in Christ—whether he was in or outside the body I do not know, God knows—who was snatched up to the third heaven...and heard secret words, words which it is not granted to man to utter."—2 Cor. 12:2-4

When the great Apostle St. Paul was snatched up and raised even to the third heaven, he did not know whether he was in or outside his body, and he affirmed that no man may or could tell what he saw there or what wonders he learned when they were shown him in his rapture. Now, if he who saw them cannot speak of them—if even after having been snatched up even to the third heaven, he dares not say a word of what he witnessed—much less should we presume to do so, we who have never been raised even to the first, or the second, let alone the third heaven.

The discourse on the Gospel [*Matt.* 17:1-9] which I am

to give you today treats of eternal happiness. I must begin
by giving you a parable. In treating of the marvellous things
of the next world in his Dialogues, St. Gregory the Great
affirms the following: "Picture a pregnant woman who is
put into prison, where she remains until the time of her deliv-
ery. She even gives birth there and is then condemned to
pass the remainder of her life in the dungeon and to bring
up her child there. As he grows older, the mother desires
to give him some idea of things in the outside world, for
having lived only in that continual darkness he has no idea
of the light of the sun, the beauty of the stars, or the loveliness of nature. Since the mother wants to teach him all these
things, they lower a lamp or a lighted candle to her. With
this she attempts to make him conceive, as best she can,
the beauty of a bright day. She tells him: 'The sun and the
stars are made like this and spread out a great light.' It is
all in vain, for the child, having had no experience of the
light of which his mother speaks, cannot understand.

"Then the poor woman tries to give him an idea of the
beauty of hills covered with trees and various fruits: oranges,
lemons, pears, apples, and the like. But the child knows nothing of all that, nor of how it can be. And although his mother,
holding in her hand some leaves of those trees, may tell him:
'My child, they are covered with leaves like these' and, showing him an apple or an orange, 'They are also laden with
fruits such as these; are they not beautiful?' the child remains in his ignorance. His mind simply cannot comprehend
what his mother wants to teach him, for all that she uses
is nothing compared to the reality itself."[1]

The limitations are the same, my dear souls, with all that
we can say of the grandeur of eternal happiness and of the
pleasure and beauties with which Heaven is filled. Indeed,
there is greater proportion between the light of a lamp and
the splendor of those great luminaries that shine upon us,
between the beauty of the leaf or fruit of a tree and the tree
itself laden with both flowers and fruit, between all that this
child comprehends of what his mother tells him and the reality

itself of the things spoken of, than there is between the light
of the sun and the splendor which the blessed enjoy in glory;
between the beauty of a meadow sprinkled with flowers in
the springtime and the beauty of these heavenly gardens; between the loveliness of our hills covered with fruits and the
loveliness of the eternal hills. But be that as it may, and we
may be certain that we can say nothing in comparison to
the reality; still we ought to say something about it.

I have already preached here many times on today's Gospel
and on this topic. Therefore I want to speak on a point which
I have never yet treated. But before beginning it, I must clarify some difficulties which might prevent you from really
understanding what I want to say. I do this eagerly because
I want this point well thought over, considered, and understood by you.

The first difficulty seen in the question is: Can the souls
of the blessed, separated from their bodies, see, hear, consider, and understand? Can they, in short, exercise the functions of the mind as freely as when they were united to their
bodies? I answer that not only can they act as before, but
much more perfectly. And to support this theory I shall give
you a story from St. Augustine, an author in whom one can
place complete trust. He relates that he was acquainted with
a physician from Carthage who was as famous in Rome as
in that city, both because he excelled in the art of medicine
and because he was a very good man, one who did many
charitable works and served the poor gratis. His charity towards his neighbor moved God to lift him out of an error
into which he had fallen as a young man. God always greatly
favors those who practice charity toward their neighbor; indeed, there is nothing that draws down His mercy upon us
more abundantly. Our Lord has declared it His own special
commandment [*Jn.* 15:12], the one He loves and cherishes
most. For after that of the love of God, there is none greater.
[*Matt.* 22:37-40].

St. Augustine recounts how this physician told him that
when young he began to doubt whether the soul, separated

from the body, can see, hear, or understand anything. One day, while in this error, he fell asleep. Suddenly, a handsome young man appeared to him in his sleep and said: "Follow me." The physician did so, and his guide led him into a large and spacious field where on one side he showed him incomparable beauties, and on the other allowed him to hear a concert of delightful music. Then the physician awoke. Some time after, the same young man again appeared to him in sleep and asked: "Do you recognize me?" The physician answered that he did indeed recognize him distinctly, that it was he who had conducted him to the beautiful field where he had heard such pleasing music. "But how can you see and recognize me?" asked the youth. "Where are your eyes?" "My eyes," he replied, "are in my body." "And where is your body?" "My body is lying in my bed." "And are your eyes open or closed?" "They are closed." "If they are closed, they can see nothing. Admit, then, since you see me even with your eyes closed, recognize me distinctly, and have heard the music even though your senses slept, that the functions of the mind do not depend on the corporal senses, and that the soul, even when separated from the body, can nevertheless see, hear, consider and understand." Then the sacred dream ended and the youth left the physician, who never after doubted this truth.

This is how St. Augustine tells it. He further mentions that the physician told him that he heard that divine music sung on his right in the field mentioned. But he firmly added: "I do not remember what he saw to his left." I mention this to point out how precise that glorious saint was, saying only what he knew to be the truth in this story. After this we must never again allow this "difficulty" entrance into our minds, namely, whether our souls, when separated from our bodies, will have full and absolute liberty to perform their functions and activities. For then our understanding will see, consider and understand not only one thing at a time, but several together; we shall be able to give our attention to several things at one time without one of them displacing any other.

Here, we cannot do that, for whoever wants to think of more than one thing at a time always gives less attention to each and his attention is less perfect in all of them.[2] It is the same with the memory; it will furnish us with many recollections, and one will not interfere with the others. Our will will also have the facility of willing many different things without being weakened or loving any one less ardently than the other. That can never be done in this life while the soul inhabits the body. Here our memory does not have complete liberty in its operation. It cannot have many recollections, at least at the same time, without one interfering with the other. Likewise, our will loves with less ardor when it loves many things together. Its desires and willing are less passionate and ardent when there are many of them.

The second difficulty concerns the opinion which many hold that the blessed in the heavenly Jerusalem are so inebriated with the abundance of divine consolation that this inebriation takes from them the power to act. They think it is the same as with the consolations sometimes received on earth. These cause the soul to fall into a certain spiritual sleep so that for a time it is incapable of moving or even of knowing where it is, just as the royal Prophet testifies in his Psalm, *In convertendo:* "We became like men comforted" [*Ps.* 125 (126):1]; or else, according to the Hebrew text and the Septuagint," "like men dreaming, when the Lord brought back the captives of Zion."[3] But it is not like this in eternal glory. There the abundance of consolation will not take away awareness or our power to act. Harmony is the excellence of our actions,[4] and in Heaven our actions will not disturb harmony but will perfect it in such a way that our actions will not be detrimental to each other, but each will aid the other to continue and persevere for the glory of the pure love of God, which will render them capable of subsisting together.

Do not imagine then, my dear souls, that our spirit will be dulled or drowsy by the abundance and joys of eternal happiness. Quite the contrary! It will be very alert and agile in its various activities. And though it is written that Our Lord will inebriate His beloved: "Drink, My friends, and be inebriated, My dearly beloved" [*Ps.* 35 (36):9; *Cant.* 5:1], this inebriation will not render the soul less capable of seeing, considering, understanding, and performing the various activities which the love of her Beloved will suggest to her, as we have just stated. It shall move the soul to increase its movements and loving glances by ever inflaming it with new ardor.

The third difficulty or misconception from which I wish to free you is the thought that in eternal glory we shall be subject to distractions just as we are while in this mortal life. No, and the reason is, as we have just said, that we shall then be capable of giving our attention to many different things at the same time, without one act interfering with the other. Rather, each will perfect the other. The many subjects we will have in our understanding, the many recollections in our memory, or the many desires of our will will not interfere with each other, nor will one be better understood than any other. Why is this? For the simple reason, my dear Sisters, that all is perfected and brought to perfection in the eternal beatitude of Heaven.

Now, what shall we say of this beatitude? The word "beatitude," or "happiness," indicates clearly what it is, for it signifies a place of consolation where all joys and blessings are found and experienced. In this world we consider as most happy a mind that can concentrate on many subjects at the same time, as is evident from the praise bestowed on that man who was able to be attentive to seven topics at the same time (cf. Pliny's *Natural History*), and as is evident from the praise given to that heroic captain who knew the hundred or fifty thousand soldiers under his command, each by name. How happy will we consider our own mind when, in beatitude, it will be able to have so many and such varied interests! But, my God, what can we possibly say of that indescribable felicity which is eternal, invariable, constant and permanent, and, as the ancient French say, *"sempiternelle"*?

I do not intend, my dear Sisters, to treat of the felicity which the blessed have in the clear vision of the face of God, whom they see, and shall forever see in His essence [cf. *1 Cor.* 13:12], for that regards essential felicity, and I do not wish to treat of that, beyond a few words at the end. Nor shall I treat of the eternity of this glory of the saints, but only of a certain accidental glory which they receive in the conversation they have together. O what divine conversation! But with whom? With three kinds of persons: with themselves, with the angels, the archangels, the cherubim, the holy Apostles, the confessors, the virgins, with the glorious Virgin, our Lady and Mistress; with the most holy humanity of Our Lord; and lastly, even with the most adorable Trinity, the Father, the Son and the Holy Spirit.

But, my dear Sisters, you must know that all the blessed will know one another, each by name, as we shall understand better from the Gospel, which shows us our Divine Master on Mount Thabor accompanied by St. Peter, St. James and St. John. While they looked upon the Saviour who was praying [*Lk.* 9:29], He was transfigured before them [*Matt.* 17:2], allowing to appear in His body a little portion of the glory which He had continually enjoyed from the moment of His glorious Conception in Our Lady's womb. He withheld this glory by a continual miracle, keeping it confined and hidden in the superior part of His soul.

The Apostles saw His face become more dazzling and brilliant than the sun. Indeed, this light and glory was spread even over His clothes to show us that it was so diffusive as to be shared by His very clothes and whatever was about Him. He shows us a spark of eternal glory and a drop of that ocean, of that sea of incomparable felicity, to make us desire it in its entirety.[5] So the good St. Peter, as head of the others, spoke for all and exclaimed in full joy and consolation: "O how good it is for us to be here!" He seems to mean: "I have seen many things, but nothing is so desirable as remaining here." The three disciples recognized Moses and Elias even though they had never seen them before, one

having retaken his body, or a body formed of air, and the
other being in the same body in which he was carried away
in the triumphal chariot. [*4 Kgs.* (*2 Kgs.*) 2:11]. Both were
talking with our Divine Master of the excess which He was
about to fulfill in Jerusalem [*Lk.* 9:31], the excess which was
the death He was about to suffer out of love. Immediately
after this conversation, the Apostles heard the voice of the
Eternal Father saying: "This is My Son, My Chosen One;
listen to Him."

Let me remark first of all that in eternal felicity we will
know each other, since in this little spark of it which the
Saviour gave to His Apostles He willed that they recognize
Moses and Elias, whom they had never seen. If this is true,
O my God, what contentment will we receive in seeing again
those whom we have so dearly loved in this life! Yes, we
will even know the new Christians who are only now being
converted to our holy Faith in the Indies, Japan, and the
Antipodes. The good friendships of this life will continue
eternally in the other. We will love each person with a special love, but these particular friendships will not cause par-
tiality because all our affections will draw their strength from
the charity of God which, ordering them all, will make us
love each of the blessed with that eternal love with which
we are loved by the Divine Majesty.

O God! What consolation we will have in these heavenly
conversations with each other. There our good angels will
give us greater joy than we can imagine when we recognize
them and they speak to us so lovingly of the care they had
for our salvation during our mortal life, reminding us of the
holy inspirations they gave us, as a sacred milk which they
drew from the breast of the Divine Goodness, to attract us
to seek the incomparable sweetness we now enjoy. "Do you
remember," they will say, "the inspiration I gave you at such
a time, in reading that book, or in listening to that sermon,
or in looking at that image?" For example, St. Mary of Egypt's
good angel will remind her of the inspiration which converted her to Our Lord and which was the foundation of her

heavenly destiny. O God! Will not our hearts melt with indescribable delight in hearing these words?

Each of the saints will have a special conversation according to his rank and dignity. One day our glorious Father, St. Augustine (of whom I speak, since I know it pleases you),[6] had a desire to see triumphant Rome, the glorious St. Paul preaching, and Our Lord among the people curing the sick and working miracles. Oh, my dear souls, what consolation this great saint now has in contemplating the heavenly Jerusalem in its triumph, the great Apostle Paul (I do not say great in body for he was small, but great in eloquence and sanctity) preaching and intoning those praises he will give throughout eternity to the Divine Majesty in glory! But what incomparable consolation for St. Augustine to see Our Lord work the perpetual miracle of the blessed's felicity which His death has acquired for us! Imagine the divine conversation these two saints might have with each other, with St. Paul saying to St. Augustine: "My dear Brother, do you not recall that in reading my epistle [*Rom.* 13:12-14] you were touched by an inspiration which moved you to be converted, an inspiration which I had obtained for you from the divine mercy of our good God by the prayer I offered for you at the very moment you were reading what I had written?" Will not this, dear Sisters, bring an incomparable sweetness to our holy Father's heart?

Let us imagine this: Suppose that Our Lady, St. Magdalen, St. Martha, St. Stephen and the Apostles were to be seen for the space of a year in Jerusalem, as for a great jubilee. Who among us, I ask you, would wish to remain here? For myself, I think we would embark at once, exposing ourselves to the peril of all the hazards which fall upon travelers, so that we might experience the grace of seeing our glorious Mother and Mistress, Magdalen, Mary Salome, and the others. After all, pilgrims expose themselves to all these dangers only to go and revere the places where these holy persons have placed their feet. If this is so, my dear souls, what consolation will we receive when, entering Heaven, we will

see the blessed face of Our Lady, all radiant with the love
of God! And if St. Elizabeth was so carried away with joy
and contentment when, on the day of Our Lady's visitation,
she heard her intone that divine canticle, the Magnificat [*Lk.*
1:39-55], how much more will our hearts and souls thrill
with inexplicable joy when we hear this sacred Chantress
intone the canticle of eternal love![7] O what a sweet melody!
Without doubt, we will be carried away and experience most
loving raptures which, however, will take from us neither
the use of reason nor of our faculties. Both will be marvelously strengthened and perfected by this divine meeting
with the holy Virgin, to better praise and glorify God, who
has given her and each of us so many graces—among them,
that of conversing familiarly with her.

But, you may ask, if it is true, as you say, that we will
converse with all those in the heavenly Jerusalem, what will
we say? Of what shall we speak? What will be the subject
of our conversation? O God! My dear Sisters! What subject?
Surely of the mercies which the Lord has shown us here
on earth and by which He has made us capable of entering
into the joy of a happiness which alone can satisfy us. I say
"alone" because in this word "felicity" every sort of good
is comprised. They are, however, but one single good, the
joy of God in eternal felicity. It is this unique good which
the divine lover[8] in the Canticle of Canticles asked from her
Beloved (she practices true wisdom here, for following the
advice of the wise man[9] [*Ecclus.* (*Sir.*) 7:40], she considers
the end, and then, in light of this, the means). "Kiss me,"
she cries, "O my dear Beloved, with the kiss of Your mouth."
[cf. *Cant.* 1:1 (2)]. This kiss, as I shall soon exclaim, is
nothing other than the happiness of the blessed.

But of what else will we speak in our conversations? Of
the death and Passion of our Lord and Master. Ah, do we
not learn this in the Transfiguration, in which they spoke
of nothing so much as the excess He had to suffer in Jerusalem, excess which was none other, as we have already seen,
than His sorrowful death?[10] Oh, if we could comprehend

something of the consolation which the blessed have in speaking of this loving death, how our souls also would expand in thinking of it!

Let us pass on, I pray you, and say a few words about the honor and grace that we will have in conversing even with our incarnate Lord. Here, undoubtedly, our felicity will reach an inexpressible and unutterable height. What will we do, dear souls, what will we become, I ask you, when through the Sacred Wound of His side we perceive that most adorable and most lovable Heart of our Master, aflame with love for us—that Heart where we will see each of our names written in letters of love! "Is it possible, O my dear Saviour," we will say, "that You have loved me so much that You have engraved my name in Your Heart?" It is indeed true. The Prophet, speaking in the name of Our Lord, says to us: "Even if it should happen that a mother forget the child she carried in her womb, I will never forget you, for I have engraved your name in the palms of my hand." [*Is.* 49:15-16]. But Jesus Christ, enlarging on these words, will say: "Even if it were possible for a woman to forget her child, yet I will never forget you, since I bear your name engraved in My Heart."

Surely, it will be a subject of very great consolation that we should be so dearly loved by Our Lord that He always bears us in His Heart. What delight for each of the blessed to see in this most sacred and most adorable Heart the thoughts of peace [*Jer.* 29:11] He had for them and for us, even at the hour of His Passion! thoughts which not only prepared for us the principal means of our salvation, but also the divine attractions, inspirations, and good movements that this most gentle Saviour wished to make use of to draw us to His most pure love![11] These visions, this gazing, these particular considerations that we will make on this sacred love by which we have been so dearly, so ardently, loved by our sovereign Master, will inflame our hearts with unparalleled ardor and delight. What ought we not do or suffer in order to enjoy these unutterably pleasing delights! This truth is shown to us in today's Gospel; for do you not see that Moses and

Elias spoke and conversed very familiarly indeed with our transfigured Lord?

Our felicity will not stop at this, my dear souls. It will pass farther, for we will see face to face [*1 Cor.* 13:12] and very clearly the Divine Majesty, the essence of God, and the mystery of the Most Holy Trinity. In this vision and clear knowledge consists the essence of felicity. There we will understand and participate in those adorable conversations and divine colloquies which take place between the Father, Son and Holy Spirit.[12] We shall listen to how melodiously the Son will intone the praises due to His heavenly Father,[13] and how He will offer to Him on behalf of all people the obedience that He gave to Him all during His earthly life. In exchange we shall also hear the Eternal Father, in a thunderous but incomparably harmonious voice, pronounce the divine words which the Apostles heard on the day of the Transfiguration: "This is My beloved Son, in whom I am well pleased." And the Father and the Son, speaking of the Holy Spirit, will say: "This is Our Spirit, in whom, proceeding One from the Other, We have placed all Our love."

Not only will there be conversation between the Divine Persons, but also between God and us. And what will this divine conversation be? Oh, what will it be indeed! It will be such as no man may speak.[14] It will be an intimate conversation so secret that no one will understand it except God and the soul with whom it is made. God will say to each of the blessed a word so special that there will be no other like it. But what will this word be? Oh, it will be the most loving word that one can ever imagine. Think of all the words which can be spoken to melt a heart, and the most affectionate names that can be heard, and then say that these words are meaningless in comparison with the word which God will give to each soul in Heaven above. He will give to each a name [*Apoc.* 2:17], will say to each a word. Suppose that He will say to you: "You are My beloved, you are the beloved of My Beloved; that is why you will be so dearly loved by Me. You are the chosen one of My Chosen One who is My Son." That is nothing, my dear souls, in comparison with the delight which will accompany this word or this holy and sacred name which the Lord will permit the blessed soul to hear.

Then it will be that God will give to the divine lover that kiss she has so ardently desired and asked for, as we have already said. Oh, how amorously she will chant her canticle of love: "Let Him kiss me," the Beloved of my soul, "with the kiss of His mouth"; and she will add: "Incomparably better is the milk that flows from His dear breasts than the most delicious wines," and the rest. [*Cant.* 1:1-3 (2-4)]. What divine ecstasies, what loving embraces between the all-sovereign Majesty and this dear lover when God gives her this kiss of peace! It will be so, and not with one lover only, but with each of the citizens of the heavenly Jerusalem, among whom there will be a marvelously pleasing conversation upon the sufferings, pains and torments which Our Lord endured for each of us during the course of His mortal life. It will be a conversation which will give such consolation, but one which the angels are not capable of (according to the opinion of St. Bernard) because although Our Lord is their Saviour and they have been saved by His death, He is, nevertheless, not their Redeemer, because He has not ransomed them as He has humankind. This is why we will receive great felicity and singular contentment in speaking of this glorious Redemption by means of which we have been saved and made like angels [*Mk.* 12:25], as our Divine Master has said.

In the heavenly Jerusalem, then, we will enjoy a very pleasing conversation with the blessed spirits, the angels, the cherubim and seraphim, the saints, with our Lady and glorious Mistress, with Our Lord and with the thrice holy and adorable Trinity—a conversation which will last forever and will be perpetually cheerful and joyous. Now if in this life we have so much pleasure in hearing that which we love spoken of that we cannot be silent about it, what joy, what jubilation will we receive in hearing chanted eternally the praises of the Divine Majesty, whom we should love, and whom we will love, more than we can comprehend in this life! If we take so much delight in the simple imagination of this unending felicity, how much more will we have in the actual possession of it! An endless felicity and glory, one that will last eternally and one which we can never lose! Oh, how greatly will this assurance increase our consolation! Let us walk gayly and joyously, dear souls, among the difficulties of this passing life; let us embrace with open arms all the mortifications and afflictions that we will meet on our way, since we are sure that these pains will have an end when our life ends, after which there will be only joy, only contentment, only eternal consolation. Amen.

NOTES

1. Cf. *Treatise on the Love of God,* Bk. VI, chap. 4.
2. Cf. *Treatise on the Love of God,* Bk. I, chap. 10.
3. Cf. *Treatise on the Love of God,* Bk. IX, chap. 12.
4. Cf. *Treatise on the Love of God,* Bk. V, chap. 3
5. Cf. *Introduction to the Devout Life,* Part III, chap. 2.
6. St. Francis de Sales and St. Jane de Chantal gave the Sisters of the Visitation the Rule of St. Augustine when the Congregation was raised to the rank of an order in the Church in 1618. This is why St. Francis speaks of St. Augustine as their "Father."
7. Cf. *Treatise on the Love of God,* Bk. V, chap. 11.
8. Here the "divine lover" is the soul who loves Our Lord; the "Beloved" is Our Lord Jesus Christ. In this book the words "lover," "beloved" and "spouse" are capitalized or not capitalized depending on whether they refer to Christ or to the faithful soul.
9. Cf. *Sermons on Our Lady,* "The Assumption," Aug. 15, 1618, p. 71.
10. Cf. p. 59 of this sermon.
11. Cf. *Introduction to the Devout Life,* Part V, chap. 13; *Treatise on the Love of God,* Bk. XII, chap. 12.
12. Cf. *Treatise on the Love of God,* Bk. III, chap. 11-13.
13. Cf. *Treatise on the Love of God,* Bk. V, chap. 11.
14. Cf. p. 52 of this sermon.

— 5 —

ELECTION AND REPROBATION

Sermon for the Thursday after the Second Sunday of Lent (coinciding with the Feast of St. Matthias), February 24, 1622, concerning the danger which all Christians live in of refusing to receive the grace of salvation, the danger of even specially favored souls falling from God and being damned, why we must always have a great fear of damnation— even in the religious life, the avarice of the evil rich man, two kinds of avarice and especially that of clinging to what we possess, using God for one's own benefit, non-material avarice, using riches vs. idolizing riches, the avarice and treachery of Judas, the beginnings of spiritual downfall, the salutary fear of sin, availing ourselves of the grace to mortify our evil inclinations, the replacement of those who die or defect from the Apostolic College or from the religious life, and the choice of St. Matthias to replace Judas.

Today I thought I would preach on some connections between what happened in the lives of the sinful rich man [*Lk*. 16:19-31] and Judas, and in the lives of Lazarus and St. Matthias. I find a great similarity between the vocation, growth and decline of the sinful rich man and of Judas, and between the vocation, growth and end of Lazarus and of St. Matthias. Such a comparison is very time-consuming. Therefore, I will concentrate principally on the vocation of St. Matthias.

We will find great reason to fear because of these words of the Gospel: many are called, the elect are few. [*Matt.* 20:16; 22:14]. We will also find here a reason for condemning those who censure and speak unjustly against Divine

Providence, and are unwilling to adore or approve its effects and events which bear upon the election of the good and the reprobation of the wicked. For when the rejection of the latter is considered, human prudence begins to search for motives and reasons for their fall, and instead of looking at the kind Providence of God, it concentrates on the lack of grace, saying, "If this sinner had received what the just received, he would not have experienced such a fall." Now, such people would be correct if they said only that grace is not offered to sinners in the same way as to the just. But if they continue and question why the first do not receive this grace in the same way as the second, certainly they would have to admit that it is not the lack of grace that is the cause of their loss, for grace is never wanting. God always gives sufficient grace to whoever is willing to receive it. This is an established truth and all theologians are in agreement with it. The Council of Trent has declared that grace is never lacking to us, but that it is we who are lacking to grace, being unwilling to receive it or to consent to it. The damned will surely have to acknowledge, as St. Denis the Areopagite writes, that it is through their own fault and not that of grace that they have been thrown down and condemned to the eternal flames, because they were wanting to grace and not because grace was wanting to them. This they will know very clearly, and this knowledge will greatly increase their torments.[1]

Now, if it is always we who are wanting to grace and never grace lacking to us, and if we see in every kind of state, condition and vocation, so many reprobate and so few elect, who among us will consider himself secure, and live without fear of losing grace or of refusing his consent to it? Who will not fear failure in rendering to God the service due to Him, each one according to his duty and obligation, when we find a Lazarus and a St. Matthias among the elect, but this rich man in the Gospel and Judas among the reprobate? Was not the sinful rich man called to the same vocation as Lazarus, and Judas to the same as St. Matthias? Yes, without a doubt. This is quite clear in the Gospel, for the sinful rich man was a Jew, since he called Abraham his father. "Father Abraham," he said, begging him to send Lazarus to him. He was circumcised, and God had shown him that He loved him by giving him the joy of great wealth, and many possessions. For the Mosaic Law is not like the Law of Grace, where poverty is so highly praised and recommended. Our Lord had not yet said, "Blessed are the poor in spirit." [*Matt.* 5:3]. So at that time God favored His friends by letting them share in riches and temporal goods, obliging them thereby to serve Him.

It is clear, then, that this rich man was called by God as Lazarus was, and that he had an even greater obligation to observe the divine commandments than Lazarus. Not that Lazarus was not also bound by them, but since the rich man had been favored with so much more wealth than he, he had a greater duty to serve his Lord. That is why if Lazarus had not served Him, he would not have been as reprehensible as the sinful rich man. Doubtless he would have been blamable, but much less so than the rich man. Nevertheless, we see in today's Gospel that of these two men, equally called by God, he who had received more and who is more obliged to serve Him, does not serve Him, but rather lives and dies miserably, while the poor Lazarus serves God faithfully and dies happily. One was carried to the bosom of Abraham, the other to the depths of Hell. But let us leave this sinful rich man there and turn our attention to the vocation of Judas and of St. Matthias, both Apostles of Our Lord.

Consider, first, how the vocation and election of Judas had more advantages than that of St. Matthias. Judas, the most wicked of men, was called to be an Apostle by the very mouth of Our Lord, who a thousand times called him by name. Like the other Apostles, he was instructed by Our Lord. He heard Him speak and preach. He was witness of the wonderful works that He did and of how He confirmed His doctrine by wonderful miracles. His dear Master had offered him many special graces which St. Matthias did not receive, who was not called to be an Apostle by Our Lord, nor during His lifetime, but rather by the Apostles after His Ascension [*Acts* 1:15-26], so that he came as one born out of due time [cf. *1 Cor.* 15:8] to succeed this miserable Judas. He was not instructed by the Saviour Himself, nor did he see His miracles, for he was not one of the Apostles who followed Him.[2] Nevertheless, he persevered faithfully and died a saint. Judas, on the contrary, the most traitorous and disloyal man there ever was, from being an Apostle became an apostate, committing the most abominable sin and the greatest treachery in selling his good Master.

All our ancient Fathers point out the seriousness and gravity of this sin. But though they stress its greatness, they can never sufficiently state its enormity. Speaking of Judas, Our Lord calls him "son of perdition" [*Jn.* 17:12], the same title St. Paul gives Antichrist. [*2 Thess.* 2:3]. This is a Hebrew phrase. When the expression "child of consolation" is used it means "of greatest consolation" or "of very great consolation"; "son of joy" means "of greatest joy" or "of very great joy." In the same way, when Judas fell into that iniquity of selling his Lord and Master and is called son or child of perdition, it means of the greatest or very great perdition, such as that of devils, for he was worse than a devil. He now burns with them in eternal flames. See how, of these two Apostles, he who had been the most favored apostatized, while the other, who was called to be an Apostle after Our Lord's death, persevered. Great reason to fear in all states and vocations, for there is danger everywhere!

When God created the angels in heaven He established them in His grace. It seems they ought never to fall from this grace. Nevertheless, Lucifer revolted. He and all his followers refused to render to the Divine Majesty the submission and obedience of their will, saying that they absolutely would not submit. This refusal was their ruin. Lucifer drew with him into Hell a third of the angels [*Apoc.* 12:4], a countless number. Those who had been in the very midst of glory itself became devils, condemned to eternal pains. You see, there was danger even in heaven.[3] And did not man fall from the earthly paradise where God had placed him in grace? Eve listened to the serpent, took the forbidden fruit and presented it to her husband. He ate it, contrary to the will of his Creator.[4] [*Gen.* 3:1-6].

Certainly, Solomon's fall is also an appalling thing—he, the wisest of all men, to whom God had so abundantly given His Spirit, His wisdom and knowledge of all things; who was able to penetrate in knowledge even to the depths of the earth, treating skillfully all that he found there; who mounted even to the heights of the cedars of Lebanon; who spoke with great wisdom, not only of material things but also of spiritual ones! [*3 Kgs.* (*1 Kgs.*) 3:11-12; 5:9-13; *Wis.* 7:7, 17-24]. We see this wisdom in that admirable Book of Ecclesiasticus [Sirach] and in Proverbs, both of which are filled with sentences of such wisdom that we can easily conclude that no one was ever as gifted as Solomon. Others may have said less with more fervor or eloquence, but he has surpassed them all in wisdom, both in passing as well as in spiritual matters. Nevertheless, he resisted grace, as we shall soon see,[5] and fell into sin, despite the fullness of the divine Spirit which he had received. [*3 Kgs.* (*1 Kgs.*) 11:1-8; *Neh.* 13:26].

Who, then, will not tremble? Will there ever be a society, religion, institute, congregation or manner of living which can be so secure and which can be said to be exempt from the fear and apprehension of falling over the precipices of sin? What company, assembly or vocation will we find exempt from danger? O God, none whatsoever![6] Everywhere there is every reason to fear and to keep oneself in great lowliness and humility. Hold fast to the tree of your profession, each one according to your calling. [*1 Cor.* 7:20]. But fail not to walk in fear, feeling your way all during your life, lest, wishing to walk with too great sureness and boldness, you fall into the ruins of sin. Job, as St. Gregory says, remaining just among the wicked, received a great grace from God, for ordinarily we are like those with whom we converse. But since God kept him good among the impious, he had great reason to praise the Lord. It is a perilous thing to live in the world and in conversation with the wicked. Thus, to remain good among them, without falling from grace, is a very special favor from God. It is for this reason, according to St. Jerome, that God calls some from the world into the desert, where they do not associate with the wicked.

Now, those whom He has placed in some good and suitable vocation truly have great reason to praise and thank Him, for they have received a special blessing in being separated from the company of the wicked and associated with the good. But are they out of danger? Oh no! Why? Because it is not enough to be in this holy vocation and to be with good people, if we do not persevere in it. [*Matt.* 10:22; 24:13; *2 Ptr.* 1:10].

Now, this grace of perseverance is very great indeed, since when we fail in grace in such a holy way of life the fall is more grave and perilous, as was that of the angels in heaven,[7] that of Adam in Paradise and that of Judas in the company of Our Lord. Extraordinary—that in the Church Triumphant (not triumphant then, but angelic), among such pure spirits, gifted with so noble and excellent a nature, among such a holy company, where there was no occasion of danger, nor temptation, nor suggestion from the wicked spirits (for they did not exist then), there should have been so small a number of angels who persevered, and that a third of them would rebel against God and be cast into Hell! Frightening also that Judas, who had been called by the Saviour Himself to be an Apostle, should have committed so abominable a sin, so strange a treason as selling his Master, and that at the very time he was in His company, hearing His preaching and seeing the marvelous works He performed! These are examples which should make all types of people tremble, no matter what may be their state, condition or vocation.

But let us consider further the similarity there is in the growth of the life of the evil rich man and of Judas. The first was rich, says the Gospel, and avaricious. To better understand this, you must realize that there are two kinds of

avarice. One is temporal, and it is that by which we are avid
to acquire wealth, honors and the goods of this life. There
are many such avaricious people in the world. They think
of amassing riches, and seem to have nothing else to do here
below: joining house to house, connecting meadow to meadow,
field to field, vineyard to vineyard, treasure to treasure. It
is to this kind of people that the Prophet says: "O fools,
do you believe that the world was made only for you?" [*Is.*
5:8]. He means: "O miserable ones, what are you doing?
Do you think you will remain forever here on earth, or that
you are here only to amass temporal goods? Oh clearly, you
were not created for that."

"What!" replies human prudence: "were not heaven, earth
and all that is in it made for man? Does not God want us
to use it?" It is true that God created the world for man,
with the intention that he use the goods he finds in it, but
not to enjoy them as if they were his final end. He created
the world before He created man for He wished to prepare
a palace, a house, a dwelling place in which man could live.
Then, He declared man master of all that is in the world,
allowing him to use it, but not as if it were his final end.
For He created him for a higher end, Himself. Nevertheless,
covetousness and greed have so confused the heart of man
that, according to St. Augustine, he has come to the point
of wishing "to enjoy that which he ought to use and to use
the things he ought to enjoy."[8]

Those who feel the pulse of the greater part of the worldly
and closely observe the movements of their hearts are moved
to compassion. For it becomes clear that they want to enjoy
the world and what it contains, but are satisfied to use God!
Hence comes all their activity for the preservation of temporal things; they do hardly anything to attain eternal happiness. If they pray at all, or if they keep the commandments
or practice some other good works, it is only because they
fear that God might chastise them with some disaster or misfortune; or it is so that God will spare them their house,
their fields, their vineyards, their wife, their children—all of

which they wish to enjoy, content to use God as a means for this or similar ones. It is from this that all our evils come. If I were preaching elsewhere I would say more on this kind of avarice, but those to whom I am speaking have nothing to do with it.

There is another kind of avarice which clings to what it has and is unwilling to part with it for anything. This is highly dangerous and steals in everywhere, even into religion and into spiritual things. We may indeed restrain ourselves from the first kind of avarice, for there are many persons who are not ambitious for amassing much property, fields and houses. But they are few who easily part with what they possess. We find married men with children and a family, for whom they should acquire some things so as to provide for their needs, but who are nevertheless not at all concerned to do this. They squander and dissipate all their substance, and remain poor, weak and miserable all their lives. Yet, they are so avaricious for their freedom, which is their treasure, their wealth, and the noblest thing they have, that they cling to it tenaciously and will surrender it for nothing else in the world. They will never give it up, but want only to enjoy it by living according to their fancies, and revel in all kinds of pleasures and luxury. There are wealthy people who do not have this first kind of avarice—to amass treasure upon treasure—but they so plunge their heart into what they have, so as better to preserve it, that it is almost impossible to detach them from it. An evil man will love sensual pleasure so much and consider it so precious that he will not quit the delight he takes in it for all the wealth and honors in the world.

There are even spiritual souls who possess what they have with such attachment and take such pleasure in seeing and reflecting on what they do, that they commit a kind of idolatry, making and adoring as many idols as they have actions. St. Gregory Nazianzen said that he easily gave up the wealth and honors of this life, so that he had neither ambition nor temptation to acquire these things. But there remained in him so great a desire to know and to study that all kinds of riches were nothing to him in comparison with the desire he had to study literature. So dear was this desire that he found nothing as difficult to give up for God. He would have more easily forsaken and more willingly surrendered all the wealth and pleasures of the world, if he had had them, than this passion for learning. It seemed as if God left it in him as the last and principal object of his renunciation. Nevertheless, so pleased was God with the resolution that St. Gregory had taken to abandon all for Him, that He placed him in a situation where he could study, and at the same time give up his desire without giving up his studies. So he dedicated himself to studies because his Sovereign Master had placed him in a situation where it was lawful for him to do so. So, in learning, he acquiesced to the divine will.

Judas and the evil rich man were avaricious with these two kinds of avarice which we have just treated. They were avid to amass riches, to obtain money and more money, but they also concealed and clung so strongly to the goods they had, and loved them so excessively, that they adored them and made them their god. Holy Scripture speaks of them in this way: The avaricious man makes a god of his gold and silver [*Eph.* 5:5; *Col.* 3:5], and the voluptuous makes a god of his body. [*Phil.* 3:19]. There is a great difference between drinking wine and becoming intoxicated, between using riches and adoring them. He who drinks wine out of necessity does no evil; but he who takes it to such an excess that he becomes intoxicated offends God mortally, loses his judgment, drowns his reason in the wine he drinks, and if he happens to die in this state, is damned. It is as if he said while drinking, "If I die I wish to be lost and damned eternally." There is also a difference between using riches and adoring them. To use riches according to one's state and condition, when it is done as it should be, is permissible.[9] But to make idols of them is to be condemned and damned. In a word, there is a great difference between seeing and regarding the things of this world, and in wishing to enjoy them as if our happiness consisted in them. The first way is good, the last damnable.

Now, that wicked man Judas (to speak only of him and to leave aside the evil rich man) was very avaricious and greedy to amass money, far beyond what was necessary for the upkeep of Our Lord and His Apostles. Very little was really needed for them, since the Saviour established His ministry on poverty and since He was to send His disciples after Him to preach His Gospel with the order to carry neither purse, nor traveling bag, nor walking staff [*Matt.* 10:9-10; *Mk.* 6:8], and to make no provision for the morrow, but rather to confide in their heavenly Father, who would nourish them by His Providence. [*Matt.* 6:25-34; *Lk.* 12:22-31]. Such was the novitiate of the Apostles, and all the rest of their life was to be founded on this beatitude: Blessed are the poor in spirit.[10] [*Matt.* 5:3].

However, since they would not be sent except after having received the Holy Spirit, and since they lived altogether with Our Lord, He permitted them to have some little things for their use to provide for their daily necessities, but not by way of private ownership. He desired rather that one of them should carry the purse and take care of the expenses. For He, who was the model of all perfection and holiness, did not involve Himself with that. Oh, no, He did not wish to think about it, nor to handle the money with His divine hands. This is what the great St. Bernard remarks when giving a word of warning to a pontiff: "Our Lord, the Sovereign Pontiff and Head of the Apostolic College," he said, "never busied Himself even with permissible material goods nor with those things necessary for His apostolate. Thus, it was necessary to have a general procurator who took care of the affairs, and this was Judas." [*Jn.* 12:6; 13:29].

The Saviour, then, handed over to him the responsibility for temporal affairs. And there would have been no wrongdoing at all in carrying the purse and managing the money if he had done as he should, but this disloyal and miserable man did not conduct himself as a faithful procurator, but rather as a thief and a miser. So he sought continually to amass money and more money, not for the support and upkeep of the community under his care, but to satisfy his avarice and cupidity. So that from being an Apostle that he was, he became a devil and sold his Master for money.

All the holy Fathers, as I have said, greatly underscore this fault, although some say that Judas did not intend, in selling Our Lord, to deliver Him to death. Although the Jews paid Judas for this purpose, nevertheless, they say, this miserable man believed that He would work a miracle to deliver Himself from their hands. By this means he thought to act like a clever thief and robber. After receiving the money from the Jews, he would mock them, since his Master would not in fact die. But it is quite certain that Judas is guilty of the greatest treachery and betrayal that could be imagined and is in no way excusable. The Saviour Himself testified to this at the Last Supper when He said of him, succinctly: One of you is about to betray Me. [*Matt.* 26:21]. And who among the Apostles will be the one to betray his Lord? It is he who keeps the purse and who, to fill it with money through ambition and avarice, will sell Him and deliver Him to death.

Now to be avaricious in the religious and apostolic life is to be like Judas; and it is the greatest defect which can be found in an ecclesiastic and in a religious, just as the greatest fault in a soldier is cowardice. He will never tolerate being called a coward. If you call him a thief, he is not offended. If you say he is debauched it does not bother him. He laughs about it. But if you call him a coward he will take offence and will not endure it, knowing well that this is the greatest injury that can be inflicted upon him, since cowardice is altogether contrary to his profession. If we accuse the wealthy of this world of being avaricious, they care little. But to see avarice in the apostolic life and to accuse a religious of this vice is a very great reproach, for to be avaricious in religion is to sell Our Lord. And why? Because avarice is altogether contrary to the religious profession.

Some ask what was the cause of the fall of Judas, and

how it began. This is my third point. It is very difficult to
declare what initiates the fall of sinners. It is nevertheless
very certain, as theologians say, that it is not that grace fails
them, but rather it is they who fail grace.[11] But to know how
they began to fail—that is very difficult.

Some ancient Fathers say that this could happen at the rejection of a warning, an inspiration. For though this rejection
may be only a venial sin, which does not take grace away,
nevertheless it places an obstacle in its course, fervor dimin-
ishes, and one grows weak in combatting vice. If today you
fail grace, refusing it your consent and committing this venial
sin, you dispose yourself to commit another very soon, and
by the multitude of venial sins to fall little by little into mortal sins, and in this way lose grace.[12] O God, how terrible
a thing is sin, however small and slight it may be! It is this
which made that great St. Bernard say, "Go forward always,
careful not to stop; always advance, for it is impossible to
remain in the same state in this life. [*Job* 14:2]. Whoever
does not advance, must of necessity go back."[13] So the Holy
Spirit gives these warnings: Let him who is standing take
care not to fall! [*1 Cor.* 10:12]. Hold fast to what you have.
[*Apoc.* 3:11]. Take care and labor, that by good works you
may make sure your calling. [*2 Ptr.* 1:10]. These warnings
ought to make us live in great fear and humility in whatsoever place and state we may be, and make us turn our
hearts often to the divine Goodness to invoke His help, raising our minds to God as often as we can, sighing after Him
with frequent prayers and supplications.

Others say we fall into the ruins of sin because of the evil
inclinations inherent in man. It is true that we all have inclinations to evil: some are prone to anger, others to sadness,
others to envy, others to vanity and vainglory, others to avarice; and if we live according to such or similar inclinations
we are lost. "But," someone will say to me, "I have a strong
inclination toward sadness." Now then, you must labor to
rid yourself of it. Another will say, "I am so joyous that
I laugh at every turn." Well, are you lacking God's grace

to mortify this inclination to laugh inordinately? Examine your heart well—it is there that these passions of joy, sadness, vanity or anger dwell. Labor with the help of God and you will arrange them all according to reason. "But I have so many bad inclinations!" And who is there who has not? Do you not have divine grace to resist them? There are others who excuse themselves because of their natural disposition. "Oh!" they say, "we can never do anything worthwhile, we have such a bad disposition." But is not grace higher than nature? St. Paul was naturally sharp, rude and harsh. Nevertheless, the grace of God transformed him and, taking hold of this natural harshness, it made him so much more resolute in the good he undertook, and so courageous and invincible in all kinds of pains and labors, that nothing could shake his courage, so that he became a great Apostle, such that we honor him today. In short, neither natural temperament nor inclinations can hinder us from arriving at the perfection of the Christian life, when we are willing to avail ourselves of the grace to mortify them and subject them to reason.[14] But when we live according to these evil inclinations, we are lost. Now Judas had, among others, that of avarice, and he was lost because he yielded to it.

Many inquire into the cause of Solomon's fall, and there are different opinions about it. Among all the reasons set down about it I am satisfied with touching on the one that he himself gave: Nothing that my eyes desired to look upon did I deny them [*Eccles.* 2:10], as if he meant: "I was a great king. I had many things which were pleasing to behold— magnificent and sumptuous palaces which belonged to me, tapestries, a variety of rich garments. In short, I refused nothing to my eyes of all they desired to see." From this we may conclude that death entered through his eyes [cf. *Jer.* 9:20] and that this was the cause of his fall, for concupiscence enters through the eyes, and with it all kinds of evil. But, O God, I think I have gone beyond the hour!

Now then, Judas fell from grace. From being an Apostle he became an apostate, and recognizing his fault, he despaired and hanged himself. [*Matt.* 27:4, 5; *Acts* 1:18]. And, like the evil rich man, he was buried in the depths of Hell. The Apostles were assembled by the order of God and, after many ceremonies, elected another to take his place. There are still four things to say about this. St. Peter, the head of the Apostles, made them reunite with the Lord's disciples, who were in all one hundred twenty. [*Acts* 1:15]. The purpose was to choose one of the one hundred twenty, or rather one of the one hundred and nine, for the Apostles who were eleven were not to be included. Then St. Peter, speaking to the disciples, said, "We must choose one of you to become an Apostle in the place of Judas, who left us and became an apostate."

We are, then, taught that although Judas left the college of the Apostles, nevertheless, the College of Apostles did not dissolve for that reason. It remains in existence always. For the College of the Apostles remained not only during the life of Our Lord, who had called them and received them; but after His death they elected another to replace the traitor. This is sufficient to confound the Huguenots, who say that the College of the Apostles dissolved when the Apostles died. This is very false, for although the Apostles died, the College of Apostles did not die. Just as St. Peter and all the other Apostles and disciples gathered together and chose one of them to succeed Judas, this one could choose another, and this other still another, and so on continuously. In this way the College of Apostles has passed down to us and will last until the end of the world. From all this we should draw a warning: to work assiduously to secure our vocation—lest, falling, another be put in our place. If you leave religion, religion will not for that reason fail, for divine Providence will send another to occupy your place. But if you do leave, where will you go? I do not know. There is a great danger that in giving up the place you had in religion you might in consequence lose that which had been prepared for you in Heaven, and, like Judas, you may have a place in Hell. For that reason, hold fast to what you have and watch, lest another take it away.[15] Preserve your call and take care that another does not take it from you. Attend to your exercises continually, observe carefully your way of life, serve God faithfully in this vocation lest it escape you. For if you lose it, it will not for that reason be lost, but another will succeed you and inherit it.

Now the Apostles nominated two: one was named Joseph, surnamed Barsabas, and the other was Matthias, who had no surname, but certainly his was a beautiful name. Joseph was just and God-fearing, a man of extraordinary holiness and purity of life, so that he was held in high esteem among the Apostles and disciples. As they were both men of singular virtue, there was a little difficulty in knowing which one they should choose; so, the better to discover what was the will of God, they cast lots. (Many things could be said about casting lots, but I will not speak of them here. I will only say that this can be done when both parties are equal or when there is no great disproportion between them, as there was none between St. Joseph, for he was a saint, and St. Matthias.) The lot fell to this latter and he became an Apostle. [*Acts* 1:23-26].

Some think that the Apostles received an inspiration or an interior word which made them understand that Matthias was chosen by God to be an Apostle, and that they all with one voice said that it should be so. Something like that happened when St. Ambrose was made bishop. The people were troubled about this election, and a little child's voice was heard to say: "Ambrose will be bishop." Then everyone cried out that Ambrose was the one. The same happened with St. Nicholas, and some others.

Now Joseph, who was just, did not lose his justice because he was not chosen to be an Apostle. His holiness remained with him to teach us that God does not always choose the holiest to govern and to have charges in His Church. Therefore, those who are called ought not to glorify themselves and presume themselves to be better or more perfect than others. And those who do not receive such offices ought not to be troubled about it, since that will not prevent them from being just and pleasing to God.

This, then, is how St. Matthias succeeded Judas, and how he became a great Apostle. And what was the end of Judas? He despaired, and, seeing what he had done, brought back the money to the priests of the Law, confessing that he had sold the Blood of the Just One. But these Mosaic priests rejected him, saying that they did not care about that, that if he had done wrong it was his damnation, but as for themselves they had nothing to do with it. [*Matt.* 27:4-5]. For with the Law of Moses it was not the same as with the law of Grace, under which we live. The priests of our time do not reject sinners when they come to them, since there is no sin, however great and grievous it may be, which cannot be pardoned in this life, if one confesses it. This is an article of faith. In short, Judas despaired, hanged himself and perished,[16] and his soul was buried in the depths of Hell with that of the evil rich man. But that of Lazarus was carried to the bosom of Abraham, and from there into Heaven, where with St. Matthias, who lived and died as a great Apostle, he will enjoy forever the eternity which is God Himself, to whom be honor and glory forever and ever. Amen.

NOTES

1. Cf. *Treatise on the Love of God,* Bk. 2, chap. 10-12; Bk. 3, chap. 4; Bk. 4, chap. 5, 6.
2. *Acts* 1:21-22 suggests the contrary: "Wherefore of these men who have companied with us all the time that the Lord Jesus came in and went out among us, beginning from the baptism of John, until the day wherein he was taken up from us, one of these must be made a witness with us of his resurrection." No doubt St. Francis means that St. Matthias was not one of the original Twelve, but rather one of those who accompanied the Twelve and Jesus.
3. The "heaven" referred to here is not the place of glory and the Beatific Vision; no sin is possible in Heaven. (Elsewhere St. Francis de Sales assures us that in Heaven we will be out of danger of sinning.) Rather, this "heaven" refers to the abode of the spirit world during their period of probation. Cf. p. 71 where St. Francis clarifies this point by stating parenthetically that before their sin the bad angels

were not yet members of the Church Triumphant. Thus they had not yet attained to the Heaven of the blessed.

4. Cf. Sermon for First Sunday of Lent, p. 24 of this volume.
5. Cf. p. 78 of this sermon.
6. Cf. *Treatise on the Love of God*, Bk. 4, chap. 1; *Spiritual Conferences*, XVII, "Voting," pp. 329-330.
7. Cf. Note 3.
8. That is, in sin, the human person confuses means and ends. The things of earth ought to be used as means to our final end, which is Heaven, not as ends in themselves; while the things of God indeed are our final end, and should not be looked upon simply as helps to make this world a more gracious place to live.
9. Cf. *Introduction*, Part III, chap. 14, 15.
10. Cf. p. 68 of this sermon.
11. Cf. p. 67 of this sermon.
12. Cf. *Treatise on the Love of God*, Bk. 4, chap. 2.
13. Cf. *Treatise on the Love of God*, Bk. 3, chap. 1.
14. Cf. *Spiritual Conferences*, XVII, "Voting"; *Treatise on the Love of God*, Bk. 12, chap. 1.
15. Cf. p. 77 of this sermon.
16. Cf. pp. 78-79 of this sermon.

6

MUTUAL CHARITY

Sermon for the Third Sunday of Lent, February 27, 1622, concerning Our Lord's commandment of love of neighbor, His desire that we be united with each other, the relationship between love of God and love of neighbor, in what way the Commandment of love of neighbor is new, Our Lord's example of love of neighbor, Our Lord's restoration of man to God's image and likeness, seeing and loving Our Lord in our neighbor, the extent to which we should love our neighbor, how it is better to be spent for our neighbor's sake than to spend ourselves for him in the way we choose, union with God and our neighbor in the Most Blessed Sacrament, love of neighbor as the Commandment which God stresses to us the most earnestly, and how we should love our neighbor with the same incomparable ardor and constancy with which Our Lord loved us on the Cross.

> *"Every kingdom divided against itself is brought to desolation."—Lk.* 11:17

In today's Gospel [*Lk.* 11:14-28], Our Lord insists that every kingdom divided against itself (not united in itself) is brought to desolation. On the other hand, the converse is true, too: all kingdoms united in concord, not permitting any division to enter, will surely be filled with consolation. For if the propositions are opposite, the consequences must be, also. These words are among the most remarkable, noteworthy and important that our Divine Master ever spoke. For this reason the ancient Fathers carefully interpreted them.

They agree that our Saviour had three kinds of concord or union in mind when He spoke, where division in any of them results in desolation. The first is the concord which should exist between a king and his subjects, making subjects submissive and obedient to his laws. The second is the union which we ought to have within, in our inner kingdom, where reason must be the king to whom are subject all the faculties of our spirit, all our senses, and even our bodies. Without this obedience and submission we cannot avoid having desolation and trouble, any more than there could be peace in a kingdom in which the subjects are not obedient to the laws of the king.

Since it would require too much time to speak of all three unions, I will dwell only on the third, that which we ought to have with each other. This union or concord has been earnestly preached, recommended and taught to us by Our Lord, equally in word and example. He does this so forcibly and in such admirable terms that He appears to forget to recommend to us the love we ought to have for Himself and for His Heavenly Father. He does this to better inculcate in us the love and union He wants us to have for one another. He even calls the Commandment of love for the neighbor *His* Commandment[1] [*Jn.* 15:12], His most cherished one. He came into this world to teach us, as our divine Master. Yet nothing is so stressed, nothing stated so completely as the observance of this Commandment. He does so with good reason, for the beloved of the Beloved, the great Apostle St. John, assures us that anyone who says that he loves God and does not love his neighbor is a liar. [*1 Jn.* 4:20-21]. On the other hand, he who says he loves his neighbor but does not love God also contradicts the truth. That simply cannot be. To love God without loving the neighbor, who is created in His image and likeness [*Gen.* 1:26-27], is impossible.[2]

But what should this union and concord be which we all ought to have? Oh! What should it be indeed! It must be such that if Our Lord Himself had not explained it, no one would have been so daring as to use the same terms as His. At the Last Supper, after He had given the incomparable pledge of His love for us men, the Most Blessed Sacrament of the Eucharist, He said: Father, My very dear Father, I beseech You that all those whom You have given Me may be one, as You and I, Father, are one. [*Jn.* 17:11-12, 21-22]. To show that He was not speaking only for the Apostles, but for all the rest of us, He added: I do not pray for them alone (that is, those He had just mentioned), but for all those who will believe in Me through their word. [*Jn.* 17:20]. Who would have dared, I repeat, to make such a comparison, or to ask that we might be united as the Father, the Son and the Holy Spirit are united?

This prayer seems at first glance too good to be true, for the union of the three Divine Persons is really incomprehensible, and no one at all can possibly imagine that simple union and that unity so unspeakably simple. Thus we cannot really hope to reach an identical union, for that is impossible, as all the ancient Fathers point out. We must be content to approach it as nearly as possible, according to our capacity. Actually, Our Lord does not call us to an identical union, but only to the quality of this union; that is, we ought to love one another and be united together as purely and perfectly as possible.

I have taken much more pleasure in preparing this subject today since I found that St. Paul recommends to us this love of the neighbor in that wonderful language he uses in the Epistle we read today at Holy Mass. To the Ephesians he writes: "Beloved, walk the way of love for one another as very dear children of God; walk in this way just as Jesus Christ walked in it, giving His own self for us, offering Himself to God His Father as a holocaust and oblation of sweet odor." [*Eph.* 5:1-2]. Oh, how lovable these words are, and worthy of reflection! These are golden words. By them this great saint helps us to understand what our concord and our dilection toward each other should be like.

Concord and dilection are the same thing. The word

"concord" signifies union of heart. "Dilection" signifies election of affections, or union of affections. He seems to want to make clear to us what the Saviour meant when He prayed to His heavenly Father that we might all be one (that is, united), as He and His Father are One. Our Lord was somewhat brief in teaching us in words how He wanted us to practice this holy and most sacred union. For this reason His glorious Apostle developed them in explaining them to us. He exhorts us to walk in the way of dilection (love) as God's most dear children. It is as if he meant: Just as God, our all-good Father, has loved us so dearly that He has adopted us as His children [*Eph.* 1:5; *1 Jn.* 3:1-2], you must show that you are truly His children by your loving one another dearly in all goodness of heart.

Lest we may walk with a child's steps in the way of dilection which God our Father has so strongly recommended to us, St. Paul adds: Walk the way Our Lord walked in it: He gave Himself for us, and so on. By this he indicates that he wants us to walk with giant strides and not with a child's little steps. Love one another as Jesus Christ has loved us [*Jn.* 13:34; 15:12], not because of any merit that may be found in us, but only because He created us in His image and likeness.[3] It is this image and likeness that we ought to love and honor in all, not anything else that may be there. For really nothing is lovable in us which is of us, since not only does it not enhance this divine image and likeness, but it actually disfigures, defiles and stains it so that we are scarcely recognizable. Now we must not love that in our neighbor, for God does not will it.[4]

Why, then, does Our Lord want us to love one another so much, and why, ask the majority of the holy Fathers, did He take so much care to equate this precept to the Commandment of the love of God? [*Matt.* 22:39]. It astonished the Fathers that these two Commandments are said to be similar to each other, because one pertains to the love of God and the other to the love of the creature: God, who is infinite, and the creature who is finite; God, who is Goodness itself and from whom all good comes to us, and man, who is full of malice, through whom so many miseries come upon us. For the Commandment to love the neighbor includes also the love of enemies. [*Matt.* 5:43, 44]. O God! What disproportion between the objects of these two loves, and yet these two Commandments are alike to such a degree that the one cannot exist without the other and must necessarily increase or perish in proportion as the other increases or perishes, as St. John declares. [*Jn.* 3:30].

Mark Antony once purchased two young slaves who were brought to him by a trader. At that time children were sometimes sold, as is still done in some countries today. There were men who supplied them and engaged in this business much as we do with horses in our country today. These two children resembled each other so perfectly that the trader tricked Mark Antony into believing that they were twins, for otherwise how could they resemble each other so perfectly? When they were separated from one another, it was particularly difficult to tell which was which. They were such a rarity that Mark Antony valued them greatly and paid dearly for them. But when he brought them to his house, he found that each spoke a different language. Pliny relates that one was from Dauphiny and the other from Asia, places incredibly distant from each other. Discovering that they were not only not twins, but not even from the same country or born under the same king, Mark Antony flew into a rage and became incensed with the person who had sold them to him. But a certain young character convinced him that their resemblance was that much more remarkable inasmuch as they were from different countries and had no connection with each other. That calmed him. He came eventually to value them so highly that he would have preferred losing all his property to losing these two children, such a rarity did he find in their resemblance.

This helps us to appreciate the fact that, in the same way, the Commandments of love of God and love of neighbor resemble each other as much as these two slaves of whom Pliny speaks, even though they too are from "countries" very remote from each other. Indeed, what could be more remote, I ask you, than the Infinite from the finite; than divine love, which relates to the immortal God, from love of neighbor, which relates to mortal man; than the one, which relates to Heaven, from the other, which relates to earth? Because of all this, this resemblance is all that much more amazing. Therefore, like Mark Antony, we should purchase both these loves as twins coming forth from the merciful Heart of our good God at the same time. For simultaneous with His creation of man in His image and likeness,[5] God commanded him to love both God and neighbor.

The law of nature has always taught these two precepts and has engraved them in the hearts of all, so that even if God had not spoken of them, nevertheless all would have known that they were obliged to keep them.[6] This seems clear in that the Lord was extremely displeased by the answer given Him by the miserable Cain who, when God asked him what he had done with his brother Abel, had the arrogance to respond that he was not obliged to watch out for him. [*Gen.* 4:9]. No one can excuse himself from this and say that he does not know that he is to love his neighbor as himself, because God has imprinted this truth in the bottom of our hearts in creating all of us in the image and likeness of each other. Bearing the image of God in ourselves, all of us are consequently the image of each other. Together we constitute the image of one portrait, that of God.

Since this is so let us see, I pray you, in what terms Our Lord has recommended the love of neighbor to us. I will make several observations. Speaking to His Apostles, He said, "I give you a new commandment: Love one another." [*Jn.* 13:34]. First of all, why does He call this Commandment *new,* since it had already been given in the Law of Moses? [*Lev.* 19:18]. As we have just seen, it had not even been ignored—but rather was recognized—in the law of nature; in fact, it had even been observed by some since the creation of man. Our Divine Master called it new because He wanted to renew it. When a quantity of new wine is put into a cask in which there is still a little of the old, we do not say that the cask contains old wine, but rather new wine, because there is such a greater quantity of the new than the old. Similarly, Our Lord called this Commandment *new* because although it had been given before, it had been observed by only a very small number of people. Because He wanted it to be so renewed that everybody would love one another, He could designate it altogether *new.*

Thus the first Christians had but one heart and one soul [*Acts* 4:32], and preserved such a union among themselves that there was never found any division among them. As a result of their concord, they enjoyed a very great consolation. The many grains of wheat are ground and kneaded together to make but one single loaf, a loaf which is made from all those grains which, though once separated, can no longer ever be separated or distinguished or recognized individually. In the same way, those early Christians had so fervent a love for each other that their wills and their hearts were all holily blended as one. But this holy blending and divine mixture presented no difficulty, for neither division nor separation was possible. The bread thus kneaded from all these hearts was infinitely pleasing to the taste of the Divine Majesty.

Many grapes are pressed together to make but one wine. It is no longer possible to distinguish what wine came forth from which cluster or which bunch. Being blended together haphazardly, they form but one wine drawn from the many clusters. In like fashion, the hearts of the first Christians, in which holy charity and dilection reigned, were only one wine though made from many hearts as from so many grapes. What built that great union among them was none other, my dear souls, than the most Holy Communion. [*Acts* 2:42; *1 Cor.* 10:17]. When later on Its reception was discontinued, or when It was rarely received,[7] charity itself, by this very fact, became cold among Christians and totally lost both its strength and its attractive sweetness.

The Commandment to love the neighbor is new, then, for the reason just given; that is, because Our Lord came to renew it, indicating that He wished it to be better observed than it had ever been before. It is new also because it is as if the Saviour resuscitated it, just as we can call a man a new man who has been restored to life from death. This Commandment had been so neglected that it must have seemed never to have been given inasmuch as there were so few who remembered it, or at least who observed it. Then Our Lord gave it again. And He wants it to be as if it were a new thing, a new Commandment, one that is practiced faithfully and fervently.

It is *new* also because of the new obligations that we have to observe it. What are these obligations that Jesus Christ brought to the world in order to render us pliant in the observance of this divine precept? They are certainly great, since He Himself came to teach them to us, not only in words but, much more, in example. This divine and most lovable Teacher did not want to instruct us how to paint until He Himself had first painted before us. Thus He gave us no precept which He Himself had not first practiced. And so, before renewing this Commandment of love of neighbor, He loved us and showed us by His example how we ought to observe it so that we would have no excuse to the effect that it is impossible to observe. He gave Himself to us in the Most Holy Sacrament and then He said: Love one another as I have loved you. [*Jn*. 15:12]. The men of the Old Law were damned if they did not love their neighbor, because either the law of nature or the Mosaic Law obliged them to it. But if, after the example Our Lord has left us of it, Christians still do not love one another and do not observe this divine precept of mutual charity, they will be condemned with a condemnation incomparably greater.

People of old (I mean those who lived before the Incarnation of our dear Saviour and Master) may have been somewhat excusable if they did not observe this Commandment well. For, though it was already known at that time that Our

Lord would unite our human nature to the divine nature and would come to repair by His death and Passion the image and likeness of God that is imprinted upon us,[8] it was only known by some of the greatest of them—the Patriarchs and Prophets, for instance. The rest were almost all ignorant of it. But now that we know, not that He *will* come, but that He *has* come, and has recommended anew this holy dilection one for another, how worthy of punishment shall we be if we do not love our neighbor!

Is it any wonder that this beloved Lover of our souls wants us to love one another as He has loved us, seeing that He has so completely restored us to that perfect resemblance to Him which we once had that it almost seems as if there is no longer any difference between Him and us? Certainly, no one can doubt that the image of God which was ours before the Incarnation of the Saviour was very far from the true likeness of Him whom we represented and whose portrait we were. For what proportion is there, I ask you, between God and the creature? The colors of this portrait were extremely faded, tarnished and discolored; there remained only some features, some small lineaments, such as we see in a portrait or picture which is only sketched, to which the last tints have not yet been added. It bears but a slight resemblance to him whom it represents. But Our Lord, in coming into the world, has so raised our nature higher than all the angels, the cherubim, and all that is not God, and has made us so like Himself, that we can say with certainty that we resemble God perfectly. In becoming man, He has taken our likeness and given us His.[9] Oh, how earnestly should we summon up our courage to live according to what we are and to imitate as perfectly as possible Him who came into this world to teach us what we need to do to preserve in ourselves this beauty and divine resemblance which He has so completely repaired and embellished in us!

Now tell me, then, how cordial ought our love to be for one another, since Our Lord has repaired us all equally, and without any exception made us like to Himself? We must

always remember, however, that we are not to love in our
neighbor what is contrary to this divine resemblance and what
could disfigure this sacred portrait. But with this one exception, my dear souls, ought we not to love dearly the neighbor, who truly represents to us the sacred Person of our
Master? And is this not one of the most powerful motives
we could have for loving each other with an ardently burning
love? When we see our neighbor, ought we not to do as the
good Raguel did when he saw the young Tobias? Tobias went
to Rages in obedience to his father [also called Tobias]. He
met there the good man Raguel. After studying him, Raguel
said to his wife: "Ah, my God, this young man reminds me
so much of my kinsman Tobias!" Then he asked the young
man where he came from and if he knew Tobias, to which
the angel who had led him answered: "Do we know him!
He to whom you are speaking is his son!" Then the good
Raguel was overcome with joy and embraced him and kissed
and caressed him very tenderly. "O my child," he cried out,
"you are the son of a good father, and how you resemble
that noble man!" Then he received him into his house and
treated him royally, in keeping with the affection which he
held for his kinsman Tobias.[10] [*Tob*. 7:1-9].

Should we not do the same when we meet one another?
We should say to our brother: "How greatly you resemble
that noble Man, for you remind me of my Saviour and my
Master!" And upon the assurance that he would give us, or
that we would give each other, that we do indeed recognize
the resemblance of the Creator and that we are His children,
how many tokens of affection ought we not to give one another!
To speak better, how lovingly and tenderly ought we to receive
our neighbor, honoring in him this divine resemblance, always tightening more closely this sweet bond of charity [*Col*.
3:14] which keeps us bound, clasped and united to each other.
Let us walk then in the way of love, as God's most dear
children, just as the holy Apostle exhorts us to do in today's
epistle.

But walk, he continues, as Jesus Christ walked. He gave

His life for us and offered Himself to His Father as an offering for us, an oblation of sweet odor. [*Eph.* 5:1-2]. From these words we learn to what degree our mutual love ought to extend and to what perfection it should reach: to give one another soul for soul, life for life—in short, all that we are and all that we have, excepting only our own salvation. For God desires only that exception. Our Lord gave Himself for each one of us; He gave His soul, He gave His body. In short, He reserved nothing. Similarly, He wants us to hold back nothing [*1 Jn.* 3:16] except our eternal salvation.

Our Divine Master gave us His life not only to heal the sick, to work miracles, and to teach us what we ought to do to be saved or to be pleasing to Him. He also spent His entire life even shaping His cross, suffering a thousand thousand persecutions from the very ones to whom He was doing so much good and for whom He laid down His life. We must do the same, says the holy Apostle, that is, we too should shape our cross in suffering for one another as the Saviour taught us; in giving our life for those very ones who would take it from us, as He so lovingly did; in spending ourselves for our neighbor, not only in agreeable things, but also in those which are painful and disagreeable such as bearing lovingly these persecutions which might in some fashion cool our heart towards our brothers.

There are some who say: "I greatly love my neighbor and would wish, indeed, to render him some service." That is very good, says St. Bernard, but it is not enough; we must go further. "Oh! I love him so much! I love him so much that I would gladly sacrifice all my possessions for him." That is going further and is certainly better, but still it is not enough. "I love him, I assure you, so greatly that I would willingly expend myself for him in whatever he wanted from me." This is certainly a very good sign of your love, but you must go still further; for there is a still higher degree in this love, as St. Paul teaches us, when he wrote: "Be imitators of me as I imitate Christ." [*1 Cor.* 11:1]. And in one of his epistles[11] he wrote thus to his most dear children:

"I am ready to give my life for you, and give of myself so completely that I make no reservation in proving to you how dearly and tenderly I love you. Yes, I am even ready to agree to all that anyone would want of me in your behalf." [*2 Cor.* 12:14-15, 19]. In this he teaches us that to spend ourselves even so far as to give our life for the neighbor is not as much as to allow ourselves to be spent at the will of others, either by them or for them.

This is what he had learned from our dear Saviour, who spent Himself for our salvation and our redemption [*Phil.* 2:8], and afterwards allowed Himself to be spent so as to perfect this Redemption and to win eternal life for us, even permitting Himself to be fastened to the Cross by the very persons for whom He died. He spent Himself during His whole life, but in His death He allowed Himself to be spent, permitting not His friends, but His enemies, to do with Him all that they wished. They put Him to death with a fury insupportably wicked. Nevertheless, He did not resist at all but allowed Himself to be pulled and turned in every direction as prompted by the cruelty of these malicious executioners. [*Is.* 50:5]. For He beheld in all this the will of His heavenly Father, which was that He should die for humankind, and to which He submitted with an incomparable love, one more worthy of being adored than imagined or understood.

It is to this sovereign degree of perfection in the love of the neighbor that religious, and we others who are consecrated to the service of God, are called, and for it we must aspire with all our strength. We must spend ourselves not only for his good and consolation, but also permit ourselves to be spent for him by holy obedience—to do, without ever resisting, whatever shall be desired from us. When we spend ourselves, what we do by our own choice or our own will always greatly satisfies our self-love. But to allow ourselves to be spent for the neighbor in things which she wishes and we do not, that is, which we do not choose, therein lies the sovereign degree of abnegation which Our Lord and Master taught us in dying. We would rather preach, but are sent to serve the sick; we want to pray for the neighbor, but are sent to serve him instead. It is always of greater value by far to do what we are made to do (I mean, of course, only in that which is not contrary to God and does not offend Him) than to do what we choose of ourselves.

Let us then love one another, says St. Paul, as Our Lord loved us. He offered Himself as a holocaust: when He was on the Cross He poured out His blood upon the earth even to the last drop, as if to make a sacred mortar [*Col.* 1:20] with which He would mortar, unite, join and attach to each other all the stones of His Church, that is, the faithful. He did this that they might be so united that there would never be any division found among them, so greatly did He fear that this division would be the cause of their eternal desolation.[12] [*Lk.* 11:14-28]. Oh, how powerful this motive is to move us to love this Commandment and to observe it exactly. We have all alike been washed with this Precious Blood, as with a sacred mortar, to bind and unite our hearts together! Oh, how great is the goodness of our God! [*Ps.* 72 (73):1].

Our Lord was offered, or rather offered Himself, for us to God His Father as an offering, an oblation of sweet odor. [*Eph.* 5:1-2]. What divine fragrance He spread before the Divine Majesty when He instituted the Most Holy Sacrament of the Altar, where He so admirably demonstrated to us the greatness of His love. This act of incomprehensible perfection, by which He gave Himself to us who were His enemies and who caused Him His death, was an infinitely sweet fragrance. At the same time He bestowed on us the means to reach the supreme degree of union which He desired for us, namely, to be made one with Him as He and His Father are One,[13] that is, one same reality. [*Jn.* 17:11-12, 21-22]. He had asked this of His heavenly Father, or rather He had desired to ask it; now in asking it He discovered at the same time how it was to be realized. O incomparable Goodness! How worthy You are to be loved and adored!

To what extent did the greatness of God lower itself for each one of us, and to what extent does He wish to exalt us? To unite us so perfectly with Himself as to make us one same thing with Him. Our Lord did this to teach us that as we are all loved with one same love by which He embraces us all in this Most Holy Sacrament, so He wishes us all to love one another with that same love, a love which tends toward union, but a union greater and more perfect than can be conceived. We are all nourished with the same bread [1 Cor. 10:17], this heavenly Bread, the divine Eucharist. The eating of It, called Communion, represents to us, as we have said, the common union that we ought to have together;[14] without this union we would not be worthy of bearing the name of "children of God," since we would not be obedient to Him.

Children who have a good father ought to imitate him and follow his commandment in all things. Now, we have a Father better than all others and from whom all good is derived. [Jas. 1:17]. His commandments can be nothing but perfect and salutary. Thus we should imitate Him as perfectly as possible, and also obey His divine ordinances. But of all His precepts, there is none which He stresses so earnestly, nor for which He has indicated that He desires so exact an observance, as that of the love of neighbor. The Commandment to love God is higher than the Commandment to love the neighbor; but since nature offers greater resistance to the love of neighbor, it was necessary that we should be encouraged in a more particular manner to its practice.

Let us love, then, to the whole extent of our hearts, in order to please our heavenly Father, but let us love reasonably; that is, let our love be guided by reason, which desires that we love the soul of the neighbor more than his body. But let us love his body also, and then, in proper order, all that pertains to the neighbo., each thing according to its merits, for the proper exercise of this love.

If we do this, oh how justly we can sing, and surely with great consolation, this Psalm which St. Augustine found such delight in reflecting upon: Behold how good it is and how pleasant where brethren dwell in holy union, concord, and peace, for they are like the precious ointment they poured out upon the head of the High Priest Aaron, which then flowed down over his beard and onto his robes. [*Ps.* 132 (133)]. Our Divine Master is the High Priest upon whom this precious and fragrant ointment of most holy charity has been poured out in measureless profusion, both toward God and toward the neighbor. We are as the hair of His head and His beard. Or else, we can consider the Apostles as the beard of Our Lord, who is our Head, and whose members we are. [*1 Cor.* 12:12, 27; *Eph.* 4:15; *Col.* 1:18]. The Apostles were attached to Him in that they saw His example and His works and received His teachings immediately from His sacred mouth. The rest of us have not had this honor. Rather, what we know we have learned from the Apostles. We are, then, like the robes of our High Priest, our Saviour, on which, nevertheless, overflowed that precious ointment of most holy charity which He so greatly prescribed and recommended to us. And so His holy Apostle has expressed this charity more in detail for us, not wanting us to busy ourselves in imitating either the angels or the cherubim in this so very necessary virtue, but rather to imitate Our Lord Himself, who taught it to us more by works than by words, especially when fastened to the Cross.

It is at the foot of this Cross that we should remain always. It is the place where the imitators of our Sovereign Master and Saviour ordinarily abide. For it is from the Cross that they receive the heavenly liqueur of holy charity. It streams out in great profusion from a divine Source, the bosom of our good God's divine mercy. He loved us with a love so firm, so solid, so ardent and so persevering that death itself could not cool it in the least. Quite the contrary, it warmed and increased it infinitely. The waters of the most bitter afflictions cannot quench the fire of His charity toward us [*Cant.* 8:6-7], so ardent is it. Even the persecutions wrought by His enemies were not powerful enough to vanquish the incomparable solidity and constancy of the love with which He loved us. Such ought to be our love for the neighbor: firm, ardent, solid and persevering.

NOTES

1. Cf. Sermon for the Second Sunday of Lent, p. 54 of this volume.
2. Cf. *Treatise on the Love of God,* Bk. X, chap. 11; *Sermons of St. Francis de Sales on Our Lady,* "The Assumption," August 15, 1618, p. 73; and "The Visitation," July 2, 1621, p. 159.
3. Cf. p. 84 of this sermon.
4. Cf. *Introduction to the Devout Life,* Part III, chap. 22.
5. Cf. p. 84 of this sermon.
6. St. Francis de Sales seems here to be expanding the parameter of the natural law from the injunction to "do good and avoid evil" to the double commandment of love of God and love of neighbor. This is just another indication of the centrality of love in his spiritual vision.
7. St. Francis de Sales is referring to a period when the frequent reception of Holy Communion had fallen into disuse; there were perhaps some who did not receive Communion at all.
8. Cf. p. 84 of this sermon.
9. Rarely has a western Doctor of the Church assessed redeemed humanity as positively as St. Francis de Sales does here. No doubt these thoughts on the grandeur of redeemed humanity contribute much to his optimistic appreciation of Christian anthropology, as well as to the attractiveness of his spirituality.
10. Cf. *Treatise on the Love of God,* Bk. X, chap. 11.
11. Cf. *Spiritual Conferences,* IV, "On Cordiality," pp. 64-65.
12. Cf. pp. 83-84 of this sermon.
13. Cf. p. 85 of this sermon.
14. Cf. *Spiritual Conferences,* VI, "On Hope," pp. 97-98.

7

PROPER CONDUCT IN ILLNESS

*Sermon for the Thursday after the Third Sunday
of Lent, March 3, 1622, concerning the cure of
St. Peter's mother-in-law, the celibacy of St. Peter,
the Communion of Saints, God's lordship over all
things, two methods of meditating, the wonderful
submission to God and resignation into the hands
of her superiors of St. Peter's mother-in-law as
she lay ill with fever, over-eagerness in seeking
cures from God, St. Bernard's words that religious
must not be concerned with their bodily illnesses,
over-eagerness in seeking remedies for illness, how
we should imitate St. Peter's mother-in-law, the
use of one's health to serve God, and the practice
of true evangelical poverty in time of illness.*

In the first part of today's Gospel [*Lk.* 4:38-44], upon which
I ought and indeed want to dwell, mention is made of the
cure of St. Peter's mother-in-law, which was brought about
by Our Lord in Capharnaum. Here are the facts of the story:
Our Divine Master was in that city, proclaiming the works
and greatness of His heavenly Father's providence. After He
had cured many people and freed a person tormented by the
devil [*Lk.* 4:33-35], He entered the house of Simon and Andrew and cured Peter's mother-in-law, who was racked with
a fever.

It happened this way. The Saviour entered the house just
before dinner. Sts. John, James and Andrew, and his brother
Peter, decided that before sitting down to dinner they would
ask Him to cure this woman. After they made their request,
Our Lord approached the patient's bed and, standing over

her, looked at her, and grasping her hand [*Mk.* 1:31], commanded the fever to leave her, or as St. Luke says, rebuked the fever and it left her. Then this good woman, feeling herself healed, got up and waited on them. First I will speak of three or four points concerning the literal meaning of this text, and then we will consider the rest.

First, the Evangelist writes that Jesus entered the house of Simon, the great Apostle St. Peter, who was the first of the Apostles to follow our dear Master, along with his brother St. Andrew. [*Matt.* 4:18-20; *Jn.* 1:41]. St. Matthew shows this clearly in his eighth chapter [*Matt.* 8:14], and St. Mark indirectly in his first chapter. [*Mk.* 1:29]. St. Luke does not mention this in today's Gospel—only that Jesus, having entered the house of Simon, cured his mother-in-law who was racked with a fever. Many superficial minds have concluded from this incident that St. Peter was not celibate at that time. The Huguenots conclude that since he had a mother-in-law, he must have been married at that time. This is certainly not so, for burdened with the duties of married life, he would not have been able to follow Our Lord.

But if they said that since he had a mother-in-law he must have had a wife at one time, and consequently a family too, that would be a different thing altogether. It would be a reasonable inference. Thus, we can conclude that although he had not always been celibate, he took on celibacy when he became a follower of the Saviour. This is clear by these words he addressed to Jesus: Here we have left all things to follow You; what can we expect from it? [*Matt.* 19:27]. "We have left all things": He did not say "in part," but "all," without any reserve whatsoever. "And since we have left all, what reward will we receive from You?" Now, had he been married, he could not have spoken in that way.

Since Our Lord chose St. Peter to be the head of all His priests, it was only fitting that he should be celibate since, as St. Jerome wrote, the virgin who marries cannot say that she belongs entirely to God. It is true that she may always recognize Him as her Lord; yet she has another lesser lord to whom she also belongs and whom she loves. Therefore her heart cannot belong entirely to Jesus Christ. It is shared, it is divided. [cf. *1 Cor.* 7:33-34]. But priests, being completely dedicated to God, should have no other lord but Him. That is why they detach themselves from the creature by renouncing marriage, the better to unite themselves more intimately to their God. The Sacrament of Matrimony is a union of creature with creature, and that of Orders is in some manner a separation of creature from creature. Thus, we must conclude that the Prince of the Apostles was a celibate and followed our dear Saviour with his whole heart.

Although it is said that Jesus entered the house of Simon, we must not think that this glorious saint had reserved a house for himself or that he still had a family. Oh no, for he had left all to follow his Master—his house, his family, his trade, and all the care and ambition that a man can have. He had had a family and a house in which his mother-in-law lived. Having left all things, he had given her the use of the house and the care of his family. Thus when it says that Our Lord entered the house of St. Peter, we must not conclude that this Apostle had one at the time, but only that it had at one time been his.

When it is written that the Apostles Peter, Andrew, John and James gathered together to ask for the cure of Simon's mother-in-law, this is a very important matter. For this request represents the Communion of Saints, by which the body of the Church is so united that all its members share in the good of one another. From this it follows that all Christians share in all the prayers and good works which are offered in Holy Mother Church. This communion exists not only here below on earth, but in Heaven as well. That position is foolish and stupid, then, which, though willing to believe in the Communion of Saints on earth, will not believe that it extends to Heaven. Certainly, people who hold that view do not believe in that article of the Apostles' Creed. It is most certain that, as we share here below in the prayers of one another, so these same prayers and good works profit

the souls in Purgatory, who can be helped by them. Moreover, they and we share in the prayers of the blessed, who
are in Paradise. It is in this that this Communion of the Saints
consists. This article of faith is symbolized by the cure of
our sick woman, who was not relieved by her own prayers,
but by those of the Apostles, who interceded for her.[1]

When Our Lord commanded the fever to leave her He
showed His omnipotence, letting it be seen that He was the
Master of sickness as well as of health, and that all things
obey Him. Angered by the evil of the fever, He rebuked it
and drove it out of her, as if He wanted to say: "How dare
it remain where the Physician and the Medicine of life is?
Why does it not flee My presence without waiting for Me
to command it?" It is written that God was angry with the
Red Sea because it had not dried up. [*Ps.* 105 (106):9]. That
seems to mean that since God's will was that the Red Sea
should be dry, He rebuked it for not being so, implying thereby
that it should have dried up even before He commanded it
to do so. So much for the literal meaning.

Let us now say something of the spiritual aspect of sickness. There are so many spiritual maladies that if I were
to begin speaking of them I would never finish. For they
are at work all year long. Although religious are exempt from
some of them, they are not exempt from all of them. But
I thought I would not treat of them today, but of bodily maladies, from which religious are no more exempt than are others.
These bodily maladies are found as much in religious houses
as in the world. And since today's Gospel deals with them,
it is very important to know how to profit from them. We
learn how to profit from them from our fever patient, who
practiced so many admirable virtues in her sickness that I
think her story ought to be written for all monastic infir-
maries, to serve as an example for all those who suffer illness and to teach them how to profit spiritually from them.
This woman practiced many virtues, but I will single out
only three for comment.

But before discussing bodily illnesses, I must cure—or at

least give the remedy proper to cure—a spiritual illness which is found in many persons. This concerns one's approach to subjects for meditation. This will serve as a preface to my discourse. I will use St. Paul's words on the subject of Melchisedech. I will use them as an "armed preface" according to St. Jerome's expression—that is, a preface which has its arms and which carries a helmet on its head. The great Apostle calls Melchisedech "king of peace" and "king of justice." [*Heb.* 7:1-3]. Then he adds that he was without father, mother or genealogy, without beginning of days or end of life. Now, many superficial and foolish minds have created heresies based on these words. They said in their false belief that Melchisedech was not a man, that he did not have a true body like ours, and they go so far as to attribute divinity to him, as if he were God—something which is manifestly false. According to St. Paul, he was a just and peaceable man, and there is no difficulty in believing that he was like all other men. In our attempt to draw different meanings from Scripture, we must never go beyond legitimate bounds in proposing our interpretations. Let us say something, then, on the correct way of meditating on Scripture.

We can consider the holy Bible, that is, the mysteries contained therein, and principally the Gospels, in two ways. The first is to use the pious considerations arranged by many of those who have had the guidance of souls. They have had beautiful insights both into the life and death of Our Lord, as well as into the other mysteries of our faith, insights which can be useful in meditation. There are still many spiritual guides today,[2] and others as well, to whom the Holy Spirit inspires holy and devout thoughts. These they arrange for our use. After all, the same God who was yesterday is still today [*Heb.* 13:8], granting as many graces and favors to us in this present time as He did to our fathers before us.

In this manner of meditating we must make good use of our imagination and reason, seeing the different thoughts or scenes from the Gospel or from the mystery upon which we are meditating, as some have done for our pious belief. For example, we can imagine the many tears shed during the Passion at the meeting of the Son and the Mother, as the Saviour carried His Cross to Mount Calvary—as well as the many tears shed at the scourging and at the foot of the Cross. In order to represent the convulsions and sorrows of the most holy Virgin, Our Lady, some have imagined her quite shocked, swooning and weakened with sorrow at the death of her Son. Our artists have depicted her thus at the foot of the Cross, as if she had been overcome by weakness or fainting. But this never happened to her, either in the life or in the death of Our Lord, for the Evangelist says that she remained firm and stood at the foot of the Cross. [*Jn.* 19:25]. Our artists have followed their imagination, which has no more truth in it than that which paints the good thief attached to the cross with nails and the bad thief with none, as if he did not deserve them. Such suppositions on Holy Scripture are really poetic license, and dangerous. We must use them soberly, as well as those regarding the three Marys.

Now[3] I do not say that we cannot use the imagination in meditating, or the pious considerations left us by the holy Fathers and by so many other good souls. Since holy and great people have written them, who will not make use of them? Who will refuse to consider or to believe piously what they have piously believed? O certainly, we may confidently follow persons of such authority. But perhaps we may not be satisfied with what they have left, and want to make many other considerations with our imagination. This is where we must be on our guard not to use the imagination carelessly in our meditation, according to our fancy, but rather we must act soberly, according to the advice of our directors and those who guide us, or according to what is written in well-approved books which keep us free from doubt and danger. So much for this first way of meditating, which is good and of which I in no way disapprove, for many great and holy persons have practiced it and still practice it. It is excellent when it is used as they have used it.

The second method is to make no use of the imagination,

but to keep to the literal meaning; that is, to be satisfied with meditating purely and simply on the Gospels and on the mysteries of our faith. Now, this way is higher and better than the first. Yes, it is simpler and safer. To return to our example, it is in this way that St. Paul speaks of Melchisedech when he writes that he was without father, mother or genealogy, without beginning of days or end of life. When he says that Melchisedech was without father and without genealogy, he does not mean that he had no father or mother as others have. Like them, he was born, and therefore had a genealogy. He was not without beginning of days, since, as man, he was born. Nor was he without end of life, since he died the same as all others do. But because nothing is mentioned in Holy Scripture of Melchisedech's father and mother, his genealogy, birth and death, St. Paul simply states nothing about them, wanting to add nothing to the letter. He wants to say only what was written. That is why he speaks thus about this holy person.

Keeping strictly to the literal meaning of the sacred text is the way I would like to speak of our fever patient. This woman is truly admirable in the way she bears her physical illness.[4] It is clear from today's Gospel that she practiced many virtues. But what I admire most is that great submission she made to God's providence and to the care of her superiors. How tranquil and peaceful she is! She has a severe fever which keeps her in bed, greatly tormenting her. This type of illness does that. Yet in all this she remains at peace, not bothering anybody. For the Gospel simply states that she was in bed with a fever. [*Matt.* 8:14-15]. Yet everyone knows how painful restlessness is. Fastidious people certainly witness to this. When they do not get their nine hours of sleep, they do nothing but complain about it. "Oh," they say, "we have been so restless." Restlessness is an evil which usually disturbs fever patients greatly. It keeps them from sleeping and makes them weary, and they find no pleasure in anything. We have to move Heaven and earth to relieve them, but even that does them no good.

The wonderful resignation of our fever patient into the hands
of her superiors is the reason why she was not disturbed
or at all restless. She was solicitous neither for her health
nor her cure. She placed herself in the care of those who
had charge of her, and was content to remain in her bed,
enduring her illness with equanimity and patience. O God,
how happy was this good woman! and how deserving to be
cared for, as Sts. Peter and Andrew and the other two Apostles, John and James, certainly did. They procured her cure.
They provided what was necessary without the patient requesting it. She did not speak to them about it. They were
simply moved by charity and pity for what she was enduring.
How happy the sick in the world would be if they simply
let themselves be cared for by those who have charge of them!
How happy religious would be if they made the great act
of abandonment into the hands of their superiors that our
fever patient made.

If it is reasonable for people in the world to give themselves into the hands of those who care for them because
of the natural love and compassion that they have for them,
it is even more reasonable for religious to do the same. After
all, they live under superiors who, through a motive of charity, serve them and provide for their needs. This charity is
stronger and more compelling than nature, sparing nothing.
It motivates the superiors of religious to provide for the needs
of those of whom they have charge. If a father of a sick
child, whom he may not actually love, nevertheless would
not fail to have him treated according to his need, urged on
only by natural compassion, what ought not to be expected
of superiors who serve us through true charity?

St. Peter's mother-in-law knew that Our Lord was in Capharnaum and that He was curing many sick people. Nevertheless, she did not anxiously send for Him to tell Him that
she was suffering, nor did she beg Him to come to her house.
But what is even more amazing is that even when they encountered one another in her house, she looked at Him and
He looked at her, but she did not say a word about her illness

so as to move Him to have pity on her; nor did she cry out, "Lord, Son of David, have pity on me" [*Matt.* 15:22]; or "Lord, say only the word and my soul will be healed" [*Matt.* 8:8; *Lk.* 7:7]—that is, I will regain life and health. She did not ask Him to approach the bed where she was lying and to place His hand on her. She was not even eager to touch His garment, nor the tassel of His cloak, as many others did, as we see in the Gospel. [*Matt.* 9:20-21; 14:36; *Lk.* 6:19]. Actually, the majority of the people who sought out the Saviour did so to be cured of bodily diseases, not of spiritual maladies. Only the Magdalen, that great saint, came to Him that He might treat her heart and cure her spiritual infirmities. She did this in a wonderful way, while still in the flower of her age.

O God, how many sick people in Capharnaum, knowing that Our Lord, the sovereign Physician, was there, displayed very great overeagerness and anxiety to make their condition known to Him whom they knew could cure them! Certainly, the centurion was truly commendable for the care he took in sending the principal people of the city to the Saviour to tell Him of his servant's illness. [*Lk.* 7:3]. He was also commendable for the lively faith by which he acknowledged that only a word from the Lord was necessary for this cure. But he demonstrated great overeagerness and anxiety for his sick servant's restoration to health. Did not the Canaanite woman do the same? How she cried out after our dear Master! How persistent she was in importuning Him to obtain what she desired! Did she not cry out after the Apostles so that they might pray for her, or at least, in seeing her persistence, be moved to do it?[5] [*Matt.* 15:22-28]. What pleadings the prince of the synagogue made in his effort to persuade Our Lord to come down to his house! [*Mk.* 5:22-23]. In a word, all of them showed great anxiety and desire for their cures.

Even today, what would our sick people not do if they learned that a man of great medical skill were here? They would beg him to visit them and cure their ills. How

impatiently they would await his coming! Oh, such disquie-
tude certainly comes from a disordered self-love, and this
is an illness to which not only the people in the world are
subject, but also those in religion. The glorious St. Bernard,
who understood this well, wrote a long letter to the Brothers
of St. Anastasius, treating at length the subject of bodily illnesses. (There are monks of the same name who live today
in Rome.) Now in this community, they were nearly all ill,
and I can indeed believe this—for there was a great number
of them, and all from different nations. Perhaps the air was
not good, or the air in Rome was polluted at that time and
caused many infirmities. Being informed of this, St. Bernard
addressed a letter to them in which he spoke as he felt necessary, scolding them rather severely. He sent them word that
the Brothers of St. Anastasius were not permitted to think
of remedies proper to recover health, still less to ask for
them. He said they ought not to know what medicine to take,
nor whether or not they needed to be bled. He added that
monks who have consecrated themselves to the service of
Our Lord ought no longer to be concerned with their bodily
illnesses, but only with their spiritual ones. They must abandon their bodily illnesses to God's providence, which permits
them, and to the care of the superiors who have charge of
them. They ought not to have recourse to either doctors or
medicines. It may be suitable for people in the world to send
for doctors with great overeagerness and to take remedies
frequently. But for monks this was not permissible. If they
were so sick that they needed something for their relief, they
could take herbs, like borage. And if their illness were serious they could be given a little wine. (This shows us that
the monks of that time used neither wine nor meat, in a
spirit of evangelical poverty.)

St. Bernard appears very austere indeed in this, but he
is still more so in what he later wrote in the same letter:
"If I seem too rigorous, let me tell you that in what I say
to you, I have the Spirit of God and it is with this spirit
that I speak to you." This is very remarkable. For if this

holy Father had told them that he had spoken to them according to his own sentiments, he would not have been so austere. But no! He assured them: "I do not speak according to my own sentiment. But in what I tell you I think I have the Spirit of God." [*1 Cor.* 7:40].

Elsewhere he replies to the objection of those who could say to him that the Apostle St. Paul, although he had the Spirit of God, commanded his disciple Timothy to drink wine, writing to him in this way: My dear son and beloved brother, we order you to stop drinking water only. Use a little wine to strengthen your stomach, which has become weak from the water you have taken. [*1 Tim.* 5:23]. This great and worthy Bishop Timothy had contracted great infirmities because of his fasts and austerities. And now, as a relief and as medicine, St. Paul counsels him to use a little wine. We see from this that up until this time the great saint drank only water. Just as St. Paul ordered his dear disciple to use wine by way of remedy, so St. Bernard ordered his religious to take wine only in case of necessity. "If you raise the objection," said St. Bernard, "that the Apostle enjoined Timothy to use wine, I will answer that he knew well that Timothy was Timothy. Give me, then, a Timothy now, and we will permit him to take wine. Indeed, we would order him to use it, and not only wine, but also 'liquid gold,' if necessary." Of course, the religious of St. Bernard, as well as other religious, are not today as they were formerly. They are not nearly as rigorous today as they were in ancient times. Each one wishes to use wine, as well as medicines and doctors.

It is true that these things are more available today than they were formerly. For at that time there were very few doctors. Sometimes there would be only one to a province, and when one was needed, people had to go from place to place to find him, at great expense. His services could not be had for less than a hundred crowns. Medicines also were very expensive. That is perhaps why religious of those times made so little use of them. But this is not true in our time. Besides drugs being less expensive, doctors are not as scarce.

Therefore we use them more freely, so that for the slightest ailment we use medicine and run in haste to call a doctor. Yet it is also true that people today are much more delicate and soft about themselves than they were formerly. Fewer would act this way if medicines and doctors were used only according to our superior's orders. But we are not satisfied with that. We wish to act in our own regard and according to our whims. We take too much care of self! We fret and anxiously try to find the means to be cured. We want to know everything, whether it is good for us or not. We wish to know about all the remedies in the world and to use them, claiming that everyone does so.

Our fever patient did not act in this way at all. She was in her bed without making any fuss whatever. It was enough for her that others knew she was ill; she was content to take what was given her for her health, not fretting over whether it would benefit her or not. She believed firmly that God was not the first, nor the second, nor the third cause of her illness, for He is not the cause of sickness in any way whatever. Since He is not the cause of sin, then He is not the cause of sickness either. But just as He permits sin, He sends infirmities to correct and purify us of it. Thus, we must be submissive to His justice as well as to His mercy, keeping a humble silence. This will make us tranquilly embrace the events of His providence, as David did, who in his afflictions said: "I suffered and was silent because I knew that it was You who sent them to correct me and purge me of my guilt." [*Ps.* 38 (39):10-12].

Our fever patient did the same. "You have sent me the fever, and I have accepted it. I have submitted myself both to Your justice and to Your mercy. Just as You sent it to me without my asking for it, so You can take it away without my asking you to do so. You know better than I do what is best for me. I have no need to trouble myself about it. It is sufficient for me that You look at me and that You know that I am sick in my bed." So, she did not say a word. She paid no attention to her illness. She did not enjoy talking about it. She suffered without being eager to be pitied or anxious to be cured. It was enough that God knew it, as well as her superiors who guided her. She was not like many people today. If they have a headache or colic everyone must try to cure it. The whole neighborhood must be told about it. Nothing less will satisfy them. Nor was she like those who for the least illness want to be sent to the infirmary so that everyone will pity them and pamper them in their pain; nor like those who run to the doctor for the least indisposition. These people are like little children who, being stung by a wasp or a honey bee, run in great haste to show it to their mother to have her blow on their finger.[6]

Our fever patient is truly remarkable, for not only did she refrain from publishing her illness, she did not delight in speaking about it, nor did she bother to send for a doctor. Even more remarkable, when Our Lord is present in her house, He who as sovereign Physician is able to cure her, she says not a word to Him about her sickness. She did not want to see Him as a doctor, but only as her God to whom she belonged both in health and in sickness. In this she made it clear that she was as content with the one as with the other, and that she had no desire to be rid of the fever except when it would please her God. Oh, if she had been a contemporary lady, what artifice would she not have used to be cured! She would have explained that she asked for good health only to be able to serve Our Lord better. Or at the very least, she would say that she could bear it better at another time; but at present, while He was in her house, she could not endure it, for she could not entertain Him well while sick in bed. And she would use other such nonsense, which our fever patient in no way used.

It is not enough to be ill because such is God's will, but we must be ill as He wills, when He wills and as long as it pleases Him,[7] entrusting our health to whatever He ordains for us, without asking for anything. It is enough that He knows it and that He sees our infirmity. We must let Him act and, without trying to foresee what is requisite for our cure, we must abandon ourselves to our superiors and leave the care of ourselves to them. We are not to concern ourselves with anything but bearing our illness as long as God pleases. This is the first point in the example of Peter's mother-in-law.

The second point relates to this woman's meekness, resignation and modesty. The third point is the attention she gave to profiting from her illness. When Our Lord dispelled the fever, she got up and waited on Him. I will say a word on these two considerations.

Great were her meekness and resignation in that she made no commotion about her illness, nor made it evident by her words. She did not say to the Saviour, nor to those who had care of her, that she desired health rather than sickness. When our purpose is to serve Our Lord better, it may be good to ask health of Him as the One who can give it to us. Yet it must be done only on this condition, that it be His will. For we ought always to say: *Fiat voluntas tua*—Thy will be done. [*Matt.* 6:10]. Nevertheless, it is much better to ask nothing of Him, and to be content that He knows our illness and the length of time that we have endured it.

There are people who when ill would like to use everyone, if they could, to be cured. They send here and there asking for prayers that God deliver them from their infirmities. Certainly, it is good to have recourse to God, but ordinarily it is done with so much imperfection that it is pitiful. Notable faults have been committed in this regard by great personages, as happened to the King of France, Louis XI. (We do no harm to the reputation of these great people when we tell the truth.) Before going off to war, the King had many prayers offered at Paris for his physical safety. One day Mass was being offered for him in the Church of St. Germain. When the good abbot, who was celebrating the Mass, came to the prayer in which he recommended the soul and spiritual health of the King to God, this prince promptly sent one of his pages to order the recommendation of his physical health, saying that his soul could be attended to later. In doing this he committed a gross imperfection; and we are quite liable to commit similar faults on such occasions.

But the great resignation of our fever patient kept her from falling into this fault, for she remained meek, modest and tranquil, asking for nothing. But moved by compassion, the Apostles very humbly spoke for her to Our Lord. The request was made secretly. When Our Lord heard it, He looked at the invalid who, in turn, was looking at Him. Then, approaching her bed, He grasped her hand and, angry with the fever, commanded it to leave her. She was cured immediately, and she got up at once and began to wait on Him.

Here is my third consideration. Certainly she manifested great virtue and the profit she had gained from her sickness. For inasmuch as she had endured her illness in resignation to Our Lord's will, so as soon as it had left her, she desired to use her health only in His service. But when did she use it? At the very moment that she recovered it. She was not like those tender and delicate women who, though ill only for several days, must take weeks and months to recuperate! So that if some did not know they were ill during their short illness, they would surely know it by the time it took them to convalesce! This would give people ample time to pity them. That is why they must be placed apart in an infirmary, be given special food, and be coddled until they are restored to health.[8] Our fever patient was not at all like that. Rather, she served Our Lord as soon as she was cured.

Now, if you wish, during this hour use your imagination to consider with what love, joy and gaiety this woman served her dear Master. Think how she kept looking at Him, how her heart was filled with His love and how many acts of love she made. How many *Benedicites* were in her mouth, praising Him who had been so good to her! Imagine also what the Apostles did who had witnessed this miracle, and you will learn how to conduct yourself during bodily illnesses, and the profit you ought to draw from them.

In conclusion, we ought to observe at these times the general rule: ask for nothing and refuse nothing.[9] Let us confide ourselves into the hands of our superiors, leaving to them the care of providing doctors, remedies and everything necessary for our health and relief. Refuse nothing—neither food, nor medicine nor any treatment that is given you—for it is in this that evangelical poverty consists. The first degree of this poverty, says St. Bonaventure, consists in having no dwelling place or house which is our own and according to our liking. The second degree is to be uncertain about having proper clothing or food in the time of health. The third degree is that, being sick, we do not know where to go, having neither lodging nor food to sustain us in our necessity nor anything according to our liking. In a word, it is to be abandoned and forsaken by all help at the end of our life and, in the midst of this, to ask for nothing for our relief, and to refuse nothing when something is given us which does not agree with us.

This has been practiced exactly in our time by two great saints: by the first one in effect, and by the other in desire and affection. I mean the Blessed Francis Xavier, who is about to be canonized for his great holiness of life. At the hour of his death he had neither house nor food to sustain him, for he died near China in a poor place, abandoned by all human help. In the midst of all that, the heart of this great servant of God melted with joy at seeing himself reduced to this state. Thinking about this, Blessed Marie of the Incarnation[10] considered his happiness so great that she said she would like to die as this blessed one did, deprived of all human support—indeed, even of divine support—being content with the ordinary grace that God gives to all His creatures. Since this great saint could not die in effect in this evangelical poverty, at least she died this way in desire and affection. To these two holy souls, as well as to all those who imitate them, we can say: Blessed are the poor in spirit, for the Kingdom of Heaven is theirs. [*Matt.* 5:3]. Amen.

NOTES

1. St. Francis de Sales is here taking issue with a view of the Reformers that since Jesus alone is the sole mediator on behalf of humanity

before God, the intercessory prayer of Christians for one another is without biblical or theological foundation. St. Francis links the efficacy of such prayer to the Communion of Saints, which he finds biblically based in this example of the Apostles interceding with the Lord on behalf of Peter's mother-in-law. Such prayer was indeed efficacious in that instance.

2. Cf. *Introduction to the Devout Life*, Part II, chap. 1.

3. Cf. *Spiritual Conferences*, XVIII, "The Sacraments and the Divine Office," pp. 362-363.

4. Cf. *Spiritual Conferences*, XXI, "On Asking for Nothing."

5. Cf. Sermon for Thursday of First Week of Lent, pp. 34-51 of this volume.

6. Cf. *Spiritual Conferences*, V, "On Generosity," p. 85.

7. Cf. *Introduction to the Devout Life*, Part III, chap. 3.

8. One can only surmise that St. Francis de Sales is speaking here on the basis of his experience of such behavior and, no doubt, with a smile on his face and tongue in cheek!

9. Cf. *Spiritual Conferences*, pp. 94, 95, 399-401, 405, 406.

10. Blessed Marie of the Incarnation (1566-1618)—known in the world as Barbe (Barbara) Acarie—was a saintly wife and mother of six children, and later a Carmelite lay sister, who at one period of her life was spiritually directed by St. Francis de Sales. Despite an attraction to the religious life, she was married at age 17 to a man of the aristocracy. As a result of visions of St. Teresa of Avila, Barbe Acarie brought the Discalced Carmelites to France by founding five Carmelite convents there; this was before she herself had entered the convent. Throughout her life she experienced visions, ecstasies and other supernatural gifts. (Barbe Acarie is not to be confused with another saintly soul also known as Blessed Marie of the Incarnation, who lived from 1599-1672. The latter was also born in France and also became a wife at age 17 and then a mother, later entering a convent. She was sent to New France, Canada, about age 40, where she taught the Indians until the end of her life. She also experienced visions; she is sometimes called Blessed Marie of the Ursulines.)

8

GOD'S SPIRITUAL PROVIDENCE

Sermon for the Fourth Sunday of Lent, March 6, 1622, concerning God's special spiritual care of those who have withdrawn from the world to follow the Saviour on the "mountain" of perfection, how God's Providence is greater in proportion to the soul's lack of anxiety for its own needs, how we must diligently use the ordinary means to attain perfection and how, if these fail, God would sooner work a miracle than leave us without assistance, how God tests souls, anxiety to be rid of spiritual pains rather than trusting God to console us as He wills, the twin virtues of humility and generosity, how Our Lord reproduced the five loaves and two fishes, how religious souls must be satisfied when God gives them only a sufficiency (or even less), and how God will continually renew the spiritual goods which we have.

"Jesus then took the loaves of bread, and having given thanks, he distributed them to those who were seated there; in the same way he gave them some fish, as much as they wanted."
—John 6:11

The narrative which Holy Church presents to us in today's Gospel [*Jn.* 6:1-15] is a picture in which are portrayed a thousand beautiful subjects helpful to us in admiring and praising the Divine Majesty. But above all else, this picture presents to us the admirable Providence, both general and particular, which God has for humanity, and especially for those who love Him and who live according to His will in Christianity.

It is true that God exercises this Providence toward all creatures, and especially toward all men and women, as much toward pagans and heretics as toward others, whoever they be. Without this Providence they would undoubtedly perish. However, it is important to know that He extends a much more particular Providence toward His children who are Christians. [*Gal.* 6:10; *1 Tim.* 4:10]. Even among these there are some, as we see in today's Gospel, who merit a more special care from Our Lord. These aspire to perfection, and, to attain it, they are not content to follow Him on the flowery plain of consolation, but courageously follow Him even in the deserts, as far as the summit of that high mountain in today's Gospel. There were many who saw the Saviour while He was going about instructing and healing people, but who did not follow Him. There were others who, thus seeing Him, did follow Him—but only as far as the foot of the mountain, content to accompany Him in the plain and through pleasant and easy paths. But a thousand times happier were those who saw Him and followed Him not only to the foot of the mountain, but, carried on by the love they bore Him, ascended with Him, divested of every care except to please Him. Thus they merited that the Divine Goodness should take care of them and even provide for them a miraculous banquet, lest they faint on the way from hunger.

It seems, indeed, that many might have been on the verge of collapse after having followed our dear Master three days and three nights without eating or drinking [Cf. *Matt.* 15:32], distracted from such activity by the wonderful delight they found in listening to His divine words. Though their needs were very great, they did not think of them. Oh! how loving these throngs were in so perfect a practice of total abandonment into the arms of Divine Providence! We need not fear that God will neglect them. He will take care of them and will have compassion on them, as we shall soon see in the continuation of our discourse. I will speak, therefore, of the confidence which those aspiring to perfection ought to have in Providence regarding spiritual necessities, just as I have spoken before, I think in this very place, of that general Providence which God has over all people and of the confidence that we ought to have in Him in temporal matters. The lessons which we shall derive from this will be very useful for our stage of spiritual development.

I will divide what I have to say into three points, in the first of which I will consider the goodness of these people who accompanied Our Lord without any care or thought of themselves, leaving their homes and all that they possessed, attracted by the affection and the satisfaction which they found in listening to His words. Oh, what a good sign it is for a Christian to take pleasure in listening to God's word [*Jn.* 8:47], and to leave all to follow Him! There is certainly no doubt that persons may aspire and attain to perfection by remaining in the world and doing carefully what pertains to their vocation. Yet it is a most certain thing that the Saviour does not exercise for them so special a Providence, nor so personal and individual a solicitude, as He does for those who abandon all care of themselves to follow Him more perfectly. [Cf. *Matt.* 19:28-29]. These have a greater capacity than the others for understanding God's word and being attracted by the charms of His loving kindness. So long as we have a care for ourselves, I mean a care full of anxiety, Our Lord permits us to act; but when we abandon all to Him, He takes a tender care of us, and His Providence for us is great or small according to the measure of our abandonment.[1]

I do not say this so much for temporal things as for spiritual things. He Himself taught this to His beloved St. Catherine of Siena: "Think of Me," He said to her, "and I will think for you." Oh, how blessed are they who so love Our Lord as carefully to follow this rule of thinking only of Him, remaining faithfully in His presence, listening to what He says to us continually in the depths of our hearts, obeying His divine attractions, movements and inspirations, breathing and aspiring unceasingly to the desire of pleasing Him and of being submissive to His most holy will! This must always be done with divine confidence in His total goodness and in His Providence, for we must always remain tranquil and not be troubled or full of anxiety in seeking the perfection which we undertake.

Consider, I beg you, this multitude who follow our dear Master, even up the mountain. See the peace and tranquility of spirit with which they follow Him. There is not one murmur or complaint, although it must have seemed that they would expire from weakness and hunger. They suffer much and yet they do not think of it, so attentive are they to their sole desire of accompanying Our Lord wherever He goes. They who follow this Divine Saviour should imitate them in this, laying aside all the many cares and anxieties for their advancement, as well as all the many complaints because they see themselves imperfect. Oh, some are so soon wearied and exhausted, although they have labored only a little! It seems to them that they will never enjoy that delicious banquet which Our Lord prepares for them up there on the summit of the mountain of perfection. We may say to these good people: Have patience, lay aside a bit that anxious care of yourselves, and have no fear that anything will be wanting to you. For if you trust in God, He will take care of you [*1 Ptr.* 5:7] and everything necessary for your perfection. No one who hoped in Him and in His Providence has ever been disappointed. [*Ecclus. (Sir.)* 2:11 (10)].

Do you not see that the birds, which neither sow nor reap, and whose only purpose is to delight us by their singing, still fail not to be nourished and sustained by the order of this divine Providence? [*Matt.* 6:26]. You know that two kinds of animals are kept in houses, some for use and others simply for amusement. For example, we have hens to lay eggs, and nightingales or other little birds in cages to sing. All are fed, but not for the same end, for some are for use and others for pleasure.[2]

It is the same among us. The Church is the house of the Father of the family, who is our Lord and Master; He takes very great care to provide for the necessities of all the faithful who are associated there—with this difference, however, that among them all, He chooses some whom He wishes to be entirely employed in singing His praises and who are therefore relieved of every other care. Therefore, He has ordained that we should be sustained and nourished by tithes which are collected without solicitude. By this I mean that we, being consecrated to His service, are the birds appointed to delight His Divine Goodness by means of our singing and the continual praises which we offer to Him.

What are religious but birds who are kept in a cage to chant unceasingly the praises of God? We might say that all the exercises of religious life are so many new canticles [*Ps.* 95 (96):1; 97 (98):1; 149:1] which make known the divine mercies to us and which continually prompt us to magnify the Divine Majesty in gratitude for the special and very particular Providence which He has had over us, in that He has withdrawn us from the rest of humankind to follow the Saviour more easily and tranquilly on the mountain of perfection.

All are called to perfection, since Our Lord was speaking to all when He said: "Be perfect as your Heavenly Father is perfect." [*Matt.* 5:48]. But, in truth, we may well say what is said in the holy Gospel: "Many are called, but the elect are few." [*Matt.* 20:16; 22:14]. There are many who aspire to perfection, but few attain it because they do not walk as they should—ardently, yet tranquilly; carefully, but confidently; that is to say, relying more on the Divine Goodness and His Providence than upon themselves and their own works. We must be very faithful, but without anxiety or eagerness; we must use the means that are given to us according to our vocation, and then remain in peace concerning all the rest.[3] For God, under whose guidance we have embarked, will always be attentive to provide us with whatever is necessary. When all shall fail us, then God will take care of us, and then all will *not* fail us since we shall have God, who must be our all.

The children of Israel had no manna until they had run

out of the flour from Egypt.⁴ This will be my second point. God would sooner work miracles than leave without assistance, either spiritual or temporal, those who trust entirely in His Divine Providence. Yet He wants us, for our part, to do all that lies in our power. That is, He wants us to use the ordinary means to attain perfection. If these should fail, He will never fail to assist us. As long as we have our rules, our constitutions and persons who tell us what we ought to do, let us not expect God to work miracles to guide us to perfection, for He will not do it.

Put Abraham with his family [cf. *Gen.* 12:1] and Elias among the prophets. The Lord will perform no prodigy to nourish them. Why not? Because He wishes Abraham to reap his grain, to have it threshed and ground and finally made into bread for his support. He has cows, he must be fed by their milk; or else, if he wishes, he may kill his fat calves and make a banquet for the angels. [*Gen.* 18:7-8]. But, on the contrary, place Elias near the torrent of Carith or in the desert of Bersabee [*3 Kgs.* (*1 Kgs.*) 17:3-6; 19:3-8], and you will see that there God supports him—in one place by the instrumentality of angels, and in the other by that of a raven, which brought him bread and meat every day for his sustenance.

Therefore, when human aid fails us, all is not wanting, for God takes over and takes care of us by His special Providence. This poor multitude who follow Our Lord today were assisted by Him only after they were all near faint with hunger. He felt an extreme pity for them because, in their love of Him, they had so forgotten themselves that none had brought provisions, except the little Martial who had five barley loaves and two fish. It is as if the Saviour, full of love for the hearts of these good people (who numbered about five thousand), said to Himself: "You have no care whatever for yourselves, but I Myself will take care of you." Therefore, He called St. Philip to Him and asked him: "These poor people will faint on the way if we do not assist them with some food, but where could we find sufficient to sustain them?" He did not ask this through ignorance, but to test him. We must not think that God tests us in order to lead us to evil, for that simply cannot be. [*Jas.* 1:13]. He tests His most beloved servants so that they might prove their fidelity and love for Him, and that they might accomplish great and shining works, as He did with Abraham when He commanded him to sacrifice his beloved son Isaac. [*Gen.* 22:1-2]. In the same way, He sometimes tests His servants in their confidence in Divine Providence, permitting them to be so languid, so dry and so full of aridity in all their spiritual exercises that they do not know where to turn for relief from the interior weariness which overwhelms them.

Our Lord tested St. Philip in this way. He was not yet confirmed in the faith and in confidence in the almighty power of his Master, and so answered Him as if rejecting His proposition: "Not even with two hundred days' wages could we buy loaves enough to give each of them a mouthful." This response symbolizes very well indeed certain souls who do not wait for Our Lord to take pity on them, but are careful to do it themselves. No one is so poor as they are; no one, they say, was ever so afflicted as they. The pains, the sorrows of each one are always the greatest. For instance, those poor women who have lost their husbands always think that their affliction is more grievous than that of all others. It is the same with purely spiritual tribulations: disgust, aridity, weariness, and that aversion and repugnance to good which souls most devoted to the service of God very often experience. "My passions disturb me greatly; I cannot bear anything without interior repugnance; everything is extremely burdensome to me; I have so great a desire to acquire humility, and yet I feel so great an aversion to being humbled; I do not have that interior tranquility which is so pleasing, since I am greatly buffeted by constant distraction. In short, I find the exercise of virtue so difficult that I no longer know what to do; my affliction is greater than I can describe, and I have no words to express the incomparable pain I am suffering."[5]

It is true that St. Andrew remarked to Our Lord: "There

is a lad here who has five barley loaves and two fish, but what are these among so many?" "Alas!" say these poor souls who pity themselves, "my affliction is so great that two hundred crowns of consolation would not suffice to relieve me. It is true that we have many good spiritual books, we have sermons, we have regular times for prayer, we even experience some consoling emotions; but what good is that? It is nothing." How strange is the human spirit: that is nothing indeed! What more would you wish? That God would send you an angel to comfort you? Oh, He will not do it; you have not yet fasted three days and three nights to follow Him on the mountain of perfection, for the attainment of which you must forget yourself, leaving to God the care to comfort you according to His good pleasure; and not troubling yourself or caring for anything but to follow after Him, while listening to His words, as these good people did.

Our Lord tested St. Philip in order to humble him—and with good reason, after Philip had given an answer so full of human prudence. It is a remarkable thing: God so loves humility that He sometimes tests us, not to make us do evil but to teach us by our own experience what we really are, permitting us to say or do some foolish thing, giving us reason to humble ourselves. Now these complaints, and this tenderness which we have for ourselves, these grievances, these difficulties in the pursuit of the good begun—truly, are they not matter fit to humble us and make us acknowledge that we are weak, and still children in what regards virtue and perfection? Oh, we must not look at ourselves so much, but we must think of God and let Him think for us.

We must indeed keep ourselves humble because of our imperfections, but this humility must be the foundation of a great generosity, for the one without the other degenerates into imperfection. Humility without generosity is only a deception and a cowardice of heart which makes us think that we are good for nothing and that others should never think of using us in anything great. On the other hand, generosity without humility is only presumption. We may indeed say:

"It is true I have no virtue, still less the necessary gifts to be used in such a charge"; but after that humble acknowledgment we must so put our confidence in God as to believe that He will not fail to give them to us when it is necessary that we have them, and when He wants to make use of us, provided only that we forget ourselves and be occupied in faithfully praising His Divine Majesty and helping our neighbor to do the same, so as to increase His glory as much as lies in our power.[6]

Notwithstanding the fact that St. Philip and St. Andrew declared that the five barley loaves and two fish were nothing for so many, Our Lord ordered them to be brought to Him, and He commanded His Apostles to make the people sit down. They all did so very simply, and in this they were certainly admirable, for they sat down to table without seeing anything on it, and there was nothing to suggest that anything could be given to them. Then Jesus took the loaves of bread, blessed them, broke them and ordered the Apostles to distribute them. When this was done, there was still some left, even though all had had enough to satisfy their need.

The question has been raised, among others, as to whether all ate of the five loaves or whether Our Lord, by His almighty power, made new ones which were distributed to the people. In speaking of another similar miracle—not the same miracle, since the number of loaves is seven, and St. John clearly relates that there were only five in the miracle of today's Gospel—St. Mark says expressly that all ate of the seven loaves and two fish. [*Mk.* 8:6-7, 20].

There is another question whose answer will help us here. At the Resurrection, how can it be that each one will rise again in his same body, since some will have been eaten by worms, others by wild beast or by birds, others will have been burned and their ashes scattered to the winds. How then can it be that at the same time the angel shall call each one to come to judgment; all, I say, in an instant, without any delay, to rise again clothed in their own flesh? [*1 Cor.* 15:52]. By the almighty power of God. I, in this same body which

I now possess, will rise again. He will reproduce it; for as it was not difficult for Him to produce it such as it is, it will not be any more difficult to produce it again.[7] Thus Our Lord made all the five thousand men eat of the same five loaves and two fish, reproducing them as often as was necessary, that each one might have a portion according to his need. All ate then of five loaves and two fish miraculously multiplied—all but St. Martial who, not participating in this miracle, ate his own bread all alone and not that of the Saviour, because he had brought his own provision. For as long as we have our own bread, God does not work prodigies to sustain us.

Let us consider, for the third point, that Our Lord, although able to make the manna fall on this mountain as formerly in the desert for the children of Israel [*Ex.* 16:14-15], nevertheless did not do it, preparing His feast instead with barley loaves. Yet these people loved Him much and did not murmur as the Israelites did who murmured even without cause—for they lacked nothing, since the manna had the taste of everything they could desire. [*Wis.* 16:20]. My God! What does this teach us? The murmuring Israelites are nourished with the bread of angels [*Wis.* 16:20; *Ps.* 77 (78):24-25], that is, with the manna which was kneaded by their hands; however, they who followed Our Lord with incomparable affection and gentle hearts, despoiled of all care of themselves, are nourished only with barley loaves. What can this mean except that worldlings, represented here by those Israelites who really aspired to reach and obtain only the earthly Promised Land—these worldlings, and those who live in the world but desire Heaven, do not fail, nevertheless, to amass for themselves and to seek unnecessary possessions and ease here below on earth. But they who aspire to follow Our Lord on the mountain of perfection must be satisfied with a sufficiency in all that regards their necessities, corporal as much as spiritual, avoiding abundance and superfluity in all things, remaining content with a simple sufficiency, or even with being deprived of what is necessary, when it pleases God that this shall happen.

As for me, I will tell you my thought on the question which
I am going to put to you, namely, which would you prefer:
to be fed with a little bread baked under the ashes with the
Prophet Elias in the desert of Bersabee, or else, with the
same prophet, with the bread and meat which he received
from the beak of a raven near the torrent of Carith?[8] [*3 Kgs.
(1 Kgs.)* 17:3-6; 19:3-8]. I cannot know your thoughts, but
as for me, I will tell you very frankly that I would prefer
the bread baked under the ashes from the hand of the angel
to bread—however white it might be—or flesh, brought to
me by the beak of a raven, a foul and repulsive bird. Better
is a morsel of barley bread from the hand of Our Lord than
the manna from that of an angel. More honored a thousand
times are these poor throngs eating a morsel of barley bread
at the table of our sweet Saviour than if they were fed with
pearls and the most delicate meats in the world at the table
of the wretched Cleopatra.

The true friends of God, and those who follow Him faithfully wherever He goes, urged on by their ardent love for
His Divine Majesty, and especially religious who make it
their profession to accompany Him through the roughest and
most difficult ways on the mountain of perfection, should
imitate these people and have only one foot on earth, keeping
their whole soul with all its powers and faculties occupied
with heavenly things, leaving all care of themselves to Our
Lord, to whose service they are dedicated and consecrated.
Therefore, they ought neither to seek nor to desire anything
but what is simply necessary, especially regarding spiritual
needs. As for temporal things, that is very clear since they
have abandoned the world and all its conveniences, where
they once lived according to their own will. God, as we have
said,[9] did not command Elias in the desert to return among
the prophets to be supported there, but Himself sent an angel
to him because he had gone there by the order of Divine
Providence. In like manner, He does not wish religious to
return to the world to seek consolation to revive their spirits,
because it was by His inspiration that they came into religion.

He will watch over them in these deserts, not of Bersabee but of His Divine Majesty.

It is true that very often He does not feed them with manna, which had the taste that each one desired. Rather, He often feeds them with a piece of bread baked under the ashes, or else with a morsel of barley bread. By this I mean that[10] Our Lord wants these souls, chosen for the service of His Divine Majesty, to be nourished always with a firm and unchanging resolution to persevere in following Him, even amid disgust, aridities, the repugnances and austerities of the spiritual life, without consolation, without relish, without tenderness, but in a very profound humility, thinking they do not deserve anything else, thus taking this bread lovingly, not from the hand of an angel, but from that of the Saviour, who gives it to us according to our need. It is certain that although it is not very agreeable to the taste, it is nevertheless extremely profitable for our spiritual health.

Our Lord gave barley bread because it was barley bread that the little Martial brought. He did not wish to change it, but He used this provision to work His miracle in order to teach us that while we have something, He wants us to offer it to Him, and that if He has to work a miracle for us, it may be with that very thing which we have. For example, if we have good desires or good instructions, and we have not sufficient strength to put them into practice, let us offer them to Him and He will make us capable of accomplishing them. If we put our confidence in His goodness, He will renew these desires as often as will be necessary to make us persevere in His service.

We say that we do not know whether the will to please Him that we now have will remain with us during our whole life. Alas! it is true, for there is nothing so weak and changeable as we are. But nevertheless, let us not be troubled. Let us, rather, frequently lay this good will before Our Lord; let us place it in His hands and He will renew it as often as is necessary that we may have enough for our whole mortal life. After this life there will be no cause for fear, nor for so many apprehensions, for with the help of God, we shall be in a safe place. There we shall never cease glorifying this Divine Majesty whom we have so dearly loved and followed according to our power, through the deserts of this miserable world to the highest summit of the mountain of perfection, to which we shall all attain by His grace, for the honor and glory of Our Lord, who is our Divine Master. Amen.

NOTES

1. Cf. *Spiritual Conferences,* II, "On Confidence," p. 24-25.
2. Cf. *Sermons of St. Francis de Sales on Prayer,* Volume I of this series, March 22, 1615, p. 4.
3. Cf. *Spiritual Conferences,* III, "Constancy," p. 48; VII, "Three Spiritual Laws," pp. 110-112; XII, "On Simplicity and Religious Prudence," pp. 220-221, 226; and *Sermons of St. Francis de Sales on Our Lady,* "The Purification," February 2, 1620, pp. 96-97.
4. *Introduction to the Devout Life,* Part IV, chap. 14.
5. Cf. *Spiritual Conferences,* VII, "Three Spiritual Laws," pp. 119-120; XIV, "On Private Judgment," p. 267.
6. Cf. *Spiritual Conferences,* V, "On Generosity."
7. St. Francis de Sales is teaching this point: just as Our Lord reproduced the same loaves as often as necessary to feed the five thousand, so He will reproduce (re-create) our same bodies when we rise on the last day.
8. Cf. p. 121 of this sermon.
9. Cf. p. 121 of this sermon.
10. Cf. *Spiritual Conferences,* II, "On Confidence," p. 24.

PROPER FEAR OF DEATH

Sermon for the Thursday after the Fourth Sunday of Lent, March 10, 1622, concerning Our Lord's raising of the son of the widow of Naim, Our Lord's motives for performing this miracle—and in this manner, burial in the Old and in the New Law, God's creative power in raising the dead, the error of some ancient philosophers who say we should not fear death, the holy Fathers' teaching that we must fear death without fearing it, how even saintly souls should fear death, St. Paul's desire for death and Job's desire for death, the secret language of love, that it is good to fear death, how this fear should be combined with confidence in God's Providence, how in order to die well we must lead a good life, how we should daily remind ourselves that we shall die, and how we should always bear in mind the account we must someday render to God and keep ourselves in the state we would wish to be found in at death.

There were in Galilee several beautiful mountains upon which Our Lord performed many miracles. Among them was one called Thabor, and another named Hermon. At the foot of this mountain was the little town of Naim. It was less than a league from Thabor. Close by, not more than two leagues further on, was the town of Capharnaum, where the Saviour made His principal residence and where He worked very great miracles. For that reason the Nazarenes reproached Him, complaining that He had not done as much in Nazareth as in Capharnaum [*Lk.* 4:23]. Now Our Lord, having honored that town by choosing it for His principal dwelling place, desired also to honor with His presence that of Naim, which, although it was small, was nevertheless very beautiful. That is why it was called "Naim," which means "beautiful." [*Ruth* 1:20].

As we read in today's Gospel [*Lk.* 7:11-16], our Divine Master entered the outskirts of this town and discovered a young man who had recently died being carried away for burial. His mother was following the litter, along with a great crowd of people. This young man was the only son of this good widow. He was not only her only son, but her only child as well. That is why she was even more afflicted at her loss and wept most bitterly.

Encountering this funeral procession at the gate of Naim, our dear Saviour desired to perform a very great miracle. He therefore stepped up to those who were carrying the body and touched the litter, commanding them to stop there and go no further, which they did immediately. With all the people watching to see what would happen, Jesus pronounced this all-powerful word: "Young man, I bid you, get up." Immediately he sat up on his litter and spoke, and Our Lord took him and gave him back to his mother. All those who saw this prodigy were filled with astonishment and began to praise and glorify God, saying that He had visited His people and that this Prophet was the Redemption of Israel. This is a summary of today's Gospel. I will not dwell long on an elucidation of the text. I will mention only three or four points for our instruction.

First, the miracle of this young man's resurrection was one of the greatest that Our Lord performed in Galilee, for He wrought it on His own initiative, being moved to do it solely by His goodness and mercy. It is true that the resurrection of Lazarus was a still greater miracle and took place with more ceremony; but the Saviour resuscitated him at the request of his sisters. [*Jn.* 11:21-33]. The daughter of the ruler of the synagogue was brought back to life through the prayers of her father, who begged Our Lord to go to his house for this purpose. [*Matt.* 9:18-19, 23-25]. In a word, all the

resurrections[1] related in the Gospel were asked for by some-
one. This is the only one which was performed by our dear
Master's desire alone, and through it He shows us that all
His works are done through His goodness alone.
This infinite goodness of our God has two hands with which
He does all things: one is His mercy, the other His justice.
All that His mercy and justice do proceeds from His goodness, for He is sovereignly good both when He uses His
justice and when he exercises His mercy. There can be neither justice nor mercy where there is no goodness. Since
God is forever Goodness itself, He is always just and merciful. It is the property of goodness to communicate itself,
for of itself it is communicative, and to this end it uses mercy
and justice: mercy to do good, and justice to punish and
uproot whatever prevents us from experiencing the effects of
this goodness of our God, this God whose mercy is His justice and whose justice is His mercy. Mercy makes us embrace good, justice makes us shun evil; the goodness of Our
Lord communicates itself through these two attributes, since
it remains equally good whether it exercises one or the other.
Urged on by this goodness alone, by which He does all things,
He raised this young man. No other motive moved or prompted
Him to it, for no one asked Him to do it.

In the second place, He touched the litter, indicating that
they should stop, because He desired to resuscitate this young
man. The Saviour's touch was not necessary for this miracle
any more than for any other. Without touching the litter He
could very well have stopped those who carried it, and without any ceremony resuscitated this youth by His almighty
power and divine virtue. But He did not choose to act thus.
Rather He made use of the imposition of His hands to show
that in the days when He was in the flesh [*Heb.* 5:7], that
is, when He conversed in His flesh with men [*Bar.* 3:38],
He mediated His virtue and divine power through His humanity. This is what St. John means in his first chapter:
The Word became flesh and dwelt among us. [*Jn.* 1:14]. The
ancients taught that God dwelt with them, and that He taught

and instructed His people to do His divine will. Yet, as our holy Fathers say, He did not dwell visibly among them, only invisibly. But from the time the Word became flesh, He conversed with us visibly. He dwelt amongst us in His flesh [*Matt.* 1:23], to show us that He wished to make use of His humanity as a tool or instrument to accomplish the works which belong to His Divinity.[2]

In the third place, let us focus on what is meant by His encountering a dead man at the gate of the town, that is, as they were carrying him out of the city. For in the Old Law they buried their dead outside the city to prevent infection from the bodies, and for fear of polluting the air. As St. Jerome writes in his letters, the custom of burying Christians in churches began only after the Incarnation of the Son of God, and was practiced only after Our Lord's death, since it was through that death that the gates of Heaven were opened for us. It seems it was not appropriate to bury in temples those whose souls were not yet in Paradise, but had descended into Hell or into Limbo. But when the gates of Heaven were opened, Christians began to be buried in churches or in cemeteries near churches.

In the fourth place, Our Lord said, "Young man, I bid you, get up." It is a little difficult to understand whom He is addressing as "young man." The deceased was certainly not so, either in body or in soul. The soul is neither old nor young. It neither grows nor recedes; it is in no way affected by time. The body was no longer young. Being dead, it was nothing but a corpse. Now inasmuch as this dead man's soul was impervious to change, and inasmuch as a body, separated from its soul, is nothing but a corpse, to whom then was Our Saviour speaking when He said, "Young man, I bid you, get up"?

Here is the explanation of this difficulty. This deceased man was not a youth either in body or in soul. Therefore, Our Lord was not speaking to him as if he were, but only as to an object to which He wished to give life. He is demonstrating here His almighty and efficacious word, a word that effects what it says. [*Ps.* 32 (33):9; 148:5]. As soon as the Saviour pronounced these words, "Young man, I bid you, get up," he who was not a youth, became one.

By an all-powerful word God created Heaven and earth. He brought forth being from non-being, since this word is efficacious, effecting what it says. By that word, it made that which is not to be that which is. [*Rom.* 4:17; *1 Cor.* 1:28]. But to whom is He now speaking? To a dead man. The dead do not hear. Who, then, will answer Him? He speaks to this dead man as if he were living, to indicate that the voice of God is heard not only by those who have ears, but also by that which is not. By this He shows that He is powerful over things both created and uncreated. So efficacious is His word that if He speaks to uncreated things, they answer Him by coming into being.

The Saviour also desires to speak to this dead man as if he were living in order to help us understand the manner in which we will rise. On the day of judgment, or shortly before, the Archangel will come. [*1 Thess.* 4:16]. By God's order he will say, "Arise, you dead, and come to judgment!" And at the sound of this voice all the dead will be raised [*1 Cor.* 15:52] to be judged. But to whom will the Archangel speak? To the entombed dead, to rotting flesh, for our bodies are nothing more than rottenness when they are separated from the soul. And why does the Archangel speak to these cadavers, which are wholly reduced to dust and ashes? Does he not know that the dead hear nothing? And if he does know it, why then does he command them thus: "Arise, you dead"? How can they arise, since they have no life? Yet it is certain that the Archangel will speak to these dead bodies. Spoken by God's order, this word is so powerful and efficacious that it gives life to those without it. Spoken, it does what it says, and from that which is not it brings forth that which is. Thus, these dead, though once reduced to ashes, will rise or be raised up in body and soul and be truly alive once again, just as Our Lord, by His own power, raised Himself up on the third day.

But how will this be done? By the power of God's word. Consider that wonderful miracle of Transubstantiation which takes place every day in the Sacrament of the Eucharist.³ In this General Resurrection there will be the transubstantiation of the ashes, found in the tombs or elsewhere, into true living bodies. These living bodies will be found in an instant in the place destined for the Last Judgment. [*1 Cor.* 15:52]. Now, if the word, not of many angels, but of a single Archangel uttered by the order of God is so effective that it gives being to that which is not, why do we not believe in every word of God? Why do we have difficulty in believing that what is spoken by Himself or by those to whom He has given the power and charge, cannot bring about that which is from that which is not, even though we may not fully grasp or understand this? What difficulty is there in this article of the resurrection of the dead, since it takes place through the almighty power of God?

There is no difficulty, then, in conceiving how this dead boy on the litter was not a youth, but became one when our Divine Master gave him this order: Young man, I bid you, get up. He resuscitated into that state by which Our Lord had addressed him.

It was, in some sense, necessary to explain the text of today's Gospel. Now I want to make two additional remarks. I do not have to tell you on what, for you no doubt have guessed that they concern death.

The first remark, then, concerns whether we must fear death or not. Some ancient philosophers maintain that we must not fear it, and that those who do lack either understanding or courage. Our holy Fathers disagree with them. Even though Christians perhaps ought not to fear death, since they ought always to be ready to die well, yet, for all that, they cannot be exempt from this fear. For after all, who is there who really knows for certain if he is in the proper spiritual condition to make this passage well, since to die well, we must be good? And who is absolutely certain of being good, that is, of having the charity to be judged such at the hour of his death? No one can know this unless he has received a special revelation. But even those so favored by God's revelation are not exempt from the fear of death.[4] The Stoics used to teach that we must not be apprehensive of death and that to fear it was a sign of lack of understanding and of courage. One wonders how they could have held such a position when the most courageous and learned philosophers among them, while on board a ship, blanched and became paralyzed with fear when they saw the waves on a storm-tossed sea and were threatened with imminent death. St. Augustine relates this, adding the words which one of them spoke on this occasion: "You others are scoundrels and have neither heart nor soul to lose, for you have already lost them; but I," he added, "I fear death because I have a soul and I fear to lose it."[5] In short, our ancient Fathers teach that we must fear death, yet without fearing it. To help you understand this, I will go on to my second point.

Those who want to cross streams or rivers on a small raft are in great danger of being lost if they wear glasses. There are two kinds of glasses: the first make objects appear larger than they are, and the others seem to make them smaller, and these latter are used by the nearsighted. Now if those who want to cross on a raft wear glasses which enlarge objects, those objects will appear much greater than they are. Thus they are in danger of their feet missing the raft and, consequently, of being lost. They step into space and fall. If they wear glasses which reduce the appearance of objects, these make the raft appear so small that they dare not try to walk on it, or if they do, they are so seized with fright as to fall. Extremes are always very dangerous and perilous. Now to avoid the anxiety associated with thoughts of death, our ancient Fathers advise us to fear it without fearing it.

We must fear it. Indeed, who would not be apprehensive about it, since all the saints have dreaded it, and even the Saint of Saints, Our Saviour? [*Mk.* 14:34]. For death is not natural to us. We are condemned to die only because of sin.

[*Gen.* 3:19; *Wis.* 2:23-24]. Since Adam's fall, all are subject to sin, and each will be judged in the state in which he dies. At that very moment, we know we must give an account [*Lk.* 16:2] of our whole life, and that we will be judged on what we have done. [*Ps.* 61:13 (62:12); *Matt.* 16:27; *Rom.* 2:6; *2 Cor.* 5:10]. For that reason we dread death. Alas! who knows whether he is worthy of love or hatred [*Eccles.* 9:1], whether he will be numbered among the elect or not? Therefore, he who does not fear death is in a very bad state and in great peril, for wherever we go after death is eternal: we will either be saved eternally or damned eternally. For this reason all the greatest servants of God have feared this passage as a very formidable one indeed.

Now do not tell me that some saints did not fear death, but on the contrary, desired it, asked for it, and even rejoiced at its approach; and that, consequently, we must no longer fear it since this fear is full of terror. It is true that there have been some saints who seem to have desired it. Yet that does not mean that they did not dread and fear it, for we can desire something we fear, and ask for something we do not like. For instance, who is the sick person who does not fear the scalpel when the surgeon needs to cut away a gangrenous member lest it infect and endanger the others? Though he fears it, he nevertheless wants it and even requests it, fearing that, without it, the gangrene will spread. For this reason he asks for the scalpel he fears, and in a certain manner rejoices at the surgeon's approach. Similarly, although there have been saints who desired and asked for death, we must not conclude from that that they were not also fearful of it. There is no one, no matter how holy, who does not justly fear it, the only possible exception being those who have had an extraordinary assurance of their salvation by very special revelations.

Since few have had such revelations, few have been exempted from fear of death. Nevertheless, let me offer you two examples of saints who have had this privilege. The first is the great Apostle St. Paul, who received such certain

assurances of beatitude that he seemed not to fear death at
all, for he himself said: I am hard pressed between two quite
contrary desires [*Phil.* 1:23-25], which trouble me unceasingly and cause me great pain. One is my desire to quit
this life, so as to go and enjoy the sweet presence and sight
of my Master. Oh! when will it be that I will see Him face
to face? [*1 Cor.* 13:12]. Oh! who will deliver me from this
body under the power of death? [*Rom.* 7:24]. With many
other similar words the great Apostle expressed the vehement passion he had to depart from this life and be separated
from the body so that his soul, inflamed with the desire to
see his Lord, would no longer be held back by its flesh.
He had an infinite longing, like a good and faithful servant
[*Matt.* 25:21, 23], to go to meet his dear Master and to enjoy
His sweet presence. And it seemed he found life insupportable because it kept him from realizing his desire.

But notice how certain he is that when he is separated
from his body of death he will see God, for the sole desire
which moved him was to see his Master. "Ah! who will permit me this good," he cries out, "that I might die and go
to see my Lord Jesus Christ!" In this he makes it clear that
he has no apprehension of being separated from Him in dying,
but rather that he is very certain that he will attain eternal
beatitude and enjoy Him. For that reason he desires and asks
to die.

Note, however, that in expressing his desire he adds one
condition—namely, only if such be God's will for him. "For,"
he says, "I am restrained by another desire, which is to remain among you, my most dear children, because I have
been sent to teach and instruct you. As long as my presence
will be in any way necessary for you, I am hard pressed
not to separate myself from you, but, for your sakes, to de-
prive myself of that incomparable and unimaginable contentment that I await after death rather than to leave you, knowing
that I can still be of use to you, and while in doing so there
remains the least bit of my Master's good pleasure. I do not
desire death in order to be delivered from the labors I endure.

Oh no, it is not that; still less to be delivered from the pain I suffer from the thirst I have to see my Lord. Rather, I desire it only so that I might see Him. For I am certain that after this life I shall see Him. Nevertheless, I have this other desire: not to die if He does not wish it. Consequently, I wish to remain among you as long as He pleases and as long as He knows that my presence will be necessary for you." If, then, this great saint sighed after death, it was only because he was certain of eternal happiness. If he asked for it, it was only on condition that such would be the will of God.[6]

There are some people who ask Our Lord that they might die, and when they are asked why, they answer: "It is to be delivered from the miseries of this life." But are you certain that when you are freed from the labors of this life you will be granted rest in the other? Oh, certainly not. Others say that they would not fret about dying, provided they were certain of going to Paradise; and they are right, for with such assurance death would not be feared. But even if you were certain of going to Paradise, it would not be appropriate either to desire or to ask for it in order simply to be delivered from the miseries of this world, but only on condition that such be God's will. In conclusion, we must neither desire nor ask for death, nor refuse it when it comes. And in this consists the summary of Christian perfection: to ask for nothing and to refuse nothing.[7]

That great character, Job, is another saint who seems to have desired death and to have considered it sweeter than life. Being reduced to so many tribulations and anguish, it seems he had stronger reasons to desire death than to continue living. Oh, what did the incredible sorrow in which he found himself immersed not make him say! Certainly, if the complaints of Job did not proceed from a heart utterly crushed with anguish, they would have been cause for great censure. Just consider these words: "Perish the day on which I was born," and those which follow. [*Job* 3:1 ff; 6:8-9; 7:15-16, 21]. These would have made him guilty if God had not taken his cause in hand and attested that he did not sin [*Job* 1:22;

42:7-8] while he was reduced on the dung hill, afflicted in every way imaginable.

These words, which seem extravagant, are really loving words and are not understood by everyone. For those who do not know what love is have not understood what this holy man meant. Love of God is similar to human love in this: it happens that foolish lovers of this world often utter words which would certainly be ridiculous if they did not come from a passionate heart. They insist that the ardor of their love forces them to use them, and that this language is understood only by those who know what it is to love.[8] It is the same with divine love. Ardor makes the lover use words which could be censured if they were not understood by those who know the language of this heavenly love.

Now, then, since Job was a great lover of God, every word he spoke on his dung hill was certainly a loving word. The flame which consumed his heart made him use foolish words. But the Lord, who penetrated the depths of his heart, saw clearly that it was neither weariness nor impatience which made him speak in this way; rather, it was love that animated him. Certainly our dear Master well knows what it is to love, and He also knows well the language of love. Therefore, He declared that Job had not sinned in anything that he said. He must have known how much this saint loved Him, since He chose to offer him to posterity as a prodigy of patience. So I think that He made Job understand that He treated him in this way so that he might be a mirror and an example of holiness for the whole world, and that the afflictions He sent him and the state to which He reduced him proceeded from the love He bore him. And this holy man understood this very well.

I wish to demonstrate this to you by an example found in the Gospel. [*Jn.* 2:1-5]. When at the wedding feast of Cana in Galilee the Holy Virgin said to Our Lord, with so much humility and charity, that the wine had failed, He seemed to reject her request, replying: "Woman, what is there between you and Me?"[9] Why do you concern yourself about that? What have I to do with it? Such questions seem implied in the answer He gave His Mother, an answer which may seem very rude and unfeeling to those who do not understand the language of love. No one who does not know what it is to love has discovered the correct interpretation of these words. Many things have been written about them which are not at all on target. But the Sacred Virgin knew what it is to love, and thus understood clearly what her Son meant, for she was very familiar with the nuance of His language.[10] She knew from experience His manner of speaking, for after all it was she who taught Him to speak.

She was in no way astonished, then, at these words by which He appeared to refuse her request. Rather, she believed that He would do all that she desired. Full of confidence, she gave this order to the waiters: "Do whatever He tells you." It was as if she meant: "If you heard my Son's answer, you will perhaps think it is very severe and that He wants to refuse me. But that is not so. I know by these very words that He desires to do all that I desire. So, do whatever He tells you, and fear nothing, for I am certain He will grant my request. Moreover, these words which seem rude at first glance are really the most gentle and obliging that a loving heart could say to a loving soul. Therefore, I repeat again, only do whatever He tells you."

Thus, love has a language which none can understand but those who know what it is to love. Now, the great St. Job speaks lovingly when he says: Perish the day on which I was born, etc. Note, however, that although by these words and similar ones he appears to desire and ask for death, still he was resigned and submissive to the divine will, for he desired only that which would please God. Yet love made him say these things, since he longed to see Him who moved him so deeply with His love. [*Job* 19:27]. Notwithstanding these two exceptions, I say in conclusion that everyone ought to fear death.

Over and above our own reflections, we see in the words that the Lord addressed to our first parents in the earthly paradise that death is naturally feared by man, for when God forbade Adam to eat the fruit from the tree of knowledge, He said to him: "I am your Lord, and therefore you must obey Me; now, as your Lord, I give you a commandment, which is: you shall not eat the fruit of that tree; for if you eat from it you will die." [*Gen.* 2:16-17]. The chastisement with which God threatened man is the harshest of all and the most contrary to his nature. This is also what Eve meant when, in response to the serpent's temptation to break the commandment, she replied: "But God has told us that if we eat of this fruit we shall die." [*Gen.* 3:1-3]. In this she clearly showed her fear of death.

Now, please do not use the approach that only when we forget death can we live joyously, because the thought of it is fearful. Since such fear is not bad, but actually good and useful, we ought sometimes to allow fear into our souls so as to move them to this wholesome fear of death on account of our sins. This should only be done with care.

But our ancient Fathers teach that we ought to fear death without fearing it. What does this mean? It means that although we must fear it, it must not be with an excessive fear, but one accompanied by tranquility; for Christians ought to walk under the standard of God's Providence and be ready to embrace all the effects and events of this kind Providence, confident that it is quite able to take very good care of us. Let us not be carried away by disturbing and morose fears, as happened to that good woman who thought of death in the morning and upset her family for the whole day so that no one had any peace with her. And why was that? Because she had thought of death, and was still all upset about it.

This is not the way to think about it. Still less should we try to know when we will die and in what place; whether it will be in the country or in the city; on horseback or at the foot of a mountain; or by some stone crushing us; or whether we will die in bed assisted by someone, or alone.[11] What does all that matter? Let us leave the care of it to Divine Providence, which looks after even the birds in the sky.

They lose not a single feather without His permission. [*Matt.*
6:26; 10:29]. Every hair of our head has been counted by
God. [*Matt.* 10:30]. He will take care of us. [*1 Ptr.* 5:7].
It is enough that I am all His, not only by right, but still
more in affection. Besides, what should I be concerned about
except to abandon myself to that caring Providence which
will never fail me, either in life or in death?

We must then fear this last passage, but without anxiety
or inner disturbance. Let us rather have a fear which keeps
us prepared and always ready to die well. And how are we
to do that? Your Father, St. Augustine,[12] tells us how in the
following words which, though simple and common enough,
nevertheless contain much instruction: "To die well we must
live well." As our life is, so will be our death. So, to sum
up this point, let us say that the general rule for a good
death is to lead a good life. It is true that even while living
well you will fear death, but your fear will be holy and tranquil, relying on the merits of Our Lord's Passion, without
which death would certainly be dreadful and terrifying. Those
who die in bed would doubtless be greatly disturbed if they
could not see the image of the crucifix, which reminds them
that the Saviour was fastened to the Cross for them, and
if they could not speak to Him or think of Him mentally.
The horror of this last passage and the sight of their innumerable sins might prompt them to despair, but the merits of
Our Lord's Passion would fill them with confidence, knowing that He has satisfied for all of our misdeeds by His death.

We must, then, fear death without fearing it, that is, we
must fear it with a fear which is both tranquil and full of
hope, since God has left us so many means to die well. Among
others He has left us that of contrition, which is so general
[that is, perfect contrition] that it can erase the guilt of all
kinds of sin. Besides that, we have the Sacraments of Holy
Church to wash us from our iniquities, for they are like chan-
nels through which the merits of the Saviour's Passion flow
into us so that through them we recover grace when we have
lost it. All this being so, what remains except to live abandoned

to the events of Divine Providence, asking Him for nothing and refusing Him nothing?[13] For, I repeat, all Christian perfection consists in this point: to ask God for nothing and to refuse God nothing. We should not ask Him for death, yet we should not refuse it when it comes. Oh, how happy are they who will continue in this holy indifference, and who, while waiting for what God has ordained for them, prepare themselves by a good life to die well!

That is what all the saints did. There are even some who have the practice of setting aside a certain time each year for a special consideration of death. Others do this once a month; still others, every week; and others every day, selecting a certain moment to think about it, in the evening or in the morning, and by this frequent remembrance they dispose themselves to make this passage well. It [death] is also a very useful thought to have every time we retire, as some do, by reminding ourselves that someday we will be lowered down into the grave. From this we come to this consideration: "So, since sleep is the image of death, it follows that when I die, I will be stretched out in the grave; and there, covered with earth, I will be reduced to dust and ashes. And I, ready to sleep in this bed tonight, do not know whether or not I will be alive tomorrow." Sometime during each day we ought to dwell on similar thoughts in order to be ready to die any day, using each day that we live as we would if we were certain that on that day we were to go forth from this world.

In this regard I will relate to you two short stories which I would not mention if I were in any other pulpit. But in this place I feel free to do so. I learned the first one from a pious man I knew. Here it is.

The King of Spain sent envoys to make a visitation of the states in a province in which all the police officers had been found guilty of something. The visitors proved very exact and severe in punishing and chastising them. They fined some, they discharged others from their offices, and they even condemned some to hard labor. In short, there was not a single one who was not reproved, except one good old man who was found reprehensible in absolutely nothing. The visitors were high in their praise of him and asked him how he had been able to remain so faithful to his prince, for they had found nothing reprehensible in his life. He answered that he had done only one thing: he kept in mind that one day they would make the visitation of the states in the province and that, without any doubt, visitors would come who would do their job very well. For this reason he had always conducted himself as he would have desired to have done when the visitors presented themselves. In this way he had protected himself, for the fear of being found in a bad state had made him live each day as if it were that day that he would have to render an account of himself.

Oh, how happy we would be if every day of our life we would seriously reflect on the account we shall have to render. We would constantly keep ourselves in the same state in which we would wish to be at the hour of death. This would be a good means of living well and of being found without reproach on that last day.

I heard the other story from a great princess. She was speaking to me one day about her affairs and told me that she once had an advisor who had retired from the court, ridding himself of all his worldly cares. "I sought him," she added, "to consult with him about one of my lawsuits, for he had the needed documents with him. While in his house I asked for him. But he sent the documents to me, informing me by note that he had relinquished all court affairs in order to take time to think of his conscience and to put his spiritual affairs in order, and that he returned my papers praying to Our Lord to grant a successful issue to my case and to protect my rights. Some time later I returned to him. He told me that he was always busy straightening out his affairs while waiting for the moment he was to render an account of them. A year later I inquired if this good lord were dead. They replied, 'No.' Then I went to see him. I found him occupied in the same way. I concluded from that that he would surely have a happy end."

How happy we would be if we thought thus of the account we must render! No longer busy with other affairs, we would always be ready for the day assigned for that. [cf. *Matt.* 25:13; *Heb.* 9:27]. We must do it, for death has cotton feet on which it comes so quietly that we scarcely perceive it, and it takes us by surprise. That is why we must be on our guard, so that when it comes it will find us ready. [*Matt.* 24:44; *Apoc.* 16:15]. Think of it without fear or excessive dread. But let us resolve to die, since it is something we must do, and with a peaceful, tranquil heart always keep ourselves in the same state in which we would wish to be found at the hour of death. It is the true means of preparing ourselves to die well. Doing this, we will reach eternity, and leaving these days of death, we will reach those of life. God grant us this grace. Amen, amen, amen.

NOTES

1. Today, theologians would tend to reserve the word "resurrection" to denote the rising of Jesus to eschatological life, thus emphasizing its absolutely unique character. St. Francis de Sales is using it in this sermon both for Jesus' rising and for those whom He raised to life. For the latter, contemporary theologians would tend to use only some other expression such as "resuscitation."
2. St. Francis is here drawing upon the ancient patristic tradition which viewed Jesus' humanity as the means by which His divine power and goodness was mediated to those on behalf of whom He ministered. As with those Fathers, St. Francis wishes to understand this humanity not as a passive, lifeless tool of His Divinity, but as the genuinely free and human response of Jesus to the will of His Father for Him in His redeeming work on behalf of the Kingdom of God.
3. Cf. Sermon for the Fourth Sunday of Lent, p. 124 of this volume.
4. St. Francis is referring to the Council of Trent's teaching that without a special grace from God, no one can be certain with the certainty of faith either that he is in the state of grace (which entails possessing the virtue of supernatural Charity) at this time (since there is always the possibility of self-deception), or that he will persevere in grace until death. Thus the Christian lives in hope and, with confidence, prays for the gift of final perseverance. Cf. also p. 136.
5. Cf. *Treatise on the Love of God*, Book 1, chap. 3.
6. Cf. *Treatise*, Book 9, chap. 4.

7. Cf. *Spiritual Conferences*, XXI, "On Asking for Nothing"; Sermon for Thursday of Third Week, pp. 113-114 of this volume.
8. Cf. *Treatise*, Book 6, chap. 1.
9. Cf. Fr. M. Manuel Miguens, O.F.M.: *Mary, The Servant of the Lord* (Boston: St. Paul Editions), p. 128.
10. There is an important footnote here in the Annecy ed.: " Faite à son jargon"; *Dictionaire de Littre*, au mot "jargon": language à double entente.
11. Cf. *Introduction to the Devout Life*, Part I, chap. 13.
12. Since the Rule of the Visitation Order is that of St. Augustine, St. Francis de Sales often refers to him as their Father when, as here, he is addressing Visitation nuns.
13. Cf. p. 138 of this sermon.

— 10 —

HEARING THE WORD OF GOD

Sermon for Passion Sunday, March 13, 1622,
concerning the goodness which should be prac-
ticed by those who preach God's word, how we
should esteem God's word even if it is taught by
a sinful person, how a person's refusal to believe
Our Lord's word proves the evilness of that
person—not of Our Lord, how all sin is a result
of defection from truth, how God's word is Truth,
how Lucifer's sin as well as that of our first par-
ents resulted from a choice of vanity over truth,
how we should remain attentive to the truths of
faith, our culpable failure to live according to the
truths of God's word, the dispositions with which
we should hear God's word, and the unimportance
of distractions and dryness in the lower part of
our soul as long as the higher part of the soul
is devoted and reverent toward God's word.

"He who is of God hears the words of God.
Therefore you hear them not, because you are
not of God."—John 8:47

A word is accepted or rejected for three reasons: because
of the person who speaks it, because of the word that is
spoken, because of those who hear it. For this word to be
honored and accepted, the one who is speaking it must be
a good man, a virtuous man, one worthy of being believed.
Otherwise, rather than being accepted, it will be rejected,
despised.[1] Further, what is said must be good and true. Finally, those who hear it must be good, prepared to receive
it; if not, it will be neither accepted, honored, nor kept.

This is what Our Lord teaches us in the Gospel Holy Church offers us today, in which He reproaches the scribes and pharisees for not receiving His words—for which they are to blame. [*Jn.* 8:46-59]. He says: "Why do you not believe the truth I teach?" Their nonbelief thoroughly astonished Him. It is as though He meant to say: "You really have no excuse, for which one of you can convict Me of sin? Why then do you not believe Me, since what I am telling you is truth itself? I cannot err. Therefore your disbelief must stem from your own wickedness and sinfulness. Certainly neither I nor the word I teach is to blame."

Thus, it is necessary that the one proclaiming God's word be irreproachable, and his life congruent with his teaching. If this is not the case, the word will be neither honored nor accepted. For this reason God forbids sinners to announce His word [*Ps.* 49 (50):16-17]. He seems to say: "Miserable one, how dare you teach My doctrine with your lips and dishonor it with your life? How can you possibly expect it to be accepted from a mouth so full of infectious sin? I will not permit such a one to proclaim My will." Thus He has forbidden sinners to announce His sacred word, fearing it will be rejected by those who hear it.

Be careful here. It is not all sinners who are forbidden to preach, but only notorious ones. Otherwise, who could announce God's word, since we are all sinners? Whoever says the contrary is guilty of grievous untruth. [*1 Jn.* 1:8]. Even the Apostles were sinners. Those who allege never to have sinned are guilty of a very great delusion indeed. The contrary is actually clear at the very moment they allege it. St. Augustine teaches this explicitly when he writes that the daily petition in the Lord's Prayer, "forgive us our trespasses" [*Matt.* 6:12], is not only a word of humility but also one of truth because, due to our frail humanity, we commit offences at every turn.

All are sinners, but not all are to be silent and refrain from teaching God's word, but only those who live a life wholly contrary to this divine word. Yet even if this word is preached to us by evildoers, we ought not reject it, but accept it, doing as the bees do who gather honey from almost all the flowers of the fields. Even though some of these flowers are harmful and poisonous, they skillfully draw out honey, a celestial dew untainted by poison.

As confirmation of what I say, I will gladly relate a beautiful example found in the life of the great St. Ephrem. He was indeed a great man, not only because he was a deacon to two illustrious Doctors of the Church, but because he too was a great Doctor, having written very beautiful teachings which truly delight those who read them. This great saint was reared very carefully and nourished from his earliest years on the eremitical life. After many years in the desert, he was inspired by God one day to go to Edessa, his native city. He had always left his heart open and receptive to the Divine Majesty, eager to receive the precious dew of heavenly inspiration, and he had always faithfully accepted them in obedience. Thus he readily embraced this one too.

He went promptly to the city. As he drew near, he was convinced that God must have something important to teach him in calling him from his hermitage. Falling on his knees, he prayed most fervently for the grace to meet someone in the city who would serve as his director and lead him to God's will. Full of confidence that the Lord would hear him, he got up. When he reached Edessa he came upon a prostitute. Disturbed, he said to himself: "My God, I asked You to let me meet someone who would teach me what Your good pleasure wants of me. Instead, I meet this unfortunate woman." Eyeing her disdainfully, he noticed that she too was looking at him attentively. Enraged at her boldness, he demanded: "Why, miserable woman, do you look at me so?" She responded very cleverly and learnedly: "I have the right to look at you, but you have no right to look at me. You know that woman was drawn from the side of man. [*Gen.* 2:21-23]. Therefore, I am only looking at the place of my origin. But man was created from the earth [*Gen.* 2:7], so why are you not continually looking down at the earth, since that is the place from which you were drawn?"

This great saint truly valued the teaching of the wretched woman, received it humbly, and even warmly acknowledged his gratitude to her. From that moment on, he so valued that lesson that not only did he always keep his bodily eyes lowered to the ground, but even more so his interior and spiritual eyes, which he kept riveted on his nothingness, his vileness and his abjection. In this way he made continual progress in the virtue of most holy humility all the rest of his life.

This story teaches us how we should honor and esteem God's word and good teachings even if they are presented by persons of ill repute. After all, the Lord desired that a prophet should be instructed by an ass [*Num.* 22:28-30], and that wicked Pilate should announce the great truth that our divine Master is Jesus [*Matt.* 1:21]—that is, Saviour—a title which he even placed above the Cross, insisting: "Such is the case, it is I who have said so." [*Jn.* 19:22]. Caiphas, the most miserable among men, pronounced this word of truth: It is expedient to have one man die for the salvation of the people. [*Jn.* 11:49-50; 18:14].

This makes it clear that although we must never esteem nor approve the evil lives of wicked and sinful people, yet we ought never to despise God's word that they may offer us. Rather, we must profit from it as did St. Ephrem. A great Doctor has taught that we ought not care whether the person who shows us the way of virtue is good or bad. All that is important is that it be indeed the true way. If so, we ought to follow it and walk in it faithfully. What does it matter whether they give us balm in an earthenware vessel or in a precious vase? It is enough that it cures our wounds.

Let us not consider the goodness or its absence in one who is our preacher or teacher, but only what he says to us. God's word is not made good or bad because of him who explains or teaches it. It is goodness itself and never partakes of the evil of him who announces it. Holy Scripture in its wisdom also teaches this when it has even beasts, be they weak or brutal, teach us what we ought to do, instructing us that we can learn even from ants how to care for what we have. [*Prov.* 6:6-8; 30:25]. They gather while the weather is good so that they might have sufficient food on those days which are not favorable for gathering. Did not Our Lord Himself tell us to imitate the prudence and cunning of the serpent and the simplicity of the dove? [*Matt.* 10:16]. Scripture gives hundreds of such examples.

All this notwithstanding, generally speaking, one who teaches ought to be good if he wants his teaching to be accepted and valued. His evil life might otherwise cause his teaching to be rejected and despised as being, like himself, bad and despicable. Surely we ought to benefit spiritually from God's word no matter who presents it. Nevertheless, hardened sinners who persevere in their wickedness offend greatly in teaching God's word and in proclaiming the praises of the Sovereign Majesty, since they lay this divine word wide open to contempt on account of their bad conduct. This is why in today's Gospel Our Lord asks the scribes and Pharisees: "Which one of you can convict Me of sin? You say that I am a Samaritan; that I eat and drink with the Publicans; that I am a drunkard; that I forbid the payment of taxes to Caesar; that I do not observe the Sabbath. These calumnies make Me out to be an imposter. But answer Me, which one of you can convict Me of sin? Why then do you not believe Me? Undoubtedly the evil is in you because there can be none at all in Me." [*Jn.* 8:48; *Matt.* 9:11; *Matt.* 11:19; *Lk.* 23:2; *Jn.* 5:16, 18; 19:16].

Our Divine Master spoke most reasonably here because it is simply not possible to join two things so contrary as God and sin. As soon as we say "God," sin is excluded forever; we cannot doubt this. Since Jesus is God He cannot sin; as man too He cannot sin because His human soul, in its high point, was glorious from the instant of His Conception in Our Lady's sacred womb. Consequently, He always enjoyed in this supreme part of His human soul the clear vision of the Divine Majesty. It is this vision which will constitute our eternal beatitude. In this vision there is no possibility of sinning, for it is impossible to see God and not love Him sovereignly, and sovereign love cannot tolerate or permit sin, which is infinitely displeasing to Him and dishonors the Divine Goodness.

Thus Our Lord said quite rightly to the Jews: "Which one of you can convict Me of sin?" He was greatly astonished that they refused to believe His words or follow His doctrine, since His life was irreproachable. He added: "If I preach the truth, why do you not embrace it? Since I am sinless, you ought to believe that I teach you only the truth and in no way deceive you." O certainly, our Divine Master cannot deceive, because He is Truth Itself. [*Jn.* 14:6; *1 Jn.* 5:6]. Those who refuse to believe will undoubtedly perish. [*Mk.* 16:16]. Our entire good consists not only in accepting the truth of God's word, but in persevering in it. Contrariwise, all human and angelic evil is a result of their defection from truth instead of perseverance in it. [*Jn.* 8:30-32].

We come to the second part of our sermon. If we want our word to be accepted, it must be the truth. But what is truth? Nothing else, my dear friends, than faith. It is written that Our Lord is full of grace and truth [*Jn.* 1:14], which means that He is full of faith and charity. It is not, of course, that He had faith for Himself, for He had the clear vision of the things taught by faith. He was said to be full of faith as its distributor to His Christian children. As I said the other day, the spouse in the Canticle of Canticles declares that her Well-Beloved, our dear Saviour, has two breasts filled with the most precious of perfumes, which permeate the surroundings with the most delightful fragrance. [*Cant.* 1:1-3]. Many have given their interpretation of this passage. I give this interpretation: these divine breasts represent grace and truth, that is, charity and faith.

Certainly He did not need this delicious milk for Himself, any more than women need the milk which is given to them by God and nature for their children's nourishment. Thus grace, still less faith, was not given to Our Lord for Himself, because He needed them. After all, He is Grace Itself, and it is His to distribute. So too for faith. It is for us that He is filled with these gifts. This was why He tried so zealously to help the scribes and Pharisees accept them and why, in anger, He asked: "Why do you not believe My words? They are not vanity, but Truth itself."

Defecting from truth, men and angels fell into vanity, as we have said. It is a truism that we do the same. When we depart from the truth, we simultaneously and increasingly choose vanity. Vanity is the absence of truth. With it we stumble into Hell. Lucifer, turning from God, who is the Eternal Truth, withdrew the eyes of his understanding from this infinitely lovable Object and lowered them at once to a consideration of his own beauty, which was solely dependent upon this Supreme Beauty. The Supreme Beauty should have been his continual focus. Considering his own beauty, this unhappy spirit admired himself and took pride in himself. This admiring pride caused his loss and his condemnation to eternal flames. In failing to persevere in truth, he perished in vanity. Faith taught him that all that he had came from God alone. Thus to God alone was due sovereign honor. He turned the eyes of his understanding away from this truth and immediately committed that act of insupportable vanity, saying: "I will ascend; I will be like the Most High"[2] [*Is.* 14:13-14]—a wicked proposition and unfortunate project that caused his eternal loss.

Our first parents also failed to remain in truth, that is, to persevere in their attentiveness to it, and thus merited to be condemned forever had not God pardoned them through the merits of His Son. Eve, walking through the Garden of Paradise and musing on idle thoughts instead of considering God's wonderful gifts and graces to them, was tempted by the evil spirit to give up her meditation of this truth: "If you eat of the forbidden fruit, you will die." What greater truth was there than this, since God Himself had spoken it? [*Gen.* 2:17]. That ancient serpent [*Apoc.* 12:9] began his entanglement of her by saying: "Do not take God's word so seriously. Surely you will not die. Do not think so much of death. It will depress you. It is a wearisome subject. . ." That poor thing listened to such trickeries and let herself be persuaded. She even led her husband into the sin of breaking God's commandment not to eat fruit from the forbidden tree. [*Gen.* 3:1-6]. How much better it would have been for her to persevere in meditation, because she would not have fallen from truth into vanity. Indeed, as is commonly taught, it was vanity that led her to sin.

Ever since, all her children have been affected by this spirit of pride which makes them skillful in pursuing honors, riches, pleasures and the rest. All such things are folly, since they make us more prone to turn from the truth than to consider it. Experience teaches us this daily. Do we not see that those who are strongly attracted to such vain and frivolous things do not think—or at least so it seems by their bad conduct— on the truth of a Paradise filled with every consolation and happiness for those who live according to God's commands and walk after Him according to His will? These commandments and God's will are wholly contrary to the life they lead. They never weary of giving themselves to low and passing pleasures, even though they know well enough that if they do not change they will be eternally denied the enjoyment of unending felicity. Do they not see, too, how full of vanity they are? If they do not remain attentive to truth there is a Hell for them where all imaginable—or rather, unimaginable—torments and misfortunes are to be found to punish those who do not fear God in this life or observe His commandments. Yet, attentiveness to this truth is extremely necessary to maintain us in our duty.

If we remain attentive to the truth of the mysteries which Our Lord teaches us in prayer, how happy we will be! When we see Him dying upon the Cross for us, what does He not teach us? "I have died for you," He says, this Sovereign Lover; "what does My death require but that, as I have died for you, you also should die for Me, or at least live only for Me?"[3] [*2 Cor.* 5:14-15]. Oh, how powerfully this truth moves our will to love dearly Him who is so lovable and so worthy of our love! Truth is the object of the understanding and love that of the will.[4] As soon as our understanding learns the truth that Our Lord died for love of us, ah, our will is immediately inflamed, conceiving great affection and desire to return this love as much as possible. These affections make us burn with the desire to please this Sacred Lover so much that nothing is too difficult to do or to suffer; nothing seems impossible; the martyrs did nothing for God in comparison with what we would now want to do. That is good. Persevere in that truth and all will be well. But we do not! From this truth, which we have learned in prayer, we turn to vanity in action. We are angels in prayer and often devils in conversation and action, offending this same God whom we have recognized as being so lovable and so worthy of being obeyed.

Similarly, we might consider how Our Lord emptied Himself [*Phil.* 2:7] and humbled Himself with such humility that it is impossible ever fully to comprehend it. Then God pronounces this truth in our hearts: if our sweet Saviour so humbled Himself to be an example for us, then certainly we ought to humble ourselves so profoundly that we would ever remain in deep acknowledgment of our nothingness. At that moment we feel we shall never experience repugnance toward humiliation. Yet when the occasion arises, we think no more of our resolution. So vain are we that the least shadow of abjection causes us to tremble, and to arm ourselves against it lest it reach us.

Our Lord taught us: "Blessed are the poor." Yet each of us rejects this truth, embracing vanity. We eagerly desire and seek to be so wealthy as to lack nothing. Our Sovereign Master said: "Blessed are the meek." Yet each wants to be feared and dreaded. "Blessed are those persecuted for justice' sake." Yet all want to be avenged and to suffer nothing, for fear of being despised. "Blessed are they who mourn." Yet everybody wants to rejoice in this mortal and passing life as if here were found our true happiness. And so on for the other beatitudes. [*Matt.* 5:3-11]. He could surely put to us the same question He put to the Jews: "Why, why do you not believe Me, since I tell you the truth?"

"We believe it indeed," we might answer, but we do not follow it. In this we are inexcusable, no different from the pagans who, though they recognized that there was a God, would not, however, honor Him. [*Rom.* 1:20-21]. We will certainly deserve great punishment if, having known that we are so dearly loved by our good Saviour, we nevertheless are so ungrateful as not to love Him with all our heart and power, nor follow with all our strength and all our care the examples He has given us in His life, Passion and Death. He will reproach us as He does in today's Gospel: "If I have taught you—I, who cannot be accused of sin; I, whose life is irreproachable; I, who preached to you the truth I learned from My heavenly Father—why then do you not believe Me? Now, if you believe that I am telling the truth, why do you not accept it and persevere in it? Why do you instead live wholly to the contrary of what is expected of you?" We will then be convicted by His Divine Majesty, and in our bafflement we will confess that the fault is our own, caused by our own malice. To avoid such a predicament, my dear souls, we must know how we are to hear and accept God's word. I turn to that consideration now.

In the first place, we must prepare ourselves to hear it with the attention it deserves, not as if it were just any other word. As a woman who did not love her husband more than her servant would not love him enough, nor as she should;[5] as a child who would love his father with a love equal only to that he bore his tutor would not love his father properly; so whoever hears a sermon with the same dispositions and attention he pays to any entertaining story or tale, does not hear it as he should. If his pleasure is the same for both, one could certainly conclude that he did not love God's word sufficiently. To dispose ourselves to understand it well we ought to open our hearts in the presence of the Divine Majesty, receptive to this heavenly dew, just as Gideon spread his fleece in the meadow so that it might be watered by the rain and dew from Heaven. [*Jgs.* 6:37-38].

With our hearts thus opened before God, and with the good disposition to profit from what He will say to us, let us remain attentive. Remember, it is His Majesty who speaks to us and makes known His will. Thus, with a spirit of devotion and attention, let us hear the truths which the preacher proposes to us.

Let us imitate the Spanish here. When they receive a letter from some important person they immediately place it on their head to show the honor they bear him who wrote it, as well as to indicate that they submit to whatever commands have been given them in the letter. Let us do the same, my dear souls, when we hear the word of God in preaching, or when we read it in a book. Let us spiritually place it on our heads. In obedience let us submit ourselves to the things that are taught us concerning God's will for our perfection and spiritual advancement. Let us listen to them and read them with the determination to profit from them. Let us never consider the quality of him who pronounces the sacred word. Remember, it matters little whether he is good or bad, provided that what he says is useful and congruent with our faith. God will not ask us if those who taught us were saints or sinners, but if we profited by what they said to us and if we received it with the spirit of humility and reverence.

The example of the great St. Charles[6] was very remarkable on this subject. He never read the Holy Bible except when kneeling, bareheaded and with very great reverence. To him it was God who spoke to him as he read. We must do the same if we really desire to read and understand the divine word well and if we really want to profit by it. Otherwise we will merit the reproach addressed to the scribes, and Our Lord will put all the blame upon us.

But before concluding, I must remove a tiny little thorn which you might get into your feet as you begin to walk in earnest in the observance of these things. You may say to me: "Good heavens! You just said that to receive the holy word well so that it leads to our profit and not to our condemnation we must hear it with attention, in a spirit of devotion and reverence. But I have never heard it in this way! Truly, I must certainly try to do so from now on. But how shall I succeed? I am usually so distracted and weighed down by dryness and a certain interior stupor that I take no pleasure in anything. My mind is so distracted during a sermon that ordinarily I have great difficulty in remaining attentive to what the preacher is saying. I seem to have no taste for devotion and almost no desire to put into practice what I learn there."

When we are taught that we must hear God's word with attention, reverence and devotion, we ought to understand this in the same way we understand what is said of prayer and of every other spiritual practice. We are not taught that we must have these feelings of devotion and of reverence in the lower part of our soul, which is the part where these disgusts and difficulties ordinarily reside. It is enough that in the higher part we hold ourselves in reverence and keep to the intention of profiting from it. Having done that, we ought not to trouble ourselves by imagining that we are not well disposed to receive this holy word. Since the preparation to hear the word was made in the will and in the higher part of our spirit, the Divine Goodness is satisfied, for He is content with little and pays no attention at all to what passes in the lower part of our spirit.[7]

Finally, we must conclude by saying that we ought never to reject God's word or the teachings Our Lord has left us because of the faults of preachers who propose them. Since our Divine Master pronounced them first with His divine mouth, we are inexcusable if we do not receive them. Even though this precious balm may be presented to us in earthen vessels, the preachers, it is nonetheless infinitely powerful to cure our wounds. It loses nothing at all of its properties and its strength because of those earthen vessels. Nor is it excusable to doubt its truth, inasmuch as Jesus Christ, who is Truth Itself, has taught us Himself and made Himself our dear Teacher. Nor must we place ourselves in danger of being lost by not persevering in the truth, that is, in not living according to it and in not making ourselves capable of understanding it well when it is proposed or explained to us in God's Name. We ought, on the contrary, to prepare ourselves well to hear it profitably. This is an excellent means of understanding it well. Understanding it well will greatly help us to keep it well. They who keep it are declared blessed in the Holy Gospel by our Lord and Saviour. [*Lk.* 11:28]. Amen.

NOTES

1. Cf. *Treatise on the Love of God,* Book VIII, chap. 1 and 5.
2. Cf. *Sermons of St. Francis de Sales on Our Lady,* "The Purification," February 2, 1620, p. 88; "The Immaculate Conception," December 8, 1622, p. 192.
3. Cf. *Treatise,* Book VII, chap. 8.
4. Cf. Sermon for Thursday of First Week, pp. 34-35 of this volume.
5. Cf. *Treatise,* Book X, chap. 6.
6. Cf. *Treatise,* Book VIII, chap. 3.
7. St. Francis de Sales distinguishes between the "higher" and "lower" parts of the soul in Book I, chap. 11 and 12 of his *Treatise on the Love of God.* He uses that distinction to help us understand how we can obediently cling to God and His will for us even if we do not always (or often!) have the feelings which one usually associates with such docility and obedience. It is enough that we do God's will, not that we feel "good" or "holy" or "consoled" in doing it. St. Francis is giving another facet of that teaching here.

11

HUMILITY AND OBEDIENCE

Sermon for Palm Sunday, March 20, 1622, con-
cerning the perfection and imperfection found in
every creature (except the Blessed Virgin)—including
the angels in Heaven and the saints, how we should
take note of and profit by the imperfections in the
lives of the saints, how we should not use the faults
of the saints to excuse our own failings, worldly
prudence vs. the folly of the Cross, fraternal cor-
rection, the ass and colt upon which Our Lord
entered Jerusalem and what they represent, Our
Lord's humility and patience and submission, per-
fect obedience vs. obedience full of worldly pru-
dence, the proper answer to make to the objections
of worldly prudence, Our Lord's confounding of
the maxims of the world, and our blessedness in
imitating Him.

Everything in the world has two faces, because everything
has two principles. The first is God, the first cause of everything that exists. The second is the nothingness from which
everything has been drawn. Now, since God is the first principle of every being, there is nothing that does not contain
something beautiful and lovable in it. But since every created
thing is drawn out of nothingness, each contains some imperfection.

The rational creature is truly created after the image and
likeness of God [*Gen.* 1:26-27], who is its first cause and
sovereign principle. Because of this it is indeed truly lovable.
Further, it is so attractive that anyone seeing a soul alive
with grace, having its Creator's image stamped upon it, would
be ravished and inflamed with love, as we are told St.

Catherine of Siena was. But because of the second principle, nothingness, we always discover some imperfection in every creature. Thus in every rational creature there is found perfection and imperfection, signs of the two principles from which it has come forth into existence.[1] Since everything that issues from God is good and lovable, it follows that everything in the creature that is good and lovable issues from God as its first source; likewise, any imperfection found there comes from the nothingness from which it has been drawn. These two faces are found not only in rational creatures but in everything created by God.

All creatures—being a mixture, as it were, of perfection and imperfection—have been used by Scripture to teach us about both good and evil. There is not one from which we cannot draw an analogy to teach us about the one or the other. All can be used to point out either good or evil. For example, in a thousand places in Holy Scripture the dove is taken to represent virtue. Our Lord made use of it Himself: Be simple as doves [*Matt.* 10:16], indicating in this way how simple He wants us to be so as to be able to draw Him into our hearts. Now, although the dove is ordinarily used to point out to us some perfection, Holy Scripture also uses it to help us understand the ugliness of vice and of sin. Speaking to the people of Ephraim, God said: You have gone astray as the dove who has no heart. [*Osee* 7:11]. Here the sacred text uses the dove to symbolize a lack of heart and courage, cowardice and a lack of generosity.

Though the serpent is a wicked reptile and seems to be good for nothing but evil, yet it is not so evil that Holy Scripture cannot use it also to symbolize good to us, for Our Lord Himself said: Be wise as serpents. [*Matt.* 10:16]. But in other places it compares iniquity to a serpent's venom [*Ps.* 139 (140):4; *Rom.* 3:13], and the sinner to its tail. [*Apoc.* 12:4; *Prov.* 23:32]. In brief, Scripture uses it to point out both good and evil.

Even the rose is not so perfect as to be without some imperfection. Though it is very beautiful in the morning, in full bloom, with a delightful and pleasing fragrance, yet in the evening it is so faded and wilted that its condition can be used to symbolize the voluptuousness and delights of a worldly life. The voluptuous say, we read in Holy Scripture: "Let us enjoy good things, let us crown ourselves with rosebuds." [*Wis.* 2:6, 8]. Elsewhere in Scripture, things with outward beauty and show, but whose life is short and fleeting, are compared to the rose which withers and fades by evening. [*Job* 14:2; *Ps.* 102 (103):15; *Is.* 40:6-8]. Yet Our Lord, who is infinite Wisdom, compared Himself to it. Speaking of Himself He said: I am like a stalk, or the branch of a rose tree. [*Ecclus.* 24:18(14)].

Thus, all creatures have something of perfection and of imperfection. This is why they can be used to provide examples of both. However, I have never found Holy Scripture to use the palm tree to represent anything but perfection,[2] or something excellent and honorable. It seems to find nothing vile or contemptible in it. Among flowers, the lily seems to have nothing abject, so I have never read in Scripture that it was used for any figure but perfection. This is not so with the rest of creatures. The palm tree and the lily are apparently the only exceptions, though they also have their origin in the same nothingness from which God created everything.

Among all rational creatures, the Blessed Virgin alone had all kinds of good, free of every trace of evil. For she alone was exempt from all spot and stain of sin and imperfection: she alone is all-pure and all-beautiful [*Cant.* 1:15; 4:1, 7], with no withering or fading.[3] I say among all pure creatures she is unique, for her Son Our Lord is not simply a creature, being God and man. Being the Source of all perfection, there can be nothing imperfect in Him. But the Holy Virgin, who, like all creatures, came from nothingness, is the only one in whom there was never any imperfection. In all others is found perfection and imperfection. He who would tell someone that he had no imperfection would be as much a liar as the one who would say he had no perfection at all. Every man has some imperfection, no matter how holy he may be—

and some perfection, no matter how wicked. Created after the image of God[4] [*Gen.* 1:26-27], from Him comes all the good that he has; created from nothingness, each retains some imperfection.

This is universally true not only among human creatures, but also among the angels, for their perfection is not free from imperfection. Iniquity was found among them, and God cast them out because they rebelled against Him. [*Job* 4:18, 15:15; *2 Ptr.* 2:4; *Jude* 6]. Imperfection was found among them not only before their confirmation in grace, but also since then. For they were not made so entirely perfect that there does not remain in them a certain negative imperfection which, however, does not render them displeasing to God. Confirmed in grace, this imperfection can no longer cause them to fall from beatitude, nor cause them to commit any sin. Their imperfection lies in the fact that, although they enjoy the clear vision of God, they do not always clearly and fully recognize His will, so that while waiting to have a clearer knowledge, they do as perfectly as they are able what they judge to be most conformable to the divine good pleasure, although at times there are different opinions among them.

It happened thus to the guardian angels of the Persians and the Jews, who debated together what should be done for the carrying out of the will of God. [*Dan.* 10:13]. In this they committed an imperfection—without sinning, however, because they could not sin. They resemble those who go contrary to God's will without knowing it or recognizing it. If they knew that what they are doing is not according to God's good pleasure, they would rather die a thousand times than do it. In His divine wisdom God has willed to leave this in the angels to show that there is no creature whatever who does not have some imperfection and who does not bear the mark of being created out of nothing.

Therefore, there is absolutely nothing wrong when one recounts the faults and sins of the saints while speaking of their virtues. On the contrary, those who write their history

do a great disservice to everyone when they conceal their
faults under the pretext of better honoring them, or in not
recounting the often sinful beginning of their lives for fear
that this would diminish or weaken the esteem one has for
their later sanctity. Oh, no! That is not right! By acting in
this manner, they do an injustice to these blessed ones and
to all posterity. All the great saints who have written the
lives of other saints have always recounted their faults and
imperfections openly and simply. They thought, and rightly
so, that such candor rendered as much service to God and
to the saints themselves, as the recounting of their virtues.
The glorious St. Jerome, in writing the epitaph, the praises
and virtues of his dear St. Paula, clearly recounted her faults
as well, after the account of her virtues. With great candor,
honesty and simplicity he condemned some of her actions
as imperfect. In recounting both her perfections and imperfections he did so in complete honesty, knowing that one
would be as useful as the other to his readers.[5]

It is good to take note of faults in the lives of the saints,
not only to recognize the goodness that God has extended
in pardoning them, but also to teach us to abhor and to avoid
them and to do penance for them, just as they did. We must
also take note of their virtues so as better to imitate them.
In fact, true Christians and true religious ought to be like
bees who fly among all the various flowers to gather honey
to nourish themselves. The great St. Antony did this when,
having left the world, he went throughout the deserts and
grottos of the anchorites—not only, like a holy honey bee,
to note and gather the honey of their virtues on which to
feed himself, but also to avoid and to guard against any evil
or imperfections in them. In doing that he became, in the
end, a great saint.

There are some souls who do just the opposite. They are
like wasps, not bees. Wasps are nasty little insects that fly
among the flowers—not to extract honey, but poison, from
them. Although they cull honey, it is only to convert it into
bitterness. There are certainly some Christians who take after

wasps. They too fly among the flowers, that is, the works and actions of their neighbors, not to gather the honey of a holy edification from a consideration of their virtues, but to extract poison[6] by taking note of their faults and imperfections—either those of the saints whose faults have been recounted in their biographies, or the faults of those with whom they live. They end by committing these same faults.

For example: they read in St. Jerome's[7] life of St. Paula of this imperfection: she so grieved over the death of her husband and children that she became sick and almost died. "Well, now," they say, "St. Paula, a great saint, grieved so excessively on being separated from her loved ones—is there, then, any reason to be astonished that I, who am in no way a saint, am unable to resign myself to the many hardships in my life, even though they are offered by Divine Providence for my good?" With such a mindset we refuse to accept any correction for a failing or imperfection, promptly objecting: "Why, such and such a saint did that too! Surely, I am no better or more perfect than he"; or, "If such a one did this, can I not do it too?" Fine reasoning, this! We are a sorry lot indeed! As if we did not have enough work to do in ourselves to correct and unravel our own imperfections and bad habits without trying to clothe ourselves as well with those we see in others!

We are so weak that instead of avoiding the failings we see in our neighbor, we use them either to add to our own or to deepen those we already have. Reading of the sharp disagreement between St. Paul and St. Barnabas [*Acts* 15:37-40], we excuse our own contentious and quarrelsome behavior with one another! "St. Peter was brusque and precipitous. Is it any wonder that I am so too? That temperament often made him commit faults; can I not be expected to do the same?" O God, what insane logic! What foolishness! Is it not clear that such people are making excuses to nourish their own imperfections and to stagnate in their bad habits?

If wasps do not find poison in flowers, they gather the

honey but convert it into poison. Such is their nature. There are people like that—so malign that, not content with observing other's faults so as to deepen themselves in their own malice, they go much further and so dwell on and interpret their neighbor's deeds that they actually change honey into poison, drawing evil from his actions. Not only this, but they prompt and provoke others to do the same, like wasps whose buzzing attracts others to the flower where he has found poison. For instance, a young man enters religion, or another does a good work. You can be sure there will be those who censure both and, by their machinations and gossip, cause many others to do so too. What St. Basil says of dogs can certainly be applied to such people: as soon as one barks and yelps, all the others bark and yelp, whether there is reason to or not, but simply because they are prompted and provoked.

But the holy Fathers teach us to continue to persevere in good despite all the barkings of such dogs. Let the world cry out as much as it wants; let human prudence censure and condemn our actions as much as it desires; we may have to listen to and suffer from all this, but let us not be frightened or give up; let us rather pursue our course firmly and faithfully. Let worldly wisdom go on constituting what it considers excellency in worldly glory if it wants to. The true Christian, or, to use the term appropriate for you, the true religious, who is tending toward Christian perfection, should, contrary to all the reasonings of human prudence, place all his perfection in the folly of the Cross [*1 Cor.* 1:18, 23], because it was in this folly of the Cross that Our Lord was made perfect. So all the saints have endeavored to become wise in this folly and, for this, suffered all the contempt, censures and humiliations which came to them from the worldly wise. Perfection of the Cross requires that we endure labors, persecutions and reprehensions for justice' sake. Blessed are those who are persecuted for justice' sake. [*Matt.* 5:10].

This wisdom is wholly contrary to that of the world. Even though Our Lord cried out again and again: Blessed are the poor in spirit, the peacemakers, the meek, they who hunger and thirst for justice[8] [*Matt.* 5:3-6], the world cannot embrace this wisdom. It cries out: "Oh! How blessed are the wealthy, the oppressors, those who take vengeance on their enemies, and those whom one dares not offend." See how the perfection of the Cross is folly in the eyes of the world precisely because it embraces what is abhorrent to human nature. It loves correction and submits to it; it not only takes pleasure in being corrected, but it has no greater pleasure than in being reproved and corrected for faults and failings. Oh, blessed are they who speak only to give fraternal correction in a spirit of charity and profound humility! But more blessed are those who are always ready to receive it with a gentle, peaceful and tranquil heart! In this, they have already made great progress. Let them be humble and faithful, and let them have good courage, because in spite of all the trickeries of human prudence, they will arrive at the highest degree of Christian perfection.

Apropos of this topic, I cannot refrain from telling you a very interesting story. The great St. Charles was once corrected by a sincere gentleman for an imperfection which he had noticed in the saint.[9] This good man, however, filtered this failing through the eye of human prudence. It happened like this. Once this glorious saint had to make a trip to Milan, and chose to go by water instead of by land in order to have more leisure for his spiritual exercises—to pray his Office, meditate for an hour, do spiritual reading and speak of spiritual matters. There was more time for such activities when traveling by boat than by horseback. Incidentally, those who have been to Milan know that the scenery is very lovely and that there are delightfully graceful canals en route.

St. Charles embarked, then, with his retinue, and as it happened, the above-mentioned gentleman made the same journey. After they had finished their accustomed prayers, St. Charles said: "Now come, let us have a little recreation." (Recreation has always been highly praised and recommended as good by the saints. It is amply provided for in all religious

communities to relax the spirit which, if always taut, leads
to one kind of trouble or other.)[10] They asked: "What shall
we do?" They certainly did not want to do something unseemly
or improper for recreation. St. Charles said: "Let us play
a game." (There was no question of cards or the like, for
this great prelate was too pious.)[11] "Let us play the game
of telling each other our faults clearly, simply, candidly—no
flattery. Each will tell these things to the one nearest him,
one after the other."

This was indeed a fine game. Not everyone knows of it
and not all like to play it! Certainly the Holy Spirit reigns
in this kind of recreation. For it is indeed the recreation of
the saints to alert one another to faults—but humbly, charita-
bly, and with great truth and simplicity. The game begins.
One says, "We have noticed that you often use duplicity; your
words are not simple; you do not perform your actions with
sincerity." Another says, "We have noticed that you are vain
and proud; you take pleasure in sporting a big mustache;
you frequently look to see if your beard is still well combed;
in short, we have noticed that you are very vain indeed."
During this game you would have seen this one blush and
that one blanche, depending upon how they reacted emotion-
ally to these corrections.

At last came the turn of the gentleman of whom we have
spoken. He was next to St. Charles and had to tell our saint
his faults. He stood with cap in hand, and St. Charles begged
him to say very simply what he had noticed in him. "Do not
spare me, I entreat you; tell me my faults. I am eager to hear
you out." Now, the gentleman had had something in his mind
for a long time and was happy with this opportunity to tell St.
Charles of it. "My lord, for a very long time we have observed
in you a great indiscretion. This has been noticed by myself
and by many others who esteem you greatly, yet think you very
inconsiderate." Raising his hat to him, St. Charles said: "Sir,
I thank you. I am sure this is the case, but please be specific.
This accusation is too general; I am waiting to hear of some
particular faults. Speak; do not spare me."

"My lord," replied the gentleman, "your great indiscretion is that you sleep in the daytime instead of at night. When you come to church for Mass, or to hear a sermon, you fall asleep. Those who see you are astonished and ask: 'Do you see our Archbishop sleeping? Would it not be better for him to sleep during the night instead of coming here to do it?' The preacher is displeased and distracted too. You ought to correct this fault by sleeping at night so that you can stay awake during the day." Now although this admonition was prompted by human prudence, St. Charles smiled and thanked the man with great affection, showing that he received it with a humble and gentle heart. Then he said, "It is very true that usually I commit this indiscretion; but I assure you, and it is true, that my body is so heavy and sluggish that even if I sleep nine hours at night I am still sleepy the next day." This is how they spent that recreation. But why did I tell you this story? I really do not know. But when something is useful to living I do not consider my purpose in saying it.

I do not well recall what I said to you in the past on this topic of Our Lord's entry into Jerusalem. [*Matt.* 21:1-9]. But I thought I would speak today on the reasons for Our Lord choosing both an ass and a colt for this royal entry. There are many, but six principal ones. I will speak of only three today as I must not speak longer than an hour. The first is the animal's humility; the second, its patience; the third, its willingness to be burdened.

However, before proceeding along these lines, I must say a word on the literal meaning of the text. I will do this briefly. The ancient Fathers are not in agreement as to whether Our Lord rode on the ass or on the colt, and there is a great diversity of opinions among the Doctors on this subject, but it is not a point to be discussed in this place. The majority of the ancient Fathers maintain that Our Lord mounted both the ass, and the colt on which no one had ever ridden. [*Mk.* 11:2]. Others disagree, and each tries to give reasons to prove his own case. For myself, I agree with those who think that our Master mounted both the ass and the colt—not both at the same time, but first one and then the other.[12] Some say that the ass represents the Jewish people, and the colt, the Gentiles. This is certainly not without foundation since, as they remark, the ass had already borne burdens and the colt had borne nothing, just as God had already "burdened" the Jewish people with His Law, while the Gentiles had not yet received it. Since Our Lord was coming to impose His yoke upon the Gentiles, He mounted the colt. [*Mk.* 11:7]. I find this very touching. But let us return to the reasons why our Saviour chose these animals to mount.

The first is because of its humility. The ass, though heavy, sluggish and lazy, has great humility. It is neither proud nor vain; in this it is unlike the haughty horse. Is not a vain and proud man compared to a horse [*Ps.* 31 (32):9], which is fiery and arrogant? Not only does it kick, but it also bites, and is sometimes so furious that none dare approach it. When the rider mounts it, it pricks up its ears, as if to hear what is said of it. It raises its head, tosses its mane and tail, and even excites vanity in the man who rides it! No sooner does he hear his horse's hoofs on the pavement than he straightens himself up proudly, raises his head, and looks around to see if there are any ladies at the windows admiring him! Indeed, which is more vain—the horse or its rider?[13] Oh, how foolish and childish all this is!

Now Our Lord, who was humble and came to destroy pride, chose not to use this proud animal to carry Him. He chose the most simple and the most humble of all animals because He so loved lowliness and humility that only a humble mount could serve Him. God dwells and abides only in the simple and humble of heart. [*Is.* 57:15]. Wishing to show His esteem for this virtue, He chose lowliness and abjection for the day of His triumph. He emptied and humbled Himself. He would not have been humiliated and despised by others except He willed it. He Himself emptied Himself, choosing abjection. He who was the Father's equal in all things, without ceasing to remain what He was, chose to be the reproach and outcast of the people. [*Ps.* 21 (22):7; *Is.* 53:3]. Though humbled in this way, He nevertheless could affirm His equality with the Father and the Holy Spirit, for He was, with them, one Substance, one Power and one Wisdom. Nor did our Blessed Saviour do a disservice to the truth when in the very depth of His contempt and humiliations He said: "The Father and I are equal in power; the Spirit and I are equal in goodness. We are but one Power, one Wisdom, and one Goodness." For in all ways They were equal. While in this glory, He humbled Himself, in entering Jerusalem not on a horse or other conveyance, but on an ass and a colt, which were covered only with the poor mantles of His Apostles.

It is of this great triumph of humility that Isaias [*Is.* 53:3; 62:11] and Zacharias [*Zach.* 9:9] sing, along with that divine poet, the royal prophet David[14] [*Ps.* 45:6, Heb. & Sept.]: He emptied and abased Himself; He humbled Himself; He came mounted upon an ass and a colt. He bent His bow and darted His arrows of love into the hearts of the people of Israel. All were moved at His coming and sang: Hosanna, blessed be the Son of David, blessed is He who comes in the name of the Lord; glory be to the Most High. [*Ps.* 117 (118):26; *Matt.* 21:9]. His gentleness and humility captivated all their hearts. Had He come on any other conveyance He would have frightened them. This is the first quality that made the ass appropriate for Our Lord's use on this occasion: its humility.

The second quality is its patience. Not only is the ass humble, it is exceedingly patient, allowing itself to be beaten and maltreated without ever forgetting its origin. [*Is.* 1:3]. It neither complains, nor bites, nor kicks. It endures all with great patience. Our Lord so loved patience that He wished to become its mirror and pattern. He endured scourging and ill treatment with invincible patience; He supported so many blasphemies, so many calumnies, without saying a word.

Now humility and patience have such an affinity with one another that one can hardly exist without the other. He who desires to be humble must be patient enough to endure the contempt, the censure, the reprehensions that the humble suffer. Likewise, he who desires to be patient must be humble, because one cannot long support the labors and adversities of this life without the humility which makes us gentle and patient. Finding these two qualities in this animal, Our Lord chose it rather than any other for His entry into Jerusalem.

The third reason is that this animal is obedient, permitting us to burden it as much as we want without offering any resistance. It carries the load with remarkable submission and suppleness. So much did our Divine Master love obedience and suppleness that He Himself chose to give us an example of it. So He bore the heavy burden of our iniquities and suffered for them all that we had merited. [Is. 53:4ff.]. Oh, how blessed are they who are supple and submissive, who allow themselves to be commanded as others wish, subjecting themselves to all kinds of obediences without reply or excuse, supporting with good heart the burden imposed on them! Only when clothed with these qualities of humility, patience and submission can we be worthy to carry Our Lord. Then the Saviour will mount upon our hearts and, as a divine riding master, conduct us under His obedience.

Having chosen the ass to carry Him into Jerusalem, Our Lord sent two of His disciples to a little village which was close by, saying: Go into the village, loose the ass and the colt, and bring them to Me; if anyone says a word to you, say, "The Lord has need of them." Hearing this, they left at once and went where their good Master had sent them. They loosed the ass and the colt and led them to Him. If you ask me who these two disciples were, I cannot tell you because the Evangelist does not tell us. Since he does not name them, neither can I. There are different opinions on this subject; some think they were St. James and St. Philip; others, St. John and St. Peter; each has his own opinion, but no one really knows who they were.

Whoever they were, I love and admire them very much because they were extremely simple and perfectly obedient in making no reply. They could have replied: "Indeed, You order us to bring You these two beasts, but how will we

know which two You want; are there only these two? Will
we be allowed to take them?" and many other such objections which human prudence could have suggested. Certainly,
there are those who make so many reflections, see so many
aspects, find so many interpretations, that they make a thousand replies to all obediences given them. We find no submission in them. They live in perpetual disturbance. On the
contrary, these Apostles went without making any reflections,
because they were obedient and loved obedience. It is a sure
indication that one does not love the command when one
reflects incessantly on it.

I have already spoken about all this at other times.[15] I
remember giving you the example of Eve, who raised so many
difficulties concerning the prohibition against eating the fruit
of the tree of knowledge. To the serpent she said: "Oh, God
has forbidden us to look at or touch this fruit" [*Gen.* 2:17;
3:1-3], implying that it was an unreasonable, harsh, and difficult command to observe. Certainly, one who has no love
for obedience never lacks reasons for avoiding its fulfillment
or for lamenting its difficulty. If a person like this is advised
to receive Communion frequently, "Oh," she will think, "what
will people say if they see me communicate so frequently,
or go to confession so often, or make meditation every day?
Oh, what will they say?" Simply go and do what the Lord
commands!

The Saviour knew, of course, that the Apostles would meet
people who would question their taking these animals and
what they were going to do with them. So it happened that
not only did the owner question them, but the neighbors med-
dled in as well. Anticipating this, Our Lord said to them:
If anyone tries to prevent your bringing them to Me, say
that the Lord needs them, and he will let them go. With
these words from their good Master, the Apostles left. To
those who tried to prevent their taking these animals they
replied: The Lord needs them; and the people let them go.
[*Mk.* 11:3-6]. Indeed, I love the people in that village for
they were very courteous; they no sooner heard that the Lord

needed their beasts than they willingly let them go.

Certainly, this answer, "The Lord needs them," is one we ought to give to anyone who tries to prevent us from doing God's will. "Why do you fast, go to confession and Communion so often?" ask the worldlywise. Answer them: "Because the Lord needs it." "Why are you entering religion? Why do you enclose yourself and bind your eyes like a falcon?" "The Lord needs it." "Why make yourself as poor as a beggar?" "The Lord needs it." In a word, we ought to make use of this reply to put in their place all those who wish to keep us from doing God's will.[16]

The Apostles led the ass and colt to Our Lord. We must note that He deliberately told them to loose them and lead them to Him. If we wish to go to our Saviour, we too must allow ourselves to be loosed from our passions, our habits, affections and the bonds of sin which keep us from serving Him. This ass and colt had only the Apostles' cloaks laid on them; then Our Lord mounted them; and in this abjection and humility He made His triumphal entry into Jerusalem. In this He confounded the world, which overthrows all the maxims of the Gospel, relishing neither humility nor abjection. It never ceases to say: "Unfortunate are the poor and suffering. But how happy that wealthy one is!" "Why do you find him happy?" "Because his barn is full of grain and his cellar is full of wine. This girl is also happy because she too is rich, well dressed and covered with jewels." Others are considered happy because their hair is well curled or daintily braided, or they have a fancy gown. How childish all this is! Nevertheless, these are the kinds of people the world considers happy and fortunate.[17]

Our Lord turns all such ideas upside down today by His entrance into Jerusalem. He in no way acts like princes of the world, who, when entering a city, do it with much pomp, show and expense. He chooses no other mount but an ass covered with the worthless and poor cloaks of His Apostles. Oh! how blessed are they whom our Divine Master chooses to carry Him, who are covered with the Apostles' cloaks, that is, clothed with apostolic virtues, which render them worthy of bearing our dear Saviour and of being led by Him. Blessed are they who conduct themselves here in lowliness and humility. They will be exalted in Heaven.[18] [*Matt.* 18:4; 23:12; *Lk.* 14:11; 18:14]. Their patience will win for them perpetual peace and tranquility; for their obedience they shall receive a crown of glory [*Tob.* 3:21; *James* 1:12]; finally, they shall be covered with the hundredfold of blessings in this life and shall bless the Father, Son and Holy Spirit eternally in the next. May God give us this grace. Amen.

NOTES

1. St. Francis de Sales is using poetic license in speaking here of nothingness as something like a co-principle of created being. As a philosopher he would agree with the classical maxim that from nothing, nothing comes.
2. Cf. *Spiritual Conferences,* XIX, p. 364, 378.
3. Cf. *Sermons of St. Francis de Sales on Our Lady,* "The Purification," February 2, 1622, pp. 177-178.
4. Cf. p. 160 of this sermon.
5. Cf. *Introduction to the Devout Life,* Part III, chap. 1, 2; *Spiritual Conferences,* XIV, pp. 261-262.
6. Cf. *Introduction,* Part III, chap. 28.
7. Cf. p. 164 of this sermon.
8. Cf. Sermon for Passion Sunday, p. 155 of this volume.
9. The editor of the Annecy edition of these sermons notes at this point that no biography of St. Charles recounts this story, and suggests that St. Francis learned of it on one of his many trips to Milan.
10. Cf. *Spiritual Conferences,* IV, p. 70; IX, p. 148.
11. It is good to be reminded here that St. Francis is giving this Lenten series to the contemplative Visitation nuns. He always has the congregation in mind when preaching and giving examples or making asides.
12. Like all the Doctors of the Church, St. Francis finds significance and spiritual value in the least detail and nuance of Scripture. In this way the Bible becomes for him an inexhaustible source for genuine wisdom and spiritual formation.
13. Cf. *Sermons on Our Lady,* "The Visitation," July 2, 1621, pp. 161-162; *Spiritual Conferences,* XVII, p. 326.
14. *Treatise on the Love of God,* Book IX, chap. 6.
15. Cf. *Sermons on Our Lady,* "The Purification," February 2, 1622, pp. 179-183.

16. Cf. *Treatise,* Book VIII, chap. 6.

17. Cf. p. 167 of this sermon.

18. Cf. *Sermons on Our Lady,* "The Immaculate Conception," December 8, 1622, p. 193.

12

THE PASSION OF OUR LORD
AND WHAT IT MEANS

Sermon for Good Friday, March 25, 1622, con-
cerning the brass serpent which saved the Israel-
ites, the sinlessness of Christ, the manner in which
He redeemed us, the two natures of Christ and
our three "natures," Our Lord as Saviour, how
our salvation comes from looking upon our Sav-
iour, Our Lord's seven last words, His prayer for
forgiveness for those crucifying Him, His pardon
of the good thief and of St. Peter, and the bad
thief's and Judas' damnation; the danger of dam-
nation and how we should both fear and hope,
Our Lord's confiding of Our Lady and St. John
to each other, the darkness on Good Friday, Our
Lord's great sorrow over those who would not profit
from His Passion, His feeling of abandonment by
His Father, His thirst, His obedience in remaining
on the Cross and how we should imitate Him, the
Cross as the one way of salvation, and Our Lord's
perfect commending of Himself into His Father's
hands and how we should do likewise, making no
reservations.

"Jesus Nazarenus, Rex Judaeorum—Jesus the
Nazarene, the King of the Jews."—Jn. 19:19

Since there are only a few hours in which to speak of the
Passion by which we have all been redeemed, I will take
for my subject only the words of the title that Pilate had
inscribed on the Cross: Jesus the Nazarene, the King of the
Jews. In this title are implied all the causes of this divine

Passion. They can be reduced to two, and these two are sig-
nified by the words: Jesus the Nazarene, the King of the
Jews. The Latin for this phrase has four words. They do
not, however, indicate four causes; His death has only two
causes, as we shall see.

"Jesus" means "Saviour!" [*Matt.* 1:21]. Now, He died because He was Saviour: to save us it was necessary for Him
to die. He was a Nazarene. This word means "flourishing,"
that is, holy and innocent, without stain or blight of sin,
but flourishing with all sorts of virtues and perfections.

"King of the Jews" means that He is both Saviour and
King. "Jews" signifies confessing: He is King, then, but only
of the Jews, that is, only of those who confess Him [cf. *Rom.*
10:9-10]; and to redeem those who confess Him, He died.
Yes, He truly died, and death on a Cross. [*Phil.* 2:8].

Here, then, are the causes of the death of Jesus Christ:
the first is that He was Saviour, holy, and King; the second,
that He wished to redeem those who acknowledge Him, which
is what the word "Jews" means that Pilate had written on
the standard of the Cross.

The Old Testament taught us this truth by many figures
and images, particularly that of the brass serpent that Moses
erected on the pole to protect the Israelites from serpent bites.
You know the whole story, I am sure, and how it happened.
[*Num.* 21:6-9]. When God withdrew His people from slavery
in Egypt to lead them to the Promised Land under the command of that great captain, Moses, a strange misfortune occurred. Small serpents came out from the earth and overran
the desert where the poor Israelites were. Their bite, though
apparently not very painful, was certainly very dangerous.
It was so venomous that all those bitten would surely have
died if, in His goodness and infinite Providence, God had
not provided a remedy.

Moved by the sight of this pitiable misfortune, Moses spoke
to God and asked for some remedy against it. The Lord commanded him to make a brass serpent and to place it on a
tall pole, promising that those bitten by the small serpents

would be cured by gazing upon it. Moses promptly did this, enjoining those bitten to cast their eyes on the brass serpent mounted on the pole. Those who did so were immediately cured. Those unwilling to gaze upon it died, for there was no other means of escaping death than that which was ordained by God Himself. "Oh! how good was the God of Israel" [*Ps.* 72 (73):1], said a great saint, "to provide Moses with such a remedy for his people's cure!"

I pray you to notice how well this incident symbolizes the cause or motivation of Our Lord's death. These children of Israel, withdrawn from slavery to Egypt, stand for the entire human race, whom God had preserved from sin and placed in the promised land of the earthly paradise, where He had established us in original justice. But in paradise a terrible thing took place: small serpents arose, and stung us in the persons of our first parents, Adam and Eve. The companions and accomplices of him who had stung our first parents so overran the desert, which is this world, that we would all surely have been bitten. I say all, because no creature can think himself exempt from such a bite, that is, from original and actual sin: Original Sin in the person of our first parents, and actual sin in our own person. If anyone says that he has been preserved from it he is certainly a liar. Indeed, as the great Apostle writes, if anyone thinks he is without sin, do not believe him, for iniquity reigns in him. [*Rom.* 3:23; 5:12, 18; *1 Jn.* 1:8-10].

I know of course that the sacred Virgin, Our Lady, was never bitten by this infernal serpent, since it is quite clear and manifest that she was without sin, either original or actual.[1] She was privileged and preferred above all other creatures, with so great and unique a privilege that no one, whatsoever, has ever received grace comparable to this holy Lady and glorious Mistress. No one has ever dared, and no one will ever dare to claim or to aspire to so unique and special a privilege. This grace was due only to her who was destined from all eternity to be the Mother of God.

This exception does not in any way lessen our assertion

that all have been bitten by the serpent. Now this bite was
so venomous that we would all have died an eternal death
if God in His infinite goodness had not provided against such
a great misfortune. He did this admirably, moved to do so
by no other motive than His pure and immense mercy. Therefore He ordained that His Son should die and Himself be
that serpent placed on the pole of the Cross to be gazed
upon by all who are bitten and sullied by sin. [*Jn.* 3:14-16].
Writing to the Galatians (and I never read these words without trembling and being seized with terror), the great Apostle said that the Son of God, who knew no sin or iniquity,
died for our redemption. [*Gal.* 3:13; cf. *2 Cor.* 5:21; *1 Ptr.*
3:18].

It is certainly true that He was sinless; moreover, He could
not sin, for He was equal to the Father in everything. His
was the same nature, substance and power. It was therefore
utterly impossible for Him to sin. Although He is all-powerful,
and can consequently do all He pleases, yet He cannot sin;
He is nevertheless still all-powerful, for to be able to sin
is not power, but powerlessness. He died for our sins without
Himself having committed any iniquity. He was, as the notice on the Cross says, a Nazarene, one flourishing in all
holiness. Nor was He a serpent, actually or figuratively, except to cure us from the stings of the true serpent. Because
of His great love for us He burdened Himself with our sins,
with our miseries and weaknesses [*Is.* 53:4ff];[2] He clothed
Himself with our plumage and shell. In short, He became
this serpent placed on the wood of the Cross to preserve
from death and give life to all who would gaze upon Him.
From Heaven He brought us Redemption, and, not only that,
He Himself was our Redemption. [*1 Cor.* 1:30]. "Oh! how
good is the God of Israel"[3] [*Ps.* 72 (73):1] to have provided
humankind with such a precious Redemption! [*Ps.* 129
(130):7-8]. Without it we would surely all have been lost.
Without this God-given remedy, all, without any exception
whatsoever, would have died, since all had sinned.

But could God not have provided the world with a remedy

other than that of His Son's death? Certainly, He could have done so, and by a thousand other means. Could He not have pardoned human nature with absolute power and pure mercy, not invoking justice or the intervention of any creature? Doubtless He could, and who would have dared to question or criticize Him? No one, for He is Sovereign Master and can do all He wills. Besides, if He had wanted some creature to undertake our redemption, could He not have created one of such excellence and dignity that, by its deeds or sufferings, it could have satisfied for all our sins? Assuredly, and He could have redeemed us in a thousand other ways than that of His Son's death. But He did not will to do so, for what may have been sufficient for our salvation was not sufficient for His love; and to show us how much He loved us, this divine Son died the cruelest and most ignominious of deaths, that of the Cross.

The implication in all this is clear: since He died of love for us, we also should die of love for Him; or, if we cannot die of love, at least we should live for Him alone.[4] [2 *Cor.* 5:14-15]. If we do not love Him and live for Him, we shall be the most disloyal, unfaithful and wretched creatures imaginable. Such disloyalty is what the great St. Augustine complained about. "O Lord," he said, "is it possible for man to know that You died for him and for him not to live for You?" And that great lover, St. Francis, sobbed, "Ah! You have died of love and no one loves You!"[5]

He died, then. But although He died for us and was lifted up on the Cross, those who refuse to look upon Him will surely die, for there is no other redemption but in this Cross. O God, how spiritually beneficial and profitable is a consideration of Your Cross and Passion! Can we contemplate our Saviour's humility on the Cross without becoming humble and having some affection for humiliations? Can we see His obedience without being obedient? Certainly not! No one has ever looked upon Our Lord crucified and remained dead or sick. On the other hand, all who have died have done so because they were unwilling to gaze upon Him, just as the Israelites died who were unwilling to gaze upon the serpent that Moses had raised upon the pole.

The fall of our first father and mother in the earthly paradise was another figure of this truth. God had given them many fruits to preserve their life; but there was one, the fruit of the tree of the knowledge of good and evil, which they were forbidden to eat under pain of death. They could therefore die or not die. They would die if they broke God's command, and not die if they kept it. But a terrible thing happened. The infernal serpent knew that they had this power of dying or of not dying, and determined to tempt them and to make them lose the Original Justice with which God had endowed and enriched them, by persuading them to eat the forbidden fruit. To accomplish this more easily, he took the scales and form of a serpent and tempted Eve. Surely, even if her heart had been flattered by this infernal spirit's words and even if, as a result, she had looked at or touched the fruit of the tree of knowledge—and indeed, even if she had picked it and offered it to Adam, her husband, they would not have died. For God had said only: if you eat of it, you will die. Thus, it was only in eating the forbidden fruit that Adam and Eve would die [*Gen.* 2:16-17; 3:1-6] and lose the life they could nevertheless have preserved if neither had actually consumed that fruit of the tree of the knowledge of good and evil.

Our Lord had two natures, human and divine. As God, He could not die. Further, He could neither suffer nor die, for God is impassible and immortal. And just as He could never sin, He also could never die, for, like sinning, dying is a lack of power. Even as man He could die or not die; for although it is a general law that all men die [*Heb.* 9:27], nevertheless He could have been exempted from that law because there was no sin in Him. Remember, it is sin that gave death entrance. [*Rom.* 5:12]. But Our Lord never chose to avail Himself of this privilege, and so took a passible and mortal body. He became incarnate in order to be Saviour. He chose to save us by suffering and dying, and to take on

Himself, in His sacred humanity, and in strictest justice, what we had merited because of our iniquities. He was so one in His divine and human natures that even though He suffered only in His humanity and not in His divinity, which is impassible, nevertheless, when one sees the manner in which He suffered, one cannot tell, so to speak, if it was God or man who suffered, so admirable are the virtues He practiced.

Even though he suffered nothing as God, yet His divinity united with His humanity gave such price, value and merit to these sufferings that the smallest tear, the smallest movement of His Sacred Heart, the smallest loving sigh was more meritorious, more precious and more pleasing to God than would have been all imaginable torments of body and spirit— more pleasing even than the torments of Hell—endured by creatures endowed with the greatest perfection. I will say even more: all the pains in a hundred thousand million Hells suffered with the greatest perfection possible to a human creature would have been nothing compared to the smallest sigh of Our Lord, to the smallest drop of the blood that He shed for love of us. For it is His divine Person, infinitely excellent and infinitely worthy, that gives price and value to such actions and sufferings. Yet His divinity is so united with His humanity that we can truly say God suffered death,[6] death on a Cross [*Phil.* 2:8], to redeem us and give us life.

Now we have, so to speak, three natures or three kinds of life, one of which is negative. The negative one we received in the person of our first father, Adam. In that one we could have either died or not died. While in the earthly paradise where the tree of life was, we could, by eating its fruit, have prevented our dying, providing that we kept from the forbidden fruit, as God had ordained. By keeping that commandment we would not have died at all, even though we would not always have remained in this life either. We would have passed to another, a better one. In our French language "death" means "passing over" from one life to the other.[7] To die is therefore to pass beyond the confines of this mortal life to the immortal. It is true that, had we not sinned, we would never have died this bodily death as we now do, but we would nevertheless have passed over to the other life. And when it pleased the Divine Majesty to withdraw us, He would have done so, either in a chariot of fire like Elias [*4 Kgs.* (*2 Kgs.*) 2:11] or in some other way pleasing to Him. It is obvious that we were also capable of dying, as we now do die, by eating the forbidden fruit, as our first mother, Eve, did.

Since Adam's sin, we possess and live the second nature. With this nature we die and can never not die, for it is now a general law that all must die. Since God pronounced the sentence of death against man, there never has been and never will be anyone who will not die. No human creature whatever can be exempted from death. We all have been soiled by original and actual sin;[8] we all shall die. [*Rom.* 5:12]. Once our sinless Lord took on our sins, He too died, as all of us sinners shall surely die.

We will possess our third nature only in Heaven, if God mercifully enables us to arrive there. In Heaven we shall live and not be able to die, for we shall enjoy eternal glory, life that was purchased for us by our Saviour's death. We shall possess it securely, without fear of losing it. Our Lord came as Saviour to save us all from dying. For His death acquired for us that life in which we shall never die, the life of glory.

Thus, it was by divine inspiration that Pilate inscribed on the Cross, "Jesus the Nazarene, the King of the Jews." It was His vocation to be Saviour. For this reason the Eternal Father gave many indications of His saving mission to men, not only from the patriarchs and prophets, but also from Himself. Indeed, strange though it seems, He even used the mouth of the impious and the most criminal, as we shall see presently, to make clear that saving mission. Finally, for this same purpose, the angel descended from Heaven to announce to the sacred Virgin the mystery of the Incarnation, telling her that He whom she would conceive would be called "Jesus," or "Saviour." [*Lk.* 1:26-31].

God the Father Himself spoke of this saving mission when

Our Lord was baptized by St. John the Baptist in the River Jordan; then they hear His voice: "This is My beloved Son, in whom I am well pleased. [*Matt.* 3:16-17]. Listen to Him." [cf. *Matt.* 17:5; *Lk.* 9:35]. As if He meant: "O poor people, you had so angered Me by your vices and iniquities that I had resolved to destroy and ruin you all. But see, I am sending My Son to reconcile you with Me, for all My delight is to look at and consider Him; and in this look I find so much pleasure that I forget all the displeasure that I receive from your sins. Therefore, listen to Him." In this word He shows that He sent Him to teach us how to "save" ourselves. "Ah, never doubt His doctrine," He wished to say, "for He is Truth itself. [*Jn.* 14:6]. Therefore, listen to Him carefully. His doctrine is all divine: and if you practice and follow it, it will lead you to eternal life."

Another such testimony was given on Mt. Thabor on the day of the Transfiguration, when they again heard the voice of the Eternal Father, who said: This is My beloved Son, with whom I am well pleased; listen to Him. [*Matt.* 17:5; *Lk.* 9:35; *2 Ptr.* 1:17]. But what will Christ say to you from this mountain? Surely, He will say nothing to you on this occasion, since He is speaking to His heavenly Father and with Moses and Elias of the suffering and death He is about to accomplish in Jerusalem. [*Lk.* 9:30-31]. You will see the glory of the Transfiguration, but like the three Apostles, you will be forbidden to report what you see. [*Matt.* 17:9]. But on Mt. Calvary, you will hear lamentations, sighs and prayers made for the remission of your sins; you will hear the words of this great doctrine of the Redemption, and you will never be forbidden to speak of what you see there. Quite the contrary, you will be commanded to speak of it and never to lose the memory of it.

Notice how eager God is to reveal the real truth of His Son's vocation. Pilate declared time and time again that Our Lord was innocent, and though he condemned Him, he knew that He was not guilty of any accusation brought against Him. [*Matt.* 27:18, 24; *Lk.* 23:14, 22; *Jn.* 18:38; 19:4-6]. Further, did not God pronounce through the high priest Caiphas—the most miserable, unfaithful, treacherous and disloyal man who ever lived—this great truth: that it was better to have one Man die so that all might be saved? [*Jn.* 11:49-50]. God went out of His way to show that His Son was truly Saviour and that it was necessary for Him to die to save us. He even revealed this truth through the most detestable high priest who ever lived on the earth.

Caiphas said it, but he did not understand that he was prophesying. Yet the Lord wished to make him a prophet on that occasion, since he was then occupying the chair of the great high priest [*Jn.* 11:51]. Certainly most of the people knew that our Divine Master was innocent. Though they asked that He be crucified, it was because of the chief priests. For you know that when a sedition arises in a city, the mob, rightly or wrongly, takes the side of those in power. Without knowing what he was doing, Pilate had it written on the Cross: Jesus the Nazarene, King of the Jews; and no matter what people said, he refused to remove it or to change its wording [*Jn.* 19:19, 22], for it was God's will that it should express the two causes of His Son's death.

Now, since God's Son was crucified for us, what remains for us at this hour but to crucify with Him our flesh with its passions and desires. [*2 Cor.* 5:15; *Gal.* 5:24]. For love is repaid with love alone. This is what we had to say about the second cause: by rendering Our Lord love for love and the praises and blessings we owe Him for His Death and Passion, we will be confessing Him as our Liberator and Saviour.

Here, where I always speak freely and frankly, I must tell you what happened to me once when I was about to preach on the Passion of Jesus Christ in one of the most famous cities of France. I needed some appropriate symbol to describe my subject more clearly. Not finding any elsewhere, I found one in a book which told of a bird which was placed on earth—I have always since thought, only as a figure of the Passion.[9] What I am going to tell you is the most wonderful and appropriate symbol to show clearly that Our Lord died for our sins. When I found this symbol, I considered it an inspiration from God, and have ever since believed it so.

This symbol, then, is the bird called the oriole in French and *icterus* in Latin. This bird is entirely yellow, but not because of jaundice. It has this special property: from a treetop, it cures those afflicted with serious jaundice, always at the expense of its own life. When the jaundiced person and this bird exchange glances, the oriole, as it were, so pities man, his good friend, that he draws to himself the man's jaundice. Then the bird's whole body turns completely yellow. His wings, which were already yellow, become more so; then his stomach, feet, all his feathers, and his little body. Meanwhile man, his great friend, becomes white, clean and completely cured. This poor bird then flies away, sighing and singing a song pitifully loving for the delight he experiences in dying to save his human friend. A truly admirable phenomenon! This bird is never afflicted with jaundice, yet he dies of it when curing a man so afflicted. Indeed, it takes pleasure in dying to save him.

Our Lord is certainly this divine Bird of Paradise, the divine Oriole, attached to the tree of the Cross to save and deliver us from the serious jaundice of sin. To be cured, however, man must look at Him on this Cross in order to move Him to pity. Then He draws to Himself all the iniquities of man and dies freely for him. If the jaundiced man does not look at the oriole, he will remain ill. Similarly, if the sinner does not look at Our Lord crucified, he will never be freed from his sins. But if he does look upon Him, the Saviour will make Himself responsible for his sins. Though our Saviour was innocent, He died for our iniquities. Indeed, He died with a holy joy at our cure, even though this was at the cost of His own life.

This truth is recognized in the words our Divine Master spoke on the Cross and in His loving tears and sighs. To say a word to you on these last words, I shall gladly take another half hour. Besides, the Office is not yet over in the

"Can a woman forget her infant, so as not to have pity on the son of her womb? and if she should forget, yet will not I forget thee. Behold, I have graven thee in my hands."   —Isaias 49:15-16

other churches. The first word, then, that Our Lord pronounced on the Cross was a prayer for those who were crucifying Him. It was of this that St. Paul wrote: In the days when He was in the flesh He offered sacrifices to His heavenly Father. [*Heb.* 5:7].

Certainly, those who were crucifying our divine Saviour did not know Him. And how could they have known Him, since the majority of those who were present did not even understand His language? (At that time all sorts of peoples and nations were in Jerusalem, and all had gathered, it seems, to torment Him.) But not one knew Him, for if they had known Him, they would never have crucified Him. [*Acts* 3:17; *1 Cor.* 2:8]. When Our Lord saw the ignorance and weakness of those who were tormenting Him, He excused them and offered for them this sacrifice to His heavenly Father, for prayer is a sacrifice. It is the sacrifice of our lips and our heart[10] [*Ps.* 26 (27):6; 115 (116):17; *Heb.* 13:15] which we present to God as much for our neighbor as for ourselves. Therefore, Our Lord made use of it by saying to His Father: Father, forgive them, for they do not know what they are doing. [*Lk.* 23:34].

Oh, how great was the flame of love that burned in the heart of our gentle Saviour, since at the height of His sufferings, at a time when the vehemence of His torments seemed to take from Him even the power of praying for Himself, He succeeded through the strength of His charity in forgetting Himself but not His creatures, and with a strong and intelligible voice uttered these words: Father, forgive them. With this prayer He wanted to make us understand the love He bore us, undiminished by any suffering, and to teach us how our heart should be toward our neighbor.

But, my God, what burning charity this was, and how powerful a prayer it must have been! Indeed, Our Lord's prayers were so efficacious and so meritorious that His Father could refuse Him nothing. For this reason, as the great Apostle says, He was heard, because of the reverence that the Father bore Him. [*Heb.* 5:7]. It is true that the heavenly

Father bore great reverence toward this Son, who as God was equal to Him and the Holy Spirit, being with Him one substance, wisdom, power, goodness and infinite immensity. That is why, looking at Him as His Word, the Father could refuse Him nothing. Now, since this divine Lord asked pardon for us, it is entirely certain that His request was granted. His divine Father honored Him too much to deny Him any request.

He was heard, therefore, not only because of the reverence the Father bore Him, but also because of the reverence He bore His Father and with which He prayed. Such reciprocal reverence as that borne between these two divine Persons is beyond imagination or human comprehension. When two equally great and powerful kings meet for discussion, they vie in honoring and respecting each other by consenting most promptly and absolutely to any request. Thus it is between the Eternal Father and His Son Our Lord, for both are equal in dignity, excellence and perfection.

Jesus Christ prayed thus to His Father—but with what reverence! Certainly, the sacred Virgin Our Lady surpassed all other creatures in the humility and respect with which she prayed and communicated with her God. All the saints prayed with great reverence. The pillars of the heavens tremble [*Job* 26:11]; the highest seraphim quiver and veil themselves with their wings for the honor they bear the Divine Majesty [*Is.* 6:2]. Yet all this humility, all this honor, all this reverence that the Virgin, the saints, all the angels and the seraphim render to God are nothing in comparison with that of Our Lord. For this reason we must never doubt that the prayers made with such great and admirable reverence, and by a Person of infinite merit and perfection, were granted at once. Therefore, if all who crucified Him did not receive the pardon the Saviour had asked for them, it was not His fault, as we shall show.

Our Lord's second word promised Paradise to the good thief. In this word, He began to hymn a different air. Whereas previously He had prayed, and prayed for sinners, now He shows that He is Redeemer. Having pardoned sins, He allows the good thief to partake even now of the fruits of the Redemption. He was crucified between two thieves, wicked men, traitors and robbers [*Matt.* 27:38; *Jn.* 19:18], one of whom blasphemed Him. The other acknowledged His innocence: "Ah, Lord, I know very well that You are not at all guilty, but I indeed deserve to be attached to this cross for my sins and crimes. For this reason I beg You to remember me when You come into Your Kingdom." [*Luke* 23:39-42].

On this subject I must say something that I have not yet said here, although I believe I have spoken of it elsewhere. During Our Lord's Passion, two great events occurred which were related to the two kinds of sinners who tormented Him grievously. There were two of each type of sinner: two Apostles and two thieves. St. Peter, one of the Apostles, wronged his Master greatly by denying Him and swearing that he did not know Him. As if that were not enough, he cursed and blasphemed Him, protesting that he did not know who He was. [*Matt.* 26:69-74]. That pierced Our Lord's heart! Alas, poor St. Peter, what are you doing; what are you saying? You do not know who He is? You are not associated with Him—you who were called with His own mouth to be an Apostle? [*Matt.* 4:18-19]. You yourself confessed that He was the Son of the living God! [*Matt.* 16:16]. Miserable man, how dare you deny knowing Him? Is this not the One who a short while ago was at your feet washing them, and feeding you with His Body and Blood? [*Jn.* 13:6]. And you declare that you are not associated with Him! Oh, how can the earth bear you? Why does it not open up and swallow you in the deepest of Hells?

The second Apostle was of course Judas, who miserably sold his Master, and at so vile a price. [*Matt.* 26:15]. O God, my dear Sisters, how terrible and appalling are the falls of God's servants, especially of those who have received great graces.[11] What greater grace could there be than that given to St. Peter and Judas? Like Peter, Judas too had been called to be an Apostle by Our Lord Himself, who preferred him to so many millions of others who would have done marvels in this ministry. The Saviour bestowed special favors upon him. Besides giving him the gift of miracles, He also foretold to him his betrayal [*Matt.* 26:21-25; *Jn.* 13:18-27] so that, being forewarned, he might avoid it. Knowing that he was attracted to dealing with and managing affairs [*Jn.* 12:6; 13:29], He made him procurator in His sacred college. He did this to gain his heart entirely and to omit nothing that could render him more devoted to His Divine Majesty. Nevertheless, this miserable Judas abused all these graces and sold his good Master.

How frightful and dangerous are the falls from the mountains! As soon as one begins to fall, one rolls inexorably to the very bottom of the precipice. Such have been the falls of several who fell away from the service of God. Frightening, indeed, that after a good beginning, even after having lived thirty or forty years in this holy service, in old age, when it is time to reap, one flings himself into the abyss and loses all. Such was the misfortune of Solomon, whose salvation is very doubtful, and of several others who deserted the right path in their last years.

What a miserable old age that is! How fearful a thing it is to fall into the hands of the living God! [*Heb.* 10:31]. How inscrutable His judgments! [*Rom.* 11:33]. Let anyone who is standing be fearful lest he fall, says the Apostle [*1 Cor.* 10:12]; let no one glory in finding himself expressly called by God to a place where there seems nothing to fear. Let no one presume on his good works and think he has nothing more to fear. St. Peter, who had received so many graces, who had promised to accompany Our Lord to prison and even to death itself [*Lk.* 22:33], denied Him nevertheless at the whimpering taunt of a chambermaid. Judas sold Him for such a small sum of money.

These falls were both very great, but there was this difference. One acknowledged his guilt; the other despaired. Yet, our Saviour had inspired in the heart of both the same *Peccavi* ("I have sinned"), that same *Peccavi* that God inspired in David's heart. [2 *Kgs.* (2 *Sm.*) 12:13]. Yes, He inspired it in both Apostles, but one rejected it and the other accepted it. Hearing the cock crow, St. Peter remembered what he had done and the word his good Master had spoken to him. Then, acknowledging his sin, he went out and wept so bitterly [*Matt.* 26:74-75; *Lk.* 22:61-62] that he received what we today call a plenary indulgence and full remission of all his sins. O happy St. Peter! By such contrition for your sins you received a full pardon for such great disloyalty!

But notice also, I pray you, that St. Peter did not become converted at all until he had heard the cock crow, as Our Lord had foretold it to him. In this one can see his remarkable submission to the means designated for his conversion. Certainly, I know that it was our Saviour's sacred glances that penetrated Peter's heart and opened his eyes to recognize his sin. [*Lk.* 22:61-62]. Nevertheless, the Evangelist tells us that he went out to weep over his sin when the cock crowed [*Matt.* 26:74-75], not when Our Lord looked at him.

From this time on, St. Peter never ceased weeping, principally when he heard the cock crow at night and morning, for he remembered this crowing as the signal for his conversion. It is also reported that he shed so many tears that they hollowed his cheeks into two furrows. With these tears he who had been a great sinner became a great saint. "O glorious St. Peter, how happy you are to have done such great penance for such great disloyalty. By it you were reinstated in grace. You who deserved eternal death became worthy of eternal life." Not only that, but St. Peter received here below special favors and privileges and was lavished with blessings on earth and in Heaven.

On the other hand, although Judas received the same inspiration for the same *Peccavi,* he rejected it and despaired. I know that efficacious and sufficient grace differ, as theologians say, but I am not here to prove and dispute whether Judas' inspiration of *Peccavi* was as efficacious as David's, or only sufficient. It was certainly sufficient.[12] This *Peccavi* sent to the heart of Judas was truly like that formerly sent to David. Why then was Judas not converted?

O miserable man! He saw the gravity of his crime and despaired. Truly, he confessed his sin, for in returning to the chief priests the thirty pieces of silver for which he had sold his good Master, he acknowledged aloud that he had sold innocent blood. [*Matt.* 27:3-5]. But these priests would give him no absolution. Alas, did not this unhappy man know that Our Lord alone could give it to him, that He was the Saviour and held Redemption in His hands? Had he not seen this truth clearly in those whose sins Jesus had remitted? Certainly, he knew it, but he did not wish nor dare to ask pardon. To make him despair, the devil showed him the enormity and hideousness of his crime and perhaps made him fear that if he asked his Master's pardon, He might impose too great a penance. Perhaps for fear of such penance, he was unwilling to ask for forgiveness. Thus, despairing, he hanged himself; and his body burst wide open, all his entrails spilling out [*Acts* 1:18], and he was buried in the deepest of Hells. These two Apostles represent the first kind of sinner.

In the second kind, we see the two thieves who were crucified with Our Lord, most evil of men who had never done any good. They were among the most criminal, perfidious and notorious robbers to be found. They were chosen to be placed on either side of our dear Saviour in order, by this means, to declare Him the master of all thieves. [*Lk.* 23:32-33]. One of these evil men turned toward Jesus and confessed Him to be innocent, while acknowledging that he was a sinner deserving the cross. Then he asked His pardon, which he received so absolutely that Our Lord promised him that he would that very day enter into Paradise with Him. [*Lk.* 23:39-43].

Strange! two robbers were crucified with our Saviour and both received the inspiration of the *Peccavi;* yet only one was converted. Certainly, neither had ever done any good, and the good thief had been one of the most vicious of robbers to be found; still, at the end of his life he looked at the Cross, found redemption there and was saved. His salvation was immediate, for Our Lord had promised that whoever looked upon His Cross, no matter how sinful he might be, even if he did so only at the end of his life, as did the good thief, would receive salvation. [cf. *Jn.* 3:14-17; 12:32]. But the other thief, even though he too was beside the sweet Jesus, was there in vain. For he would not look upon the Cross. Despite the many inspirations he received, despite the drops of this divine Blood with which he was sprinkled, despite our dear Saviour's frequent secret and loving promptings to look upon this sacred wood and at the mystic Serpent attached to it, so as to obtain his cure, he was unwilling to do so. Because of his refusal, he obstinately died in his sin and was miserably lost.

Here, then, my dear Sisters, are the two kinds of sinner— which should make us live in great fear and trembling [*Ps.* 2:11; *Phil.* 2:12], but also in great hope and confidence, because of these two kinds, one was saved and one damned. From the first kind one was saved, the glorious St. Peter, and one damned, Judas—both Apostles of Our Lord. Certainly, there are souls who fail even after having served God for a long time, and even after having attained the mountain of perfection. "We have seen," says the great St. Augustine, "stars falling from Heaven," who afterward became obstinate and died without repenting. Others, who fall in the same manner after having received equal graces, yet repent like St. Peter. What great reason for fear and hope! There are also some who have never done any good and who, at the end of their life, find pardon and mercy, while others persevere in their iniquities.

O God! with how much humility and spiritual abasement ought we to live on this earth! But also what great reason to anchor our hope and confidence completely in Our Lord! For if even after having committed sins such as denying Him, persevering and spending one's life in horrible crimes and iniquities, one can find forgiveness when one returns to the Cross to which our Redemption [*1 Cor.* 1:30] is attached, why should a sinner of either kind fear in life and in death to return to his God? Will he still listen to that evil spirit who tries to convince him that his faults are unpardonable? Ah, let him answer boldly that his God died for all [*2 Cor.* 5:15], and that those who look upon the Cross, no matter how sinful they are, will find salvation and redemption.

What may we not hope for from this Redemption, which is so plenteous [*Ps.* 129 (130):7] that it overflows from all sides? Let us consider that now. O God, how often our divine Saviour offered it to Judas and to the bad thief! With what patience He waited for both! What did this dear Saviour's Sacred Heart not do for Judas? How many impulses and secret inspirations He gave him, both at the Supper when He was on His knees before him, washing his feet, and in the Garden of Olives, when He embraced and kissed him [*Matt.* 26:49-50]; and along the road; and in the house of Caiphas, where Judas, that unhappy man, went to confess his crime.[13] But he was unwilling either to ask pardon or to hope to receive it.

What did this same Saviour's Heart not do for the bad thief all the while He was on the Cross? How often did He look at him, inviting him to return His look, permitting His Precious Blood to fall on him that it might soften and purify his soul! Alas! in refusing salvation, did this miserable man not deserve that God should hurl him instantly into Hell? But He did not do that; rather, He waited for his repentance until he expired. Therefore, if Our Lord so liberally remits such great and enormous sins—indeed, if He offers pardon even to the obstinate and waits for their repentance with such patience [*Rom.* 2:4], O God! what will He not do for him who asks it of Him, and with what heart will He not receive the contrite penitent.

Our Lord's third word was one of consolation. He spoke it to His sacred Mother who was at the foot of the Cross, pierced by a sword [*Lk.* 2:35] of sorrow, but certainly not swooning nor with faint heart, as artists have falsely and impertinently painted her. The Evangelist clearly says the contrary, insisting that she remained standing with an incomparable firmness.[14] [*Jn.* 19:25]. That courage did not keep her from the grieving which she endured with the generous and magnanimous heart belonging to her alone. O God! what agonies were hers! They are inexplicable and inconceivable. Her heart was crucified with the same nails that crucified Our Lord's body, for now she would be without both Child and husband.

Seeing her in this distress, our dear Saviour said a word of consolation to her. But this consoling and tender word was not given to lift her heart from such great desolation. The heart of this perfectly submissive and resigned holy Virgin needed to be extremely strong, and Our Lord, who knew her so well, dealt with her accordingly.[15] Indicating St. John, His Heart's beloved disciple, He said: Woman, there is your son. [*Jn.* 19:26]. He gave him to her to care for her, for this holy Virgin was not thinking of herself at all. Her every thought was centered around her divine Son's sorrows, sorrows that she herself pondered in her soul [cf. *Lk.* 2:35, 51] while at the foot of His Cross. But her dear Child, about to die, knew that as widow and alone, she would not know where to go, so He wished to provide for her in her desolation by giving her, as the most precious thing He could leave her when dying, His disciple as son. For John was the disciple whom He loved [*Jn.* 13:23; 19:26; 21:7, 20], and in whom He inspired a true son's love for His Mother. With this love he would care for her with even greater solicitude.

As He was dying He rejoiced to leave, as pledge of His love, the sacred Virgin as Mother to St. John, and to His holy Mother, the disciple of His Heart as son. Dying men who want to favor their children or heirs tell them something like: "Go to such a cupboard; you will find there so many thousand crowns." And mothers near death glory in saying to their daughters, "Go to such a chest; you will find the dress in which I was married, still perfectly new; you will also find there my chains and rings that I have saved for you, and other jewelry." Perhaps this seems nothing but folly and nonsense. Yet they take pride in being able to bequeath such things when they are near death. But our dear Saviour left nothing like that to St. John and to His Mother. He left a far greater treasure.

True, Our Lady sorrowed at the time. After all, what comparison would there be between Our Lord and His disciple? She nevertheless docilely accepted John with a gentle and tranquil heart. Her divine Son in turn gave her a more tender love for St. John than all mothers together ever had or would have toward their children. This sacred Virgin knew that Our Lord, in giving her St. John for son, was giving her as Mother to all Christians as children of grace, for "John" means grace. She loved this holy Apostle with great love, but not in the same way she loved her divine Son. Him she loved not only as her Son, but also as her God. What great love that Virgin's most holy heart had for that of Our Lord! Since her love for Him was measureless, the pain in leaving Him and in seeing Him die, the pain of being deprived of His bodily presence, was unspeakable.

I do not think I ever pointed out before that as soon as the Saviour gave His Mother and the disciple to one another, the sun withdrew its light and darkness was over the whole earth. [*Matt.* 27:45; *Lk.* 23:44-45]. So thick was that darkness that it was terrifying. Theologians dispute about whether this darkness covered all the earth or only a part of it; I have often seen both opinions. They also question whether this eclipse was natural or supernatural, and whether or not the sun behaved as normal. This is hardly the time for settling that dispute.

Personally, I agree with those who hold that darkness was over the whole earth, for the great St. Denis the Areopagite, who was then in Egypt, mentions it, and several historians do as well. There is no doubt at all that this eclipse was supernatural and that in it the sun suffered no change. The eclipse occurred at high noon and when the moon was full. St. Denis, who only later was converted by the preaching of the great Apostle St. Paul and came here as the Apostle of France, wrote that at the time he saw only two possible meanings in this prodigy: "Either the God of nature is suffering, or the end of the world is approaching." He went on: "This eclipse is entirely supernatural, since it is occurring both at high noon and during the full moon. Besides, it is lasting longer than ordinary eclipses (three whole hours)." Certainly, he spoke the truth. Darkness fell because the God of nature was suffering in Jerusalem.

What was Our Lord doing during those three hours? He was offering sacrifices of praise. It was particularly during those hours that He did what St. Paul wrote: He prayed, He lamented, He complained with strong cries in the days when He was in the flesh[16] [*Heb.* 5:7]; that is, during those three hours He complained to His Father, He wept and cried, trying to move all hearts to repentance. O God! how many loving tears He shed during those three hours of meditation, how many sighs and sobs! How many and what kinds of pains pierced through the Sacred Heart of my Saviour! No one can imagine but He who suffered them, and perhaps the sacred Virgin Our Lady, who was standing at the foot of the Cross. To her He communicated them, and she pondered them within her heart.[17]

Since I have spoken with you several times on this subject I will mention now only what I feel to be the greatest sorrow the Sacred Heart of Our Lord then endured: the ingratitude of those Christians who, scorning His Death and not profiting from His painful and sorrowful Passion, were lost because they were unwilling to take advantage of it. But these particular sorrows were known only to Him who suffered them and to His holy Mother, to whom He communicated them. But wanting to make known to everyone that He really was suffering, He cried out in a loud voice to His Eternal Father so that He was heard by all: My God, My God, why have You forsaken Me? [*Matt.* 27:46; *Ps.* 21 (22):1].

This was the fourth word Our Lord uttered on the tree of the Cross. O God, how great was His most holy soul's anguish in being forsaken not only by all creatures, but also by the Eternal Father, who for a time had withdrawn His face from His beloved Son! [cf. *Ps.* 131:10]. He did not, of course, suffer this privation in the superior part of His soul, for it always enjoyed the clear vision of the Divinity, and thus of beatitude, from the first instant of its creation. It was never deprived of that glory. But the inferior part was bereft of all human and divine aid. It was deprived of all consolation, experiencing bodily and spiritual pains with all the bitterness and rigor imaginable. So He cried out: "My God, My God, why have You forsaken Me?" that all might understand the vehement pain He was then enduring.

But, alas! the misunderstanding of these words was a further pain to Our Lord. [*Matt.* 27:47-49; *Mk.* 15:35-36]. Some thought He was praying to Elias. These were almost Christians in that they already had some disposition to receive grace, since they believed in the invocation of the saints. Elias had died many years before—at least he was not of this world, but had been carried off in a fiery chariot by angels.[18] [*4 Kgs.* (*2 Kgs.*) 2:11]. They thought that, in His great affliction, our dear Master was calling Elias to His aid. They believed, then, that Elias could help Him. There were others who said: He is invoking Elias, but what can he do? He cannot deliver Him. These were evil people who did not believe that the saints can do anything for those who are afflicted, nor for those who invoke them. Therefore they were like today's Huguenots because they denied the power of the saints before the Divine Majesty.[19] The rest, laughing, said: See how He is calling aloud on Elias for help; now let us wait and see, I pray you, whether Elias comes to His rescue. They said this to mock Him. Others murmured among themselves: If He is as holy as they say, let Him save Himself! He saved so many others [*Matt.* 27:40-42; *Mk.* 15:29-32]; He is a fool if He does not do for Himself what He has done for others. During those three hours our good Saviour suffered all possible injuries and calumnies.

They also made the most attractive suggestions and offers for Him to prove Himself. For example, some cried to Him [*Matt.* 27:40-42; *Mk.* 15:29-32]: "You boast of being God's Son; come down then from that Cross and we will adore You and acknowledge You as such. You have said that You would destroy the temple. All right, then, perform some miracle for Your deliverance, and we will acknowledge You as our God. Yes, if on Your own power You can come down from that Cross we all will believe in You. Otherwise we shall consider You an evil man. We will neither believe in You nor be converted." What an offer to the Heart of our gentle Saviour, which was so aflame with desire for our salvation! Several blasphemed against Him, calling Him a sorcerer and enchanter, attributing this darkness to some magic trick; others said that it was not darkness, but their eyes were blinded and dazzled by His spells. From such as these, Our Lord's most Sacred Heart suffered incomparable torments.

Knowing that a multitude would be lost and would take no profit from the Redemption of the Cross and be saved, He pronounced the fifth word, one of complaint and lamentation: *Sitio*—"I thirst." [*Jn.* 19:28]. This word can mean His bodily thirst caused by the extreme torments He had suffered all night. It was so great a dehydration that it burned and consumed His lungs and would certainly have killed Him if God had not reserved for Him greater sufferings. Never was hart, pursued by dogs and huntsmen, so parched and desirous of coming upon a fountain of fresh water as was our Saviour in His bodily thirst. Therefore, with good reason He said: I thirst.

Yet, this was nothing compared to the spiritual thirst which oppressed His soul. With an insatiable ardor He desired that everyone be converted at the price of His Passion. Seeing how many souls would not, He cried out: I thirst! He also knew that some would ask for a means other than that of His Passion for salvation, as did for instance this crowd, which cried out for Him to descend from the Cross so they could believe in Him. They seemed to say to our blessed Saviour: "If You are so athirst for our salvation, come down from that Cross and we will believe in You. Thus You will be able to slake Your thirst." So infinitely did Our Lord desire our salvation that He offered to die for us. [*Is.* 53:10-12]. Yet, He did not want to descend from the Cross, because

such was not His Father's will. Rather, it was that will that
kept Him attached to this wood.

Miserable people, what do you mean by asking our dear
Saviour and Master to descend from this gibbet? He will
certainly not do so, for as St. Paul says, He humbled Himself, obediently accepting even death, death on a Cross.[20] He
mounted the Cross through obedience and died on it through
obedience. All those who are willing to be saved through
the Cross will find salvation there. But those who desire to
be saved without it will perish miserably. There is no salvation except in this Cross. "Ah, miserable ones," says our
Saviour, "you are asking Me to descend from this wood that
you may believe in Me, you want a means of redemption
other than the one My Father has ordained from all eternity,
one foretold by so many prophets and announced by so many
figures. You intend then to be saved according to your will
and not as God wills. That is not right, and for it you will
die obstinate in your sins [*Jn.* 8:21, 24], and you will not
find any pardon; even though the pool is prepared for you,
you refuse to cast yourself into it. [cf. *Jn.* 5:4]. Redemption
is open and so abundant that it overflows on all sides, yet
you do not wish to wash yourself in it!" [cf. *Zach.* 13:1].

Listen to this dear Saviour, who cries out that He is thirst-
ing for our salvation, who awaits and invites us to it. "Come,"
He says to us, "if you wish; for if you do not come, you
will not find salvation anywhere else." Why do some ask
for a redemption other than that of the Cross? Is the Cross
not sufficient? It is more than sufficient. A single tear, a
single loving sigh from this Sacred Heart could have redeemed
millions of thousands of sinful human and angelic natures.
Nevertheless, He did not redeem us with just a single sigh,
just a single tear, but with many, many labors and pains,
with all His precious Blood outpoured. This Redemption is
so plenteous[21] [*Ps.* 129 (130):7] that it could never be exhausted, not only after millions of years, but even after millions of millions of centuries.[22] It was to perfect this
Redemption that Our Lord chose not to descend from the

Cross. As the great Apostle says, He was truly obedient, even unto the Cross, for He truly died the death of the Cross through a great obedience.

There are several kinds of obedience. They can all be understood in two ways. The first is speculative, that of theologians when they declare and explain the excellence of this virtue. Thus some value it greatly; they read what is written about it with great relish. "Oh how happy are the obedient!" they say. They speak eruditely of the five degrees of obedience. Yet in all this they do no more than the theologians who discourse about it so excellently. But to speak well about it is not enough. We must come to the second way of understanding this virtue, which is to practice it in the small and great occasions that present themselves. Some want to obey, but only on condition that no one asks anything difficult of them. Others want to obey provided no one contradicts them in their capriciousness. This person will submit to this one, but not to another. It takes little to assess the virtue of such persons: they obey in what *they* want, but not in what *God* wants.[23]

Now, such obedience is not pleasing to Our Lord. One must obey equally in great and little things, in easy and in difficult ones, and remain firm, that is, attached to the cross where obedience has placed us, without accepting or admitting any condition which tries to make us descend from it, no matter how fine it may appear. Therefore, if any inspirations or movements come to you that would withdraw you from obedience, reject them boldly and never follow them.[24]

Let married people remain on their cross of obedience, which is in marriage. It is the best and most practical cross for them and one of the most demanding, in that there is almost continual activity—and occasions for suffering are more frequent in this state than in any other. Do not desire, therefore, to descend from this cross under any pretext whatever. Since God has placed you there, remain there always.

Let not the prelate or the priest desire to be detached from his cross because of the turmoil of a thousand cares and hindrances he encounters there. Let him attend to his duties of state, taking care of the souls that God has confided to him, instructing some, consoling others, sometimes speaking, sometimes keeping silent, giving time to action and to prayer. This is the cross to which God has attached him. He must remain there firmly, without believing in anything that might induce him to leave it.

Let the religious remain constantly and faithfully nailed to the cross of his vocation, never permitting the least thought that might divert him or make him change the resolution he has made to serve God in this way of life, and still less even listening to what would lead him to do anything contrary to obedience. And do not say to me: "O God! if only I had my way, I would pray for hours and receive so many consola tions that I might even experience being enraptured.[25] If I could only pray at *this* hour, I could easily wrest the very Heart of God and place it in my own, or soar up to the Cross and place my hand in the Saviour's side, taking away His Heart. If I could only pray *now,* I would pray so fervently that I would be raised right off the ground." All this is nothing but the *appearance* of virtue. We must reject all that is contrary to obedience, never permitting such movements and inspirations. Simply obey. God does not ask anything else of you.

Thus Our Lord in no way desired to descend from the Cross. He asks, "Do you want Me to descend from it? No! For all is finished." [*Jn.* 19:30]. This was the sixth word He pronounced: *Consummatum est*—"All is finished." "O My Father, I have accomplished in every detail all that was Your will. Nothing more remains for Me to do. Behold the work of Redemption finished and perfected." [*Jn.* 17:4]. O God! these words provide material for an infinity of very useful reflections, but I have spoken of them to you before.

Let us come to His last word: Father, into Your hands I entrust My spirit. [*Lk.* 23:46]. Here again, many considerations present themselves. This word contains all Christian perfection. In this word is found Our Lord's perfect abandonment into His Heavenly Father's hands, without any reserve whatever. "I entrust My spirit into Your hands." Note here His humility, His obedience, and His true submission. "While I lived, O Father, I gave You My body and My soul without reserve; now, having accomplished all that You asked of Me, nothing more remains but to entrust My spirit into Your hands."

Here is the quintessence of the spiritual life—this perfect abandonment into the hands of the heavenly Father and this perfect indifference in whatever is His divine will.[26] "All is accomplished, but if it would please You that My spirit should remain still longer in this body that it might suffer more, I entrust it into Your hands. If You wish Me to pass from this life and so to enter My glory, I entrust My spirit into Your hands. In short, O Father," our dear Master would say, "here I am entirely ready and resolved to do all that pleases You."

Ah! my dear Sisters, if when we consecrate ourselves to God's service we begin by absolutely and unreservedly entrusting our spirit into His hands, how happy will we be! Any delay in our perfection comes from this lack of self-gift. Truly we must begin, pursue, and complete the spiritual life with this self-gift, in imitation of the Saviour, who did so with admirable perfection at the beginning, during the course, and at the end of His life.

On entering God's service many lay down conditions, saying: "I do entrust my spirit into Your hands, but with this reservation, that You nourish my heart with delights and consoling feelings, and that I never suffer either aridity or dryness. I entrust into Your hands my spirit, but only on condition that no one thwarts my will; or only on condition that You give me a superior according to my heart, or according to my liking and inclination. I entrust into Your hands my spirit, but please provide that I am always dearly loved by those who direct me, by those into whose hands I deliver myself for love of You. Please make sure that they approve and value all I do—at least the greater part of it, for not to be loved and not to feel this love is intolerable."

Is it not clear to you that you are not entrusting your spirit into God's hands as Our Lord did? Certainly, it is in this that all our ills, our troubles, our disquietudes and other such nonsense originate. As soon as things do not happen as we had expected or as we had promised ourselves, desolation seizes us. We are not yet perfectly indifferent, totally surrendered into the divine hands. Oh, how happy we would be if we thoroughly practiced this point. It is the abridgement and quintessence of the spiritual life! We would reach the high perfection of a St. Catherine of Siena, or a St. Francis, or a Blessed Angela of Foligno, or of many others who were like balls of wax in the hands of Our Lord and of their superiors, receiving all the impressions given them.[7]

Therefore, my dear Sisters, act accordingly, and say indifferently in all things, with our dear Master: "Into Your hands, O my God, I entrust my spirit. Do You wish me to be in dryness or in consolation? Into Your hands I entrust my spirit. Do you wish me to be contradicted, to experience repugnances and difficulties, to be loved or not, to obey this one or that one, and in whatever it may be, in great things or small? Then into Your hands I entrust my spirit." Let those, therefore, who are engaged in the activities of the active life not desire to leave it in order to devote themselves to the contemplative until God so ordains it; and let contemplatives not give up contemplation until God commands it. Let us be silent when we should, and speak when the time for it comes. [*Eccles.* 3:7].

If we act thus, we will indeed be able to say at the hour of our death, as did our dear Master: "All is consummated, O God; in everything I have accomplished Your divine will. What remains now for me except to entrust my spirit into Your hands at the end of my life, just as I entrusted it to You at its beginning and during its course." But so that we might live this way, my dear Sisters, let us use the three hours of the darkness of this life as did our dear Saviour and Master. Let us remain on the cross where God has placed us; let us pray on it; indeed, let us complain to Him of our afflictions and aridities; and when appropriate, let us say words of consolation to our neighbor. Finally, let us be consumed on this cross and accomplish all that God wills, so that at the end we will receive from this great God—as I pray Him with all my heart, and for myself in particular—the grace to entrust our spirit into His hands. He will receive it as He did that of His dear and only Son, to make it rejoice in Heaven, where we will bless Him eternally for the glory that He won for us by His Death and Passion. May God indeed give us this grace! Amen.

NOTES

1. Cf. Sermon for Palm Sunday, p. 162 of this volume; *Treatise on the Love of God,* Book 2, chap. 6.
2. Cf. Sermon for Palm Sunday, p. 172 of this volume.
3. Cf. p. 179 of this sermon.
4. Cf. Sermon for Passion Sunday, p. 154 of this volume; *Treatise,* Book 7, chap. 8.
5. Cf. *Treatise,* Book 6, chap. 14.
6. Here St. Francis de Sales is making use of the ancient patristic teaching on the *communicatio idiomata.* In the Incarnation we recognize the union, in the Person of the Logos, of both the divine and human natures. Thus, the properties or characteristics of either divinity or humanity can be predicated of the divine Person who is the subject of the Incarnation. In this way, even though it is only characteristic of *humanity* to die, death can nevertheless be predicated of the one God-man in light of the hypostatic union. Since Jesus is a divine Person, we can truly say that God suffered and died. The patristic tradition, and here St. Francis de Sales, made use of this doctrine to show the loving involvement of God, through the Incarnation, in our human predicament of suffering and dying. God, Love Itself, is not aloof or indifferent to our human suffering and dying; He is there with us in Jesus.
7. Cf. *Treatise,* Book 9, chap. 13.
8. Our Lady was an exception; cf. p. 179 of this sermon.
9. Here, as in countless other instances, St. Francis de Sales will use something borrowed from Pliny's *Natural History.* It was an endless source for many of the images he used to clarify some article of faith or spiritual principle. St. Francis knew well that much of what Pliny wrote was simply no longer tenable according to the view of

natural science in his day. Still, it served his purposes well.

10. Cf. *Treatise*, Book 5, chap. 8.

11. Cf. Sermon for Thursday of Second Week, pp. 66-82 of this volume.

12. Theologians use the distinction between sufficient and efficacious grace to help explain how God's universal salvific will (God "will have all men to be saved. . .'—*1 Tim.* 2:24) is reconciled with the fact that some apparently are not saved. St. Francis was very familiar with that issue and even contributed to the solution of the *De Auxiliis* controversy, but he chose not to deal with theological subtleties during a Good Friday sermon.

13. Cf. pp. 192-193 of this sermon.

14. Cf. Sermon for Thursday of the Third Week, p. 104 of this volume.

15. Cf. Sermon for Thursday of the Fourth Week, pp. 139-140 of this volume.

16. Cf. pp. 187-188 of this sermon.

17. Cf. p. 196 of this sermon.

18. Cf. p. 184 of this sermon.

19. St. Francis de Sales is here alluding to the teaching of the Reformation on the mediatorial function of Jesus alone: Jesus, and only He, can intercede on behalf of the human family before God; one does not need to use saints for this purpose. The Catholic teaching sees the intercession of the saints in terms of Jesus' identity with His people (i.e., the Body of Christ), and of the People of God's share in Jesus' priestly office. Their intercessory role is joined with His mediatorial role and derives all its efficacy from it.

20. Cf. p. 178 of this sermon.

21. Cf. p. 195 of this sermon.

22. Cf. p. 183 of this sermon.

23. Cf. *Sermons on Our Lady*, "The Purification," February 2, 1622, p. 184; and "The Presentation of Our Lady," November 21, 1620, pp. 129-130.

24. Cf. *Treatise*, Book 8, chap. 13; *Spiritual Conferences*, X, "Obedience"; XI, "Virtue of Obedience."

25. Cf. *Sermons on Our Lady*, "The Purification," February 2, 1622, pp. 181-182.

26. Cf. *Treatise*, Book 9, chap. 4.

27. Cf. *Treatise*, Book 9, chap. 4; *Spiritual Conferences*, XII, "Simplicity," pp. 226-230.

INDEX
Topical Index

Abandonment. See also Providence.
quintessence of spiritual
   life....................204
to God..110-111, 123, 203-206
superiors..........106, 111
Abraham
  no miracle...............121
  tested by God........121-122
Adam. See also Sin, Original.
  could die or not die......182
  feared death..............141
Adultery
  committed by David........16
  shunned by Joseph.........16
Ambition.............28-30, 32
  St. Peter renounced.......101
Ambrose, St.
  on fasting.................4
  election as bishop..........80
Ananias and Saphira..........17
Ancient Fathers' teachings
  ass and/or colt............169
  concord or union...........84
  dwelling of God with men..132
  fall from grace.............77
  fasting with humility.........4
  fear of death.....134-135, 141
  Judas................68, 76
  perseverance in good......166
  union in Trinity............85
Andrew, St.
  on dissatisfaction......122-123
Angela of Foligno, Bl........205
Angels
  conversing in Heaven.......59
  confirmed in grace........163
  established in grace.........69
  evil spirit..............41, 43
  fall from grace 69, 71, 152, 163

Angels (cont.)
  guardian of Persians, Jews.. 163
  imperfection of, negative...163
  lower than Sacred Humanity. 91
  minister to Christ..........31
  not our models in love......97
  "of light"..............30-31
  saved but not redeemed.....64
Antichrist...................69
Antony, St..............24, 164
Anxiety
  Canaanite woman.........107
  centurion 107
  concerning death..........142
  in illness.................110
  pursuit of perfection   118,
  ....120, 122-123
  prince of synagogue.......107
Apostolic College.........75, 79
Attachment..................73
Attentiveness. See also Faith.
  of Canaanite woman.....41-42
  to follow Christ...........119
Augustine, St.
  on common life...........8, 9
  dying well............142
  enjoying creatures....60, 72
  fasting with humility......4
  grace, falls from......194
  ingratitude of man......181
  Our Father...........148
  Psalm 132 (133)........97
  Stoics 135
Avarice
  cause of Judas' loss........78
  in religious and ecclesiastics..76
  St. Gregory Nazianzen......73
  spiritual........28-30, 32, 72
  Judas and Dives.........74

Avarice (cont.)
temporal
Judas and Dives..........74
to increase possessions..71-72
maintain possessions....73
Basil, St...................166
Beatitude. See Glory.
Beatitudes   68, 75, 114,
............155-156, 166-167
Beauty..................34-35
Bernard, St., teachings
angels not redeemed.......64
charity towards neighbor....93
Christ and temporal affairs...75
fasting..................2-3
letter on physical
illness.............108-109
progress in spiritual life.....77
Psalm 90....19, 21, 27, 28, 30
reward for works...........40
wine...............108, 109
Bonaventure, St.
on poverty..............114
Bread
barley..................126
of the angels............126
Saviour...........127
Burial of Dead............132
Cain & Abel. See Law of Nature.
Canaanite Woman
anxiety of..............107
attentiveness of.........41-42
confidence of.............44
humility of..........48, 50
patience of..............48
perseverance of..........45
prayer of.............43
Capuchins.................30
Cardinal virtues..........39-41
Cassian
on purity of heart.........11
Catherine of Genoa, St........28
Catherine of Siena, St.
.........18, 118, 161, 205

Celibacy
in the priesthood......100-101
of St. Peter.............100
Centurion
anxiety of...............107
lively faith of............107
Charity
affinity with humility........5
always active...........36, 48
grace...................152
more compelling than
nature.................106
necessary for meritorious
works...................5
Sermon 6.............83-97
toward neighbor...........54
vivifies faith...........36, 48
Charles Borromeo, St.
fraternal correction 167-169
Chartreuse.................30
Christian Life
combatants.............17, 31
continual penance.........25
symbolized by Lent........31
Cicero....................46
Commandments of love, two
dissimilar..............86-87
similar................87-88
love of God, the greater.....96
love of neighbor, greater
emphasis...............96
proceed from Heart of
God....................88
Common Life
exceptions to
St. Paul the first hermit....8
St. Simon Stylites........9
value of................8-9
Communion of Saints. See also
Prayer, intercessory.
article of Creed on.....101-102
nature of.............101-102
Complaining to God
Christ on the Cross........198

Complaining to God (cont.)
  in our prayer............205
  with self-pity............122
Concupiscence
  combated by fasting.........2
Confidence in God   17, 18, 21,
  ....22, 25, 27, 28, 43
  measure of faith............44
Consolations
  and false generosity. .22-23, 26
  noonday devil..........30
  penance (Magdalen). .26-27
  misuse of.................31
  of eternal glóry, effect
    on soul...............56-57
  worldly..................126
Contrition
  at moment of death........142
  of good thief.............193
  St. Peter...........191-192
Conversations
  in Heaven..............58-65
  between God and us.....63
  Within Holy Trinity......63
  on mercies of the Lord...61
    Passion, death....59, 61
  with the angels..........59
    each other..........59
    Our Lady..........60
  of desert Fathers...........10
Correction, fraternal.....26, 167
Council of Trent
  on grace..................67
Creation
  man for God, world for man. 72
  perfection and
    imperfection in......160-163
Cross
  folly of..............166-167
  Good Friday Sermon...180-181
  of obedience of priests,
    married, religious....202-203
  perfection of..........166-167
  place of our abode........97

Crown of glory......17, 32, 175
David
  overcome by temptation.....15
  peccavi of...............191
  submission to Providence...110
Death
  contrary to nature........141
  fear of...............134-138
    Adam 141
    Christ 135
    exceptions to........136-140
    Sermon 9...........129-146
  fruit of sin...............135
  God suffered.............183
  preparation for............143
  relying on merits of the
    Passion in 142
  submission to God's will in.138
Denis the Areopagite, St.
  Apostle of France........197
  converted by St. Paul......197
  on the damned............67
  darkness over the earth. .197
Desert Fathers
  conversations of...........10
Discouragement   19, 28, 45,
  ....119, 122, 204
Dives (sinful rich man)   66, 67,
  ....74, 75
Doctrine
  God never teaches a useless...2
Ecclesiastics
  avarice greatest evil in......76
  called to perfection of love
    of neighbor.............94
  cross of care of souls.....202
  fasting.....................
  supported by tithes........120
Edification
  obligation.................7
Election. See also Vocation.
  Sermon 5..............66-82
Elias   58-59, 62-63,
  ....121, 126, 184, 199

Ephrem, St.
   accepting word from sinner
  149-150
Eternity
   enjoyment of....32, 50, 65, 81
Eucharist, Holy
   frequent 173
   model of charity...........90
   pledge of love.............85
   rarely received............89
   source of union............89
      with neighbor........89, 96
      Our Lord........95-96
   transubstantiation..........134
Extreme Unction............142
Faith. See also Truth.
   and cardinal virtues......39-41
      truth.................151
   attentive............41-43, 50
   attentiveness to.......153, 154
   avarice, sensuality obstacles
      to attentiveness to........42
   believing all truths of necessary
      for salvation...35-36, 39, 40
   birth of..................35
   dead..................36-37
   defined 34-35
   dormant 38
   dying...................36
   governs other virtues.......38
   "great faith"........35-36, 37
   living 36
   object of.................34
   Sermon 3..............34-50
   vigilant............38-39, 41
Fasting
   divine institution............2
   expiation for Adam's sin....12
   fruits of fasting.............2
   in secret..............7-8, 11
   kinds
      exterior (of the body).2-4, 6-7
      interior (of the spirit)..2-4, 7
   not a virtue in itself.........1

Fasting (cont.)
   of philosophers, pagans, sinners
      ....1, 5
   of religious..............2, 8
   on Saturdays...............6
   penitential aspect............3
   religious under special
      obligation of..............2
   Sermon 1...............1-14
   through vanity............4-7
   virtuous fast—3 conditions of
      humility............4-11, 14
      purity of heart.....11-12, 14
      wholehearted and
         universal 2-4, 14
Fear
   in eternity, none......127, 184
   every state and vocation
      ...69, 70, 77, 190, 191, 194
   of chastisements...........72
      children 21-22
      damnation..........94, 191
      death (See also Death.)129-146
         Stoics on...........135
      God..............154, 191
      losing grace........67, 191
      not consenting to grace...67
      slothful 19-21
      weak................25-27
Fortitude
   accompanies vigilant faith...39
Francis (of Assisi), St.
   grieved that God not loved..181
Francis Xavier, Blessed (St.)
   died in effective poverty....114
Friendship
   in Heaven.................59
Generosity
   and humility..............123
   false...................22-23
Gideon 156
Glory, Eternal. See also
   Conversations.
   accidental 58

Glory, Eternal (cont.)
  acquired for us by Christ...184
  beatitude..........57, 151-152
  essential felicity of...58, 61, 63
  faculties perfected in....56, 61
  mutual recognition of souls58-59
  no distractions in...........57
God
  attributes of: goodness, mercy,
    justice.................131
  perfection and purity.......27
Good
  object of will...........34-35
  eternal felicity one single....61
Grace
  charity.................152
  Council of Trent on.......67
  the damned had sufficient....67
  fear of losing or refusing....67
  fall from.....70, 77, 191, 194
  God gives sufficient.67, 78, 192
  just.....................67
  mortal sin causes loss of....77
  of Judas and of St. Peter...192
    sinners.................67
  venial sin weakens.........77
Gregory the Great
  Dialogues of—Parable on eternal
    happiness...............53
  on Job...................70
Gregory Nazianzen, St.
  renunciation...........73-74
Happiness, Eternal
  Sermon 4..............52-65
Holiness
  and ecclesiastical office.....80
Holy Scripture
  and temptation.........18, 24
Holy Spirit
  and temptation15, 16, 17, 18, 29
Hope..........18, 28, 119, 194
Huguenots.........79, 100, 199
Human nature
  evil inclinations of..........77

Human nature (cont.)
  passions of...........78, 122
  of St. Paul................78
  three natures
  —negative nature—from
    Adam............183-184
  —sinful nature............184
  —glorified nature..........184
Human spirit
  defected from truth........152
  dissatisfaction of..........123
  inconstant..........46-47, 127
Humility
  and confidence............194
  faith..................50
  fasting...............4-5
  fear...............70, 77
  generosity............123
  patience..............171
  confounds the world...174-175
  dependence of on charity.....5
  false.................49, 123
  God tries us to increase our.123
  loved by Christ...........170
  of Canaanite woman.....49-50
  Our Father expresses......148
  penitents lacking in........50
  pleasing to God........49, 123
  triumph of...........171-174
Idleness
  and temptation.........16, 21
Idolatry
  of avarice.............73, 74
    Judas and Dives.........74
Image & likeness of God
  defiled by ourselves........86
  motive for love of neighbor..86
  rational creatures created
    after..............160, 163
  restored by Incarnation......91
Imagination
  in prayer.......103-104, 113
Imperfections
  involuntary........25, 27, 119

Imperfections (cont.)
  of saints
    recounting of.......163-164
    used to excuse our own..165
Incarnation
  known in Old Law.......90-91
  purpose—for Our Lord to be
    Saviour...............182
  raised our nature above
    the angels..............91
  restored the image
    of God................91
Indulgence, Plenary.........192
Inspirations
  contrary to obedience......203
  obedience to..............118
  of angels..................59
    Holy Spirit............103
    Sacred Heart............62
    saints..................60
  particular..................8
  rejection of...........77, 193
  to religious vocation.......126
Jerome, St.
  "armed preface"..........103
  on burial of dead..........132
    desert calling...........71
    virginity..............100
  recounted imperfections of
    St. Paula...............164
Jesuits.....................30
Jesus Christ
  acts through goodness
    alone..................131
  anger of..................102
  comes to Gentiles through
    His Apostles..........48-49
  compassion of............121
  concealing His glory........41
  exemplar of charity
    ....90, 93, 94, 97, 188
  death of
    feared.................135
    true..............178, 181

Jesus Christ (cont.)
  equal to the Father
    ....170-171, 180, 188, 189
  faith of...............19, 152
  glorious from conception
    ....58, 151, 198
  humility of..155, 170-171, 181
  impeccable...........151, 180
  knowledge................19
  model of holiness, poverty...75
  natures, two
    human—could die or not
    die..................182
    Divine—impassible,
    immortal, impeccable...182
  obedience of. See also
    Obedience......63, 181, 201
  omnipotence of
    ....102, 122, 124, 180
  in creation..........132-133
  resurrection
    —Christ's..............133
    —general......124, 133-134
  resuscitation........132-133
  transubstantiation........134
  Passion and Death of
    causes of...............178
    contains all Christian
    perfection.........203-206
    darkness over the earth
    during...............197
    His prayers during..188, 198
    seven last words.....187-206
    title of Christ on Cross—
    interpretation..........178
    what it won for us......62
  pleasing to the Father...63, 185
  prayer of
    efficacious.............188
    for Apostle and us.......84
    for His crucifiers........187
  promised only to Jews......48
  revered by His Father..188-189
  revered His Father........189

Jesus Christ (cont.)

  Saviour, Christ's mission as,
indicated by Eternal Father,
patriarchs and prophets,
Himself, the impious, angel
of the Incarnation....184-186

  soul of.................198

  source of all perfection.....162

  Sovereign Pontiff & head of
Apost. College.......75, 97

  temporal affairs of..........75

  tempted......15, 16, 19, 24-25

  tested St. Philip...........121

  theandric actions of....131-132

    infinite merit of.........183

  the Truth.........18, 152, 185

Job

  did not fear death.138-139, 140

  remained just among sinners..70

John, St.

  beloved disciple....84, 196-197

  filial love for Mary........196

  means "grace"...........197

  on love of neighbor.........84

Joseph Barsabas.............80

Joseph in Egypt

  and temptation..........16-17

Joy......................113

Judas

  apostate...............69, 78

  avaricious...........74-75, 78

  betrayal of Christ
........69, 71, 76, 190-191

  cause of his fall.........76-77

  despair of.....78, 81, 191-193

  idolatrous................75

  procurator................75

  Sacred Heart and..........195

  "son of perdition".........69

  vocation of...........66, 67

Judgment

  at moment of death........136

  greater or lesser severity
of...............68, 90-91

Judgment (cont.)

  of God.................191

Justice, Original.........24, 182

Language of love

  understood by Job.....139-140

  understood by Our Lady
at Cana...........139-140

Law, Mosaic

  and wealth, possessions.....68

  commands love of neighbor
...................88, 90

  rejected sinners........81, 193

Law of Grace

  pardons all sinners if
they confess.............81

  poverty praised in..........68

Law of Nature

  Cain, Abel obliged to obey..88

  commands love of God and
neighbor...............88

  commands love of neighbor
...................88, 90

Lazarus.................66, 67

Lent—symbol of Christian
life.....................32

Looking on Our Lord...102, 110,
113, 187, 180-182, 193-195

Louis XI of France

  anxiety for physical health..112

Love

  for God, who loves us.181, 186

  object of the will..........155

  of God for us.62, 154-155, 156

  ours for God in return..154-155

Love of neighbor

  clergy called to perfection of.94

  concord among early
Christians..............89

  concord or union—defined
...................85-86

  degree of perfection of...93, 94

  exceptions

    giving up eternal salvation.93

    offense against God.......94

Love of Neighbor (cont.)
in superiors' care of sick...106
love only the good in
neighbor.............86, 92
motive:
avoid division and damnation94
example of Christ..90, 93, 97
neighbor bears image of
God, Christ..84, 86, 91-92
resemblance to Christ.....92
"My commandment".......84
new commandment.....88-90
practiced by Raguel.........92
quality of, unity of the
Divine Persons........85-86
religious, called to perfection
of.....................94
with reason, proper order....92
Lucifer
perished in vanity.........153
revolt of..................69
Magdalen.........25, 26-27, 60
only person who sought
spiritual cure...........107
Magnificat..................61
Maladies, physical
anxiety about.........107, 110
artifice in requesting cure...111
caused by sin, not God.....110
profiting spiritually from...102
proper conduct in.......99-115
purpose of..............110
resignation in....105, 106, 111
St. Bernard on........108-109
submission in
to God's mercy and
justice.........105, 110
others.....105-106, 110
too much seeking for cure
of.................110-112
virtues to practice during
abandonment............111
profiting from cure......113
resignation.........112-113

Malady, a spiritual
regarding meditation.......103
Manna
bread of angels...........125
in the desert........120, 125
murmuring Israelites.......125
Marie of the Incarnation
died in affective poverty....114
Martha...............25-26, 60
Martial, St........121, 125, 127
Martyrdom
religious life is a..........47
Mary, Blessed Virgin
at Cana..............139-140
foot of the Cross....195-198
fasting on Saturday to honor..6
foot of the Cross..1-4, 195-198
heart of..............195-197
honor given to..............6
Mother of all Christians....197
never swooned......104, 195
no imperfection in.........162
preserved from all sin......179
spiritual communication with
Christ on the Cross......198
Mary of Egypt..............59
Matrimony.................101
Matthias, St.
chosen by lot..............80
vocation of.............66-67
Maxims
"Ask for nothing"   111, 112,
..........113, 114, 138, 143
of the world.........155, 174
Melchisedech
a true man..........103, 105
heresies concerning........103
Miracles
confirm doctrine..........42
cure of St Peter's mother-in-law
...................99-102
granted when ordinary means
fail..............121, 125
no miracle for Abraham..121

Miracles (cont.)
    loaves and fish 121-124
    manna in desert . . 120, 121, 125
    material for 127
    raising of son of widow of Naim.
      See also Resuscitation. 130-134
Moses 58-59, 62-63, 178-179
Naim
    honored by Christ 130
    "beautiful" 130
    raising of son of widow of . . 130
Name
    the new received in Heaven . . 63
    our engraven in His palms . . . 62
Nicholas, St.
    election as bishop 80
Obedience 84
    deliberation, too much 12-14, 173
      Adam 12
      disciples in John 6 12
      Eve 173
      Life of St. Pachomius 84
    of Christ. 63, 172-173, 175, 201
    simple 124
    speculative and practical: the
      married, prelates, priests,
      religious 201-202
Original Justice 179, 182
Our Father 45-46, 148
Pachomius, St.
    fought vanity of monk 10-11
    mocked the devil 24
    perseverance of 44
Palm Sunday, symbolism
    ass—Jews 170
    colt—Gentiles 170
    ass—qualities: humility,
      patience, willingness to be
      burdened 169, 172
Patience
    affinity of with humility 171
    and prayer 43, 48
      tranquility 48, 175
    of the ass 171

Patience (cont.)
    Christ 171
Paul, St.
    did not fear death 136-138
    disagreement of with
      St. Barnabas 165
    ecstasy 52
    fasting, instructions on 4-5
    harsh temperament of 78
    on edification 7
    love of neighbor . . . 85, 93-94
    Melchisedech 103, 105
    wine 109
    temptations of 17
Paul, St., the first hermit 8
Paula, St. 164
Peace of soul 26, 27
Penance
    life of perfect Christian a
      continual 25
    this life the place of our 25
Penance, Sacrament of . . 142, 173
Perfection, Universal Call to . . 120
Perfection, pursuit of. See also
    Religious Life.
    abandonment to Providence
       . . . . 117, 126
      measure of perfection 118
    quintessence of spiritual
      life 204
    aridity   23, 26, 44-45, 46
       . . . . 122, 127, 204, 205
    discouragement. See
      Discouragement.
    evil inclinations cannot hin-
      der us from attaining . . . 77-78
    false generosity 22-23, 26
    grace makes possible 78
    importance of love 95
    Providence, Divine
       . . . . 117, 119, 120-121
    self-forgetfulness
       . . . . 118, 121, 123, 125
    simplicity in 29

Perfection, pursuit of (cont.)
  temptations 23
  testings by God 122
  vain hopes 90
  worldly consolations 126
Perseverance
  Adam and Eve failed in 153
  fasting 4-7
  final 44
  in prayer 44, 47-48
    the truth . . 152, 153, 155, 165
  religious life . 47, 70, 71, 127
  of Canaanite woman 44
Peter, St.
  celibacy of 100
  confidence in God, lack of . . . 44
  first Apostle to follow Christ
    100
  generosity and fear of . . . 22, 23
  head of the Apostles 58, 79
  head of all priests 100
  imperfections of 165
  mother-in-law of 99-102
  no possessions 100
  plenary indulgence gained by 192
  Prince of Apostles 101
  repentance of 191-192
Philip, St.
  tested by Christ 122
  not confirmed in faith 122
  human prudence of 123
Poverty
  affective—Marie of the
    Incarnation's 114
  effective—St. Xavier's 114
  evangelical 114
  not highly praised under
    Mosaic Law 67
  of Apostolic College 75
  poor in spirit 68, 75, 114
Prayer
  Canaanite woman's 43
  confidence 43
  consolations 28, 44-45

Prayer (cont.)
  contemplation 42-43
    of Jesus crucified 181
  humility 43
  intercessory   60, 99, 106, 113,
    . . . . 178, 199
  is a sacrifice 188
  meditation
    using imagination 103-104
    without imagination 105
  Our Father 45-46
  patience 43, 48
  perseverance 43
Preachers
  notorious sinners unqualified
    . . . . 148, 151
  of irreproachable life . . 148, 151
  qualities of 157
Precious Blood
  poured out on the Cross 201
  sacred mortar 95
  sprinkled on the Cross . 194, 195
Presumption . 17, 18, 70, 123, 191
Pride and vanity 154-155
  fasting through 5-6, 8
Priests
  avarice greatest evil in 76
  called to perfect
    love/neighbor 94
  celibacy of 101
  crosses of 202
  special obligation to fast 2
  St. Peter head of all 100
  complete dedication to God . 101
Providence, Divine
  abandonment to 143
  adoring 67
  and our death 141-142
  censured by human
    prudence 66-67
  David's submission to 110
  in the desert 178-179
  in hardships and sickness
    . . . . 105, 165

Providence, Divine (cont.)
    preached by Christ.........99
    replaces defections.......79-80
    testings..................122
    toward all creatures....116-117
        ordinary Christians..117, 118
        pagans and heretics......117
    those pursuing perfection
        ....117, 118, 119, 120-121
    when human aid fails...120-121
Prudence
    and faith...............39-40
    human
        ....39-40, 66, 166, 167, 173
Purgatory..................102
Purity of heart
    and fasting.............2, 11
    Cassian..................11
Red Sea...................102
Redemption
    Christ died of love........181
    God suffered death....183, 201
    motivated by mercy/love
        alone.............. 180,181
    only in the Cross..........201
    other ways of God could have
        chosen............. 180-181
    superabundant....180, 195, 201
    through obedience of Christ.201
Religious life
    aridity   23, 26, 44-45, 46,
        ....122, 127
    avarice, greatest evil in.....76
    defections.............. 79-80
    discouragement   19, 28, 45,
        ....119, 122, 204
    dress....................47
    fasting....................2
    food....................47
    making reservations........204
    martyrdom................47
    miraculous interventions....121
    paradise.................47
    perfection of love/neighbor..94

Religious life (cont.)
    perseverance............. 127
    regularity................47
    vocation................126
    worldly consolations.......126
Repentance
    always possible.......142, 194
    of Good Thief............193
    St. Peter...........191-192
Reprobate..............67, 70
Reprobation and Election
    (Sermon 5).............66-82
Resurrection
    of Christ.................133
    the dead......124, 133-134
Resuscitation
    Jairus' daughter...........130
    Lazarus..................130
    widow's son..............130
    one of greatest miracles..130
    Christ's motivation......130
Reverence
    in prayer.................189
    of Father for Son.........188
    of Son for the Father......189
Sacraments. See individual
    Sacraments.
Sacred Heart
    and consolations.......31, 203
    appeals to Judas and
        bad thief..............195
    disciple of...........196-197
    infinite merit.........183, 201
    lesson in love of neighbor..188
    love of us...........62, 188
    our names engraven on......62
    patience of..............195
    pierced by ingratitude   190,
        ....198, 200
Salvation
    faith and obedience to the
        commandments, the
        requirements for........40
    only in the Cross.........201

Satan..................24, 182
Self-Knowledge..............26
Sermon on the Mount. See also
Beatitudes.
 fasting.....................2
Simon Stylites, St.............9
Sin
 ability to implies
  powerlessness...........180
 actual 179
 all can be forgiven
  if confessed.............81
 cause of death....182, 183-184
 even slight sin is terrible....77
 impossible in Christ...151, 180
 impossible in God.........151
 mortal causes loss of grace..77
 of the senses and the spirit....3
 original   12, 24, 69-70,
  ....179, 182
 venial, effects of...........77
Sinners
 all men are.148, 179, 180, 184
  exception: Our Lady.....179
  taught by St. Augustine...148
 comparison between Judas
  and Peter, and the good and
   bad thieves.......190, 194
 impossible in beatific vision.152
 notorious may not preach word
  of God...........148, 151
Sloth
 of David..................16
Solomon
 fall from grace of......78, 191
 wisdom of................70
Soul
 faculties of limited by body..56
 faculties of perfected in
  glory................57, 61
 faculties of separated from
  body................54, 55
 higher part of.............158
 not affected by time.......132

Soul (cont.)
 of Christ.................198
  St. Augustine.........54-55
Symbols
 ants.....................151
 apostles' cloaks...........174
 ass and/or colt........169-170
 ass—Jews................170
 colt—Gentiles.............170
 bees..................9, 164
 birds 119
 bread.....................89
  barley 125
 dove................151, 161
 grapes....................89
 hens 119
 horse....................170
 lily 162
 nightingales 119
 oriole—the Passion........187
 palm tree................162
 portrait...................91
 Psalm 132 (133)........... 97
 rose 161-162
 St. Peter's mother-in-law...102
 serpent
  ..151, 161, 178-179, 181-182
 spiders 9
 tree, dying or dead........37
 vinegar 47
 wasps..............164, 166
Temptation
 and idleness...............16
  obedience...16, 17, 18, 29
  servants of God.15, 17, 20
 of Ananias and Saphira......17
  Christ as example....15, 16
  David 16-17
  Joseph in Egypt...16-17, 29
  St. Paul...............17
 Sermon 2.............15-32
 through Bethsabee..........16
 to be avoided.......15, 17, 18
 universal..........15, 17, 23

Temptation (cont.)
found in Apostolic College.24
—Eden........24, 182
—heaven...........24
—where Christ is...24
weapons against 17, 18, 20,
...............21, 22, 25
Teresa (of Avila), Mother.....28
Testings by God
purpose of.......121-122, 123
Timothy, St.
and wine.................109
Thomas, St.
and fasting..............4, 11
Tobias & Raguel.............92
Tranquility of Heart 25-27, 110,
..............118, 119, 120
in face of death
.........141, 142, 145, 175
Transfiguration
spark of eternal glory.......58
testimony of the Father.....185
Trinity
conversations of Persons of
in Heaven...............63
model of our union......85-86
unity of Persons in.........85
equality of Persons in
.............170-171, 189
Truth (Faith)
and beauty...............35
as weapon
......18, 25, 27, 28, 31, 32
believing all the truths of faith
necessary for salvation.39, 40
expressed in Our Father....148
in the spiritual life..........35
is faith.................152
leads us to salvation.......154
object of understanding
.................154-155
the valor of faith...........39
Union or Concord.
See Love of Neighbor.

Vanity
absence of truth...........153
fasting through............4-7
human race subject to..154-155
in action.................155
led to sin.............152-153
Lucifer perished in........153
of man and his horse......170
performs works to
be seen.............10-11
Virginity
St. Jerome on.........100-101
Vocation and Election
of Dives.................68
Judas 68
Lazarus 68
Matthias............68-69
preserved by good works
.................77, 79-80
St. Jerome on.............71
Wine
and evangelical poverty....108
intoxication through........74
Word of God. See also Preachers.
is goodness itself; does not
partake of the evil of the
speaker..........150, 158
hearing it:
in self-forgetfulness......123
with attention, reverence,
devotion......156-158
pleasure 118
understanding.......118
omnipotent 133-134
proclaimed by Caiphas, Pilate,
an ass.................150
rejected by Scribes, Pharisees
.........148, 151-152, 153
rejection due to sinfulness151, 155
Sermon 10..........147-159
should always be honored and
esteemed. (See St. Ephrem)
....................149

Index to the Scriptural References

Gen. 1:26-27 . . . . .84, 160
2:7 149
2:16-17 . . . . .141, 182
2:17 . . . . .153, 173
2:21-23 149
3:1-3 . . . . .141, 173
3:1-6 . . . .12, 70, 154, 182
3:19 . . . . .3, 136
4:9 88
12:1 121
18:7-8 121
22:1-2 122
37:28 16
39:7-12 17
Ex. 16:14-15 125
Lev. 19:18 88
Num. 21:6-9 178
22:28-30 150
Jgs. 6:37-38 156
Ruth 1:20 130
2 Kgs. (2 Sam.) 11:1-4 16
12:13 192
3 Kgs. (1 Kgs.) 3:11-12 70
5:9-13 70
11:1-8 70
17:3-6 . . . . .121, 126
19:3-8 . . . . .121, 126
4 Kgs.(2 Kgs.)2:11 . .59,184,199
3 Esd. 4:35 39
2 Esd. (Neh.) 13:26 70
Tob. 3:21 175
7:1-9 92
Job 1:22 139
3:1ff 138
4:18 163
6:8-9 138
7:15-16, 21 138
14:2 . . . . .77, 162
15:15 163
19:27 140
26:11 189

Job 42:7-8 139
Ps. 2:11 194
17 (18):30 18
21 (22):1 198
21 (22):7 170
26 (27):6 188
31 (32):9 170
32 (33):9 133
35 (36):9 57
38 (39):10-12 110
43 (44):6-7 18
45:6 (Heb. & Sept.) 171
49 (50):16-17 148
61:13 (62:12) 136
72 (73):1 . . . . . .95, 179, 180
77 (78):24-25 125
90 (91) 18
90 (91):5-6 31
95 (96):1 120
97 (98):1 120
102 (103):15 162
105 (106):9 102
115 (116):17 188
117 (118):26 171
122 (123):2 40
125 (126):1 56
129 (130):7 . . . . . . .195, 201
129 (130):7-8 180
131 (132):10 198
132 (133) 97
139 (140):4 161
148:5 133
149:1 120
Prov. 6:6-8 151
6:9 21
23:32 161
30:25 151
Eccles. 2:10 78
3:7 205
9:1 136
Cant. 1:2 61

Cant. 1:1-3 152
  1:2-4 64
  1:15 162
  4:1, 7 162
  5:1 57
  5:8 31
  8:6-7 97
Wis. 2:6, 8 162
  2:23-24 136
  7:7, 17-24 70
  16:20 (2 refs.) 125
Ecclus. (Sir.) 2:1 15
  2:11 (10) 119
  3:27 16
  7:40 61
  24:18 (14) 162
Is. 1:3 171
  5:8 . . . . 30, 72
  6:2 189
  14:13-14 153
  40:1-2, 10-11 48
  40:6-8 162
  49:15-16 62
  50:5 94
  53:3 . . . . 170, 171
  53:4ff 172, 180
  53:10-12 200
  57:15 170
  61:1 48
  62:11 171
Jer. 9:20 78
  29:11 62
Bar. 3:38 131
Dan. 10:13 163
Osee 7:11 161
Zach. 9:9 171
  13:1 201
Mal. 4:2 30
Matt. 1:21 . . . . 150, 178
  1:23 132
  3:16-17 185
  4:1 15
  4:2 24
  4:3-10 25

Matt. 4:11 31
  4:18-19 190
  4:18-20 100
  5:3 . . . . 68, 75, 114
  5:3-6 167
  5:3-11 155
  5:10 166
  5:43-44 87
  5:48 120
  6:9-13 45
  6:10 112
  6:12 148
  6:16-18 . . . . 2, 7
  6:25-34 75
  6:26 . . . . 119, 142
  8:8 107
  8:14 100
  8:14-15 105
  8:24-26 44
  9:11 151
  9:18-19, 23-25 130
  9:20-21 107
  10:9-10 75
  10:16 (2 refs.) . . . 151, 161
  10:22 71
  10:29 142
  10:30 142
  11:19 151
  14:29-31 22
  14:36 107
  15:21-28 34
  15:22 107
  15:22-28 107
  15:28 34
  15:32 117
  16:16 190
  16:26 39
  16:27 136
  17:1-9 52
  17:2 58
  17:5 (2 refs.) 185
  17:9 185
  18:4 175
  19:16-17 40

Matt. 19:27 100
       19:28-29 118
       20:16 . . . . .66, 120
       21:1-9 169
       21:9 171
       22:14 . . . . .66, 120
       22:37-40 54
       22:39 86
       23:12 175
       24:13 71
       24:44 145
       25:13 145
       25:21, 23 . . . . .40, 137
       25:30 41
       26:15 190
       26:21 76
       26:21-25 191
       26:31-35 22
       26:49-50 195
       26:69-74 190
       26:74-75 (2 refs.) 192
       27:3-5 193
       27:4-5 . . . . .78, 81
       27:18, 24 185
       27:38 190
       27:40-42 (2 refs.) 199
       27:45 197
       27:46 198
       27:47-49 199
Mark 1:12 15
       1:29 100
       1:31 100
       5:22-23 107
       6:8 75
       7:24-29 41
       8:6-7, 20 124
       11:2 169
       11:3-6 173
       11:7 170
       12:25 64
       14:27-31 22
       14:34 135
       15:29-32 (2 refs.) 199
       15:35-36 199

Mark 16:16 . . . . .40, 152
Luke 1:26-31 184
       1:39-55 61
       2:35 195
       2:35, 51 196
       4:1 15
       4:2-13 25
       4:18-21 48
       4:23 129
       4:33-35 99
       4:38-44 99
       6:19 107
       7:3 107
       7:7 107
       7:11-16 130
       7:37-39 27
       9:29 58
       9:30-31 185
       9:31 59
       9:35 (2 refs.) 185
       10:39-40 26
       11:2-4 45
       11:14-28 . . . . .83, 95
       11:14-22 185
       11:17 83
       11:28 159
       12:22-31 75
       12:37 40
       14:11 175
       16:2 136
       16:19-31 66
       18:14 175
       22:33 . . . . .22, 191
       22:61-62 (2 refs.) 192
       23:2 151
       23:14, 22 185
       23:32-33 193
       23:34 188
       23:39-42 190
       23:39-43 193
       23:44-45 197
       23:46 203
John 1:14 . . . . .131, 152
       1:41 100

John 2:1-5 139
3:14-16 180
3:14-17 193
3:30 87
5:4 201
5:16, 18 151
6:1-15 116
6:11 116
6:61-67 12
8:21, 24 201
8:30-32 152
8:46-59 148
8:47 . . . . 118, 147
8:48 151
9:16 151
11:21-33 130
11:49-50 . . . . 150, 186
11:51 186
12:6 . . . . 75, 191
12:32 193
13:6 190
13:18-27 191
13:23 196
13:29 . . . . 75, 191
13:34 . . . . 86, 88
13:37 22
14:6 . . . . 18, 152, 185
15:12 . . . . . 54, 84, 86, 90
17:4 203
17:11-12, 21-22 . . . . . 85, 95
17:12 69
17:20 85
18:14 150
18:38 185
19:4-6 185
19:18 190
19:19 177
19:19, 22 186
19:22 150
19:25 . . . . 104, 195
19:26 (2 refs.) 196
19:28 200
19:30 203
21:7, 20 196

Acts 1:15 79
1:15-26 69
1:18 . . . . 78, 193
1:21-22 81
1:23-26 80
2:42 89
3:17 188
4:32 89
5:1-3 17
15:37-40 165
Rom. 1:20-21 156
2:4 195
2:6 136
3:13 161
3:23 179
4:17 133
5:12 . . . . 182, 184
5:12, 18 179
7:24 137
10:9-10 178
11:33 191
13:11 21
13:12-14 60
14:1-6 6
1 Cor. 1:7-8 20
1:18, 23 166
1:28 133
1:30 . . . . 180, 194
2:8 188
7:20 70
7:33-34 101
7:40 109
10:12 . . . . 77, 191
10:13 17
10:17 . . . . 89, 96
11:1 93
12:12, 27 97
13 4
13:12 . . . . . . 58, 63, 137
15:8 69
15:52 . . . . . 124, 133, 134
2 Cor. 1:7 31
5:10 136
5:14-15 . . . . 154, 181

2 Cor. 5:14-15, 19 94
      5:15 . . . . .186, 195
      5:21 180
      11:14 31
      12:2-4 52
      12:7 17
      12:14-15, 19 94
Gal. 3:13 180
      5:6 36
      5:24 186
      6:10 117
Eph. 1:5 86
      4:5 36
      4:15 97
      5:1-2 . . . . .85, 93, 95
      5:5 74
      6:11-16 21
Phil. 1:23-25 137
      2:7 155
      2:8 . . . . .94, 178, 183
      3:19 74
      4:5 7
      2:12 194
Col. 1:18 97
      1:20 95
      3:5 74
      3:14 92
1 Thess. 4:16 133
      5:8 18
      5:24 20
2 Thess. 2:3 69
1 Tim. 2:4 35
      4:10 117
      5:23 109

2 Tim. 2:5 17
Heb. 5:7.131, 188 (2 refs.), 198
      7:1-3 103
      9:27 . . . . .145, 182
      10:31 191
      11:6 40
      11:33-34 18
      13:8 103
      13:15 188
Jas. 1:12 . . . . .17, 175
      1:13 121
      1:17 96
      2:14-15 . . . .(Note 2) 50
      2:14-26 36
1 Ptr. 3:18 180
      5:7 . . . . .119, 142
2 Ptr. 1:10 . . . . .71, 77
      1:17 185
      2:4 163
1 Jn. 1:8 148
      1:8-10 179
      2:16 3
      3:1-2 86
      3:16 93
      4:20-21 84
      5:4 18
      5:6 152
Jude 6 163
Apoc. 2:17 63
      3:11 77
      12:4 . . . . .69, 161
      12:9 153
      16:15 145

If you have enjoyed this book, consider making your next selection from among the following . . .

Confession of a Roman Catholic. Paul Whitcomb................. 1.25
The Catholic Church Has the Answer. Paul Whitcomb............. 1.25
The Sinner's Guide. Ven. Louis of Granada...................... 8.00
True Devotion to Mary. St. Louis De Montfort................... 5.00
Life of St. Anthony Mary Claret. Fanchón Royer................. 8.00
Autobiography of St. Anthony Mary Claret...................... 8.00
I Wait for You. Sr. Josefa Menendez............................ .50
Words of Love. Menendez, Betrone, Mary of the Trinity............ 3.00
Little Lives of the Great Saints. John O'Kane Murray..............12.00
The Rhine Flows into the Tiber. Fr. Ralph Wiltgen................ 8.00
Prayer—The Key to Salvation. Fr. Michael Müller................ 5.00
Sermons on Prayer. St. Francis de Sales........................ 3.00
Sermons on Our Lady. St. Francis de Sales...................... 7.00
Sermons for Lent. St. Francis de Sales......................... 8.00
Passion of Jesus and Its Hidden Meaning. Fr. Groenings, S.J.........9.00
The Victories of the Martyrs. St. Alphonsus Liguori.............. 5.00
Canons and Decrees of the Council of Trent. Schroeder........... 8.00
St. Dominic's Family. Sr. Mary Jean Dorcy......................20.00
Sermons of St. Alphonsus Liguori for Every Sunday...............10.00
What Faith Really Means. Fr. Henry Graham..................... 2.00
A Catechism of Modernism. Fr. J. B. Lemius..................... 3.00
What Catholics Believe. Fr. Lawrence Lovasik................... 2.50
Alexandrina—The Agony and the Glory. Johnston................. 2.50
Blessed Margaret of Castello. Fr. William Bonniwell.............. 4.00
The Ways of Mental Prayer. Dom Vitalis Lehodey................ 8.00
Who Is Teresa Neumann? Fr. Charles Carty..................... 1.25
Summa of the Christian Life. 3 Vols. Granada...................24.00
Fr. Paul of Moll. van Speybrouck.............................. 6.00
St. Francis of Paola. Simi and Segreti.......................... 4.50
Communion Under Both Kinds. Michael Davies.................. 1.00
Abortion: Yes or No? Dr. John L. Grady, M.D................... 1.00
The Story of the Church. Johnson, Hannan, Dominica.............12.50
Religious Liberty. Michael Davies............................. 1.00
Hell Quizzes. Radio Replies Press............................. .60
Indulgence Quizzes. Radio Replies Press........................ .60
Purgatory Quizzes. Radio Replies Press......................... .60
Virgin and Statue Worship Quizzes. Radio Replies Press........... .60
The Holy Eucharist. St. Alphonsus............................ 5.00
Meditation Prayer on Mary Immaculate. Padre Pio............... .75
Little Book of the Work of Infinite Love. de la Touche............ 1.50
Textual Concordance of The Holy Scriptures....................30.00
Douay-Rheims Bible. Leatherbound............................35.00
The Way of Divine Love. Sister Josefa Menendez................12.00
The Way of Divine Love. (pocket, unabr.). Menendez............. 5.00
St. Pius V—His Life, Times, Miracles. Anderson................. 2.00
Mystical City of God—Abridged. Ven. Mary of Agreda............15.00
Beyond Space—A Book About the Angels—Fr. Parente............ 4.50

Prices guaranteed through December 31, 1987.

Miracles of the Eucharist. Joan Carroll Cruz 10.00
Martyrs of the Coliseum. Fr. O'Reilly 12.50
How Christ Said the First Mass. Fr. Meagher 12.00
Too Busy for God? Think Again! D'Angelo 2.50
St. Bernadette Soubirous. Trochu 12.00
Passion and Death of Jesus Christ. Liguori 5.00
Treatise on the Love of God. 2 Vols. St. Francis de Sales 10.00
Confession Quizzes. Radio Replies Press .60
St. Philip Neri. Fr. V. J. Matthews 3.00
St. Louise de Marillac. St. Vincent Regnault 3.50
The Old World and America. Rev. Philip Furlong 12.00
Prophecy for Today. Edward Connor 3.00
The Active Catholic. Fr. Gabriel Palau 4.00
What Will Hell Be Like? St. Alphonsus Liguori 40
The Book of Infinite Love. Mother de la Touche 3.00
Chats With Converts. Fr. M. D. Forrest 5.50
The Church Teaches. Church Documents 10.00
Conversation with Christ. Peter T. Rohrbach 5.00
Purgatory and Heaven. J. P. Arendzen 2.00
What Is Liberalism? Sarda y Salvany 3.00
Spiritual Legacy/Sr. Mary of the Trinity. van den Broek 6.00
The Creator and the Creature. Fr. Frederick Faber 9.50
Radio Replies. 3 Vols. Frs. Rumble and Carty 27.00
Convert's Catechism of Catholic Doctrine. Fr. Geiermann 2.00
Incarnation, Birth, Infancy of Jesus Christ. St. Alphonsus 5.00
Light and Peace. Fr. R. P. Quadrupani 3.50
Dogmatic Canons & Decrees of Trent, Vat. I. Documents 5.00
The Evolution Hoax Exposed. A. N. Field 3.00
The Primitive Church. Fr. D. I. Lanslots 5.50
The Priesthood. Bishop Stockums 7.00
The Priest, the Man of God. St. Joseph Cafasso 7.00
Blessed Sacrament. Fr. Frederick Faber 11.00
Christ Denied. Fr. Paul Wickens 1.25
New Regulations on Indulgences. Fr. Winfrid Herbst 1.50
A Tour of the Summa. Msgr. Paul Glenn 12.50
Spiritual Conferences. Fr. Frederick Faber 9.00
Latin Grammar. Scanlon and Scanlon 9.00
A Brief Life of Christ. Fr. Rumble 1.50
Birth Prevention Quizzes. Radio Replies Press 60
Marriage Quizzes. Radio Replies Press 60
True Church Quizzes. Radio Replies Press .60
St. Lydwine of Schiedam. J. K. Huysmans 5.00
Mary, Mother of the Church. Church Documents 2.00
The Sacred Heart and the Priesthood. de la Touche 5.00
The Passion and Death of Jesus Christ. Liguori 5.00
Revelations of St. Bridget. St. Bridget of Sweden 2.00
Magnificent Prayers. St. Bridget of Sweden 1.00
The Happiness of Heaven. Fr. J. Boudreau 6.00
St. Catherine Labouré of the Mirac. Medal. Dirvin 7.50
The Glories of Mary. (pocket, unabr.). St. Alphonsus Liguori 5.00

Prices guaranteed through December 31, 1987.

Raised from the Dead. Fr. Hebert............................12.00
Love and Service of God, Infinite Love. Mother Louise Margaret..8.00
Life and Work of Mother Louise Margaret. Fr. O'Connell........8.00
Autobiography of St. Margaret Mary.......................... 3.00
Thoughts and Sayings of St. Margaret Mary................... 2.50
The Voice of the Saints. Comp. by Francis Johnston............ 4.00
The 12 Steps to Holiness and Salvation. St. Alphonsus.......... 6.00
The Rosary and the Crisis of Faith. Cirrincione & Nelson....... .75
Sin and Its Consequences. Cardinal Manning.................. 5.00
Fourfold Sovereignty of God. Cardinal Manning............... 4.50
Catholic Apologetics Today. Fr. Most....................... 6.00
Dialogue of St. Catherine of Siena. Transl. Algar Thorold...... 6.00
Catholic Answer to Jehovah's Witnesses. D'Angelo............. 5.50
Twelve Promises of the Sacred Heart. (100 cards).............. 4.00
St. Aloysius Gonzaga. Fr. Meschler........................ 7.00
The Love of Mary. D. Roberto............................. 5.00
Begone Satan. Fr. Vogl.................................. 1.50
The Prophets and Our Times. Fr. R. G. Culleton.............. 6.00
St. Therese, The Little Flower. John Beevers................. 3.50
St. Joseph of Copertino. Fr. Angelo Pastrovicchi.............. 3.00
Mary, The Second Eve. Cardinal Newman................... 1.50
Devotion to Infant Jesus of Prague. Booklet................... .40
The Faith of Our Fathers. Cardinal Gibbons.................. 9.00
The Wonder of Guadalupe. Francis Johnston................. 5.00
Apologetics. Msgr. Paul Glenn............................ 6.00
Baltimore Catechism No. 1................................ 2.00
Baltimore Catechism No. 2................................ 3.00
Baltimore Catechism No. 3................................ 5.00
Bethlehem. Fr. Faber...................................10.00
Bible History. Schuster.................................. 8.00
Blessed Eucharist. Fr. Mueller............................ 9.00
Catholic Catechism. Fr. Faerber.......................... 3.00
The Devil. Fr. Delaporte................................. 4.00
Dogmatic Theology for the Laity. Fr. Premm.................12.50
Evidence of Satan in the Modern World. Cristiani.............. 5.50
Fifteen Promises of Mary. (100 cards)....................... 4.00
Life of Anne Catherine Emmerich. 2 vols. Schmoger...........33.00
Life of the Blessed Virgin Mary. Emmerich..................10.00
Manual of Practical Devotion to St. Joseph. Patrignani.......... 9.00
Pere Lamy. Biver....................................... 6.00
Prayer to St. Michael. (100 leaflets)....................... 4.00
Prayerbook of Favorite Litanies. Fr. Hebert.................. 7.50
Preparation for Death. (Abridged) St. Alphonsus.............. 5.00
Purgatory Explained. Schouppe........................... 8.50
Purgatory Explained. (pocket, unabr.). Schouppe.............. 5.00
Fundamentals of Catholic Dogma. Ludwig Ott................15.00
Spiritual Conferences. Tauler............................. 7.00
Trustful Surrender to Divine Providence. Bl. Claude............ 3.00
Wife, Mother and Mystic. Bessieres........................ 5.50
The Agony of Jesus. Padre Pio............................ 1.00

Self-Abandonment to Divine Providence. Fr. de Caussade, S.J.... 12.50
The Song of Songs—A Mystical Exposition. Fr. Arintero, O.P.... 15.00
Prophecy for Today. Edward Connor........................ 3.00
What Will Hell Be Like? St. Alphonsus Liguori............... .40
A Year with the Saints. Anonymous........................ 5.00
Saint Michael and the Angels. Approved Sources.............. 3.50
Dolorous Passion of Our Lord. Anne C. Emmerich............10.00
Modern Saints—Their Lives & Faces. Ann Ball................10.00
Our Lady of Fatima's Peace Plan from Heaven. Booklet......... .40
Divine Favors Granted to St. Joseph. Pere Binet............... 3.00
St. Joseph Cafasso—Priest of the Gallows. St. J. Bosco........ 2.00
Catechism of the Council of Trent. McHugh/Callan............15.00
The Foot of the Cross. Fr. Faber...........................10.00
The Rosary in Action. John Johnson........................ 5.00
Padre Pio—The Stigmatist. Fr. Charles Carty.................. 8.50
Why Squander Illness? Frs. Rumble & Carty.................. 1.50
The Sacred Heart and the Priesthood. de la Touche............ 5.00
Fatima—The Great Sign. Francis Johnston.................... 6.00
Heliotropium—Conformity of Human Will to Divine............ 8.50
St. Rose of Lima. Sister Alphonsus......................... 8.00
Charity for the Suffering Souls. Fr. John Nageleisen............10.00
Devotion to the Sacred Heart of Jesus. Verheylezoon............ 8.50
Who Is Padre Pio? Radio Replies Press...................... 1.00
Child's Bible History. Knecht.............................. 2.00
The Stigmata and Modern Science. Fr. Charles Carty.......... .75
The Incorruptibles. Joan Carroll Cruz....................... 8.00
The Life of Christ. 4 Vols. H.B. Anne C. Emmerich...........67.00
The Life of Christ. 4 Vols. P.B. Anne C. Emmerich............40.00
St. Dominic. Sr. Mary Jean Dorcy......................... 5.00
Is It a Saint's Name? Fr. William Dunne.................... 1.25
St. Anthony—The Wonder Worker of Padua. Stoddard.......... 2.50
The Precious Blood. Fr. Faber............................. 7.50
The Holy Shroud & Four Visions. Fr. O'Connell.............. 1.50
Clean Love in Courtship. Fr. Lawrence Lovasik............... 1.50
The Prophecies of St. Malachy. Peter Bander................. 3.00
St. Martin de Porres. Giuliana Cavallini..................... 7.00
The Secret of the Rosary. St. Louis De Montfort.............. 1.00
The History of Antichrist. Rev. P. Huchede.................. 2.00
The Douay-Rheims New Testament. Paperbound.............. 8.00
St. Catherine of Siena. Alice Curtayne...................... 7.50
Where We Got the Bible. Fr. Henry Graham................. 3.00
Hidden Treasure—Holy Mass. St. Leonard................... 2.50
Imitation of the Sacred Heart of Jesus. Fr. Arnoudt............10.00
The Life & Glories of St. Joseph. Edward Thompson.......... 9.00
An Explanation of the Baltimore Catechism. Fr. Kinkead....... 8.50
Humility of Heart. Fr. Cajetan da Bergamo.................. 4.50
The Curé D'Ars. Abbé Francis Trochu......................15.00
Love, Peace and Joy. St. Gertrude/Prévot.................... 4.00
Three Ways of the Spiritual Life. Garrigou-Lagrange............3.00

At your bookdealer or direct from the publisher.

Prices guaranteed through December 31, 1987.